Undergraduate Topics in Computer Science (UTiCS) delivers high-quality instructional content for undergraduates studying in all areas of computing and information science. From core foundational and theoretical material to final-year topics and applications, UTiCS books take a fresh, concise, and modern approach and are ideal for self-study or for a one- or two-semester course. The texts are all authored by established experts in their fields, reviewed by an international advisory board, and contain numerous examples and problems. Many include fully worked solutions.

For further volumes:
www.springer.com/series/7592

Gilles Dowek

Proofs
and Algorithms

An Introduction to Logic and Computability

 Springer

Gilles Dowek
École Polytechnique
Palaiseau
France
gilles.dowek@polytechnique.edu

Based on course notes by Gilles Dowek, published simultaneously in French by École Poly-technique with the following title: "Les démonstrations et les algorithmes". The translator of the work is Maribel Fernandez.

ISSN 1863-7310
ISBN 978-0-85729-120-2   e-ISBN 978-0-85729-121-9
DOI 10.1007/978-0-85729-121-9
Springer London Dordrecht Heidelberg New York

British Library Cataloguing in Publication Data
A catalogue record for this book is available from the British Library

Printed on acid-free paper

Springer is part of Springer Science+Business Media (www.springer.com)

Acknowledgements

The author would like to thank René Cori, René David, Maribel Fernández, Jean-Baptiste Joinet, Claude Kirchner, Jean-Louis Krivine, Daniel Lascar, Stéphane Lengrand, Michel Parigot, Laurence Rideau and Paul Rozière.

Contents

Introduction

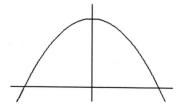

There are several ways to find the area of the segment of parabola depicted above. One method consists of covering the area with an infinite number of small triangles, proving that each of them has a specific area, then adding together all the areas of the triangles. This is *grosso modo* the method that Archimedes used to show that this area is equal to 4/3. Another method, which gives the same result, has been known since the 17th century: the area can be obtained by computing $\int_{-1}^{1}(1-x^2)dx$. To integrate this polynomial function we do not need to build a proof, we can simply use an algorithm.

Building a proof and applying an algorithm are two well-known mathematical techniques; they have co-existed for a long time. With the advent of computers, which allow us to implement algorithms at a scale that was unimaginable in the past, there has been a renewed interest in algorithmic methods.

The co-existence of these two problem-solving techniques leads us to question their relationship. To what extent the construction of a proof can be replaced by the application of an algorithm? This book describes a set of results, some positive and some negative, that provide a partial answer to this question. We start by giving a precise definition of the notion of a proof, in the first part of the book, and of the notion of an algorithm, in the second part of the book. A precise definition of the notion of proof will allow us to understand how to prove independence theorems, which state that there are certain problems for which no proof can provide a solution. A precise definition of the notion of an algorithm will allow us to understand how to prove undecidability theorems, which state that certain problems cannot be solved in an algorithmic way. It will also lead us to a better understanding of algorithms, which can be written in different ways (for instance, as a set of rewriting rules, as terms in the lambda-calculus, or as Turing machines), and to the discovery that behind this apparent diversity there is a deep unifying notion: the idea that a computation is a sequence of small steps.

The third part of the book focuses on the links between the notions of proof and algorithm. The main result in this part is Church's theorem, establishing that provability is an undecidable problem in predicate logic; Gödel's famous theorem is a corollary of this result. This negative result will be counterbalanced by two positive results. First, although undecidable, this problem is semi-decidable, and this will lead us to the development of algorithms that search for proofs. Second, by adding axioms to predicate logic we can, in certain cases, make the problem decidable. This will lead us to the development of decision algorithms for specific theories.

The final chapter of the book will describe a different link between proofs and algorithms: some proofs, those that are said to be *constructive*, can be used as algorithms.

Over the next chapters we will explore the deep connections that exist between the concepts of proof and algorithm, and unveil the complexity that hides behind the apparently obvious notion of truth.

Part I
Proofs

Chapter 1
Predicate Logic

What are the conditions that a proposition should satisfy to be true? A possible answer, defining a certain notion of truth, could be that a proposition is true if it can be proved. In this chapter, we will analyse this answer and give a definition of the concept of provability. For this, we will first define the set of *propositions*, and then the subset of *theorems*, or *provable propositions*.

Since in both cases we will be defining sets, we will start by introducing some tools to define sets.

1.1 Inductive Definitions

The most basic tool to define a set is an *explicit definition*. We can, for example, define explicitly the set of even numbers: $\{n \in \mathbb{N} \mid \exists p \in \mathbb{N} \; n = 2 \times p\}$. However, these explicit definitions are not sufficient to define all the sets we need. A second tool to define sets is the notion of an *inductive definition*. This notion is based on a simple theorem: the fixed point theorem.

1.1.1 The Fixed Point Theorem

Definition 1.1 (Limit) Let $\leq$ be an ordering relation, that is, a reflexive, antisymmetric and transitive relation, over a set E, and let $u_0, u_1, u_2, \ldots$ be an increasing sequence, that is, a sequence such that $u_0 \leq u_1 \leq u_2 \leq \cdots$. The element l of E is called *limit* of the sequence $u_0, u_1, u_2, \ldots$ if it is a least upper bound of the set $\{u_0, u_1, u_2, \ldots\}$, that is, if it is an upper bound:

- for all i, $u_i \leq l$

and it is the smallest one:

- if, for all i, $u_i \leq l'$, then $l \leq l'$.

G. Dowek, *Proofs and Algorithms*, Undergraduate Topics in Computer Science,
DOI 10.1007/978-0-85729-121-9_1, © Springer-Verlag London Limited 2011

If it exists, the limit of a sequence $(u_i)_i$ is unique, and we denote it by $\lim_i u_i$.

Definition 1.2 (Weakly complete ordering) An ordering relation $\leq$ is said to be *weakly complete* if each increasing sequence has a limit.

The standard ordering relation over the real numbers interval $[0, 1]$ is an example of a weakly complete ordering. In addition, this relation has a least element 0. However, the standard ordering relation over $\mathbb{R}^+$ is not weakly complete since the increasing sequence $0, 1, 2, 3, \ldots$ does not have a limit.

Let A be an arbitrary set. The inclusion relation $\subseteq$ over the set $\wp(A)$ of all the subsets of A is another example of a weakly complete ordering. The limit of an increasing sequence $U_0, U_1, U_2, \ldots$ is the set $\bigcup_{i \in \mathbb{N}} U_i$. In addition, this relation has a least element $\emptyset$.

Definition 1.3 (Increasing function) Let $\leq$ be an ordering relation over a set E and f a function from E to E. The function f is *increasing* if $x \leq y \Rightarrow fx \leq fy$.

Definition 1.4 (Continuous function) Let $\leq$ be a weakly complete ordering relation over the set E, and f an increasing function from E to E. The function f is *continuous* if for any increasing sequence $\lim_i (f \ u_i) = f \ (\lim_i u_i)$.

Proposition 1.1 (First fixed point theorem) *Let $\leq$ be a weakly complete ordering relation over a set E that has a least element m. Let f be a function from E to E. If f is continuous then $p = \lim_i (f^i \ m)$ is the least fixed point of f.*

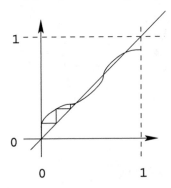

Proof First, since m is the smallest element in E, $m \leq fm$. The function f is increasing, therefore $f^i m \leq f^{i+1} m$. Since the sequence $f^i m$ is increasing, it has a limit. The sequence $f^{i+1} m$ also has p as limit, thus, $p = \lim_i (f \ (f^i \ m)) = f \ (\lim_i (f^i \ m)) = f \ p$. Moreover, p is the least fixed point, because if q is another fixed point, then $m \leq q$ and $f^i m \leq f^i q = q$ (since f is increasing). Hence $p = \lim_i (f^i \ m) \leq q$. $\square$

The second fixed point theorem states the existence of a fixed point for increasing functions, even if they are not continuous, provided the ordering satisfies a stronger property.

Definition 1.5 (Strongly complete ordering) An ordering relation $\leq$ over a set E is *strongly complete* if every subset A of E has a least upper bound, denoted by $\sup A$.

The standard ordering relation over the interval $[0, 1]$ is an example of a strongly complete ordering relation. The standard ordering over $\mathbb{R}^+$ is not strongly complete because the set $\mathbb{R}^+$ itself has no upper bound.

Let A be an arbitrary set. The inclusion relation $\subseteq$ over the set $\wp(A)$ of all the subsets of A is another example of strongly complete ordering. The least upper bound of a set B is the set $\bigcup_{C \in B} C$.

Exercise 1.1 Show that any strongly complete ordering is also weakly complete. Is the ordering

weakly complete? Is it strongly complete?

Proposition 1.2 *If the ordering $\leq$ over the set E is strongly complete, then any subset A of E has a greatest lower bound, inf A.*

Proof Let A be a subset of E, let B be the set $\{y \in E \mid \forall x \in A \ y \leq x\}$ of lower bounds of A and l the least upper bound of B. By definition, l is an upper bound of the set B

$- \ \forall y \in B \ y \leq l$

and it is the least one

$- \ (\forall y \in B \ y \leq l') \Rightarrow l \leq l'.$

It is easy to show that l is the greatest lower bound of A. Indeed, if x is an element of A, it is an upper bound of B and since l is the least upper bound, $l \leq x$. Thus, l is a lower bound of A. To show that it is the greatest one, it is sufficient to note that if m is another lower bound of A, it is an element of B and therefore $m \leq l$. □

The greatest lower bound of a set B of subsets of A is, of course, the set $\bigcap_{C \in B} C$.

Proposition 1.3 (Second fixed point theorem) *Let $\leq$ be a strongly complete ordering over a set E. Let f be a function from E to E. If f is increasing then $p = \inf\{c \mid fc \leq c\}$ is the least fixed point of f.*

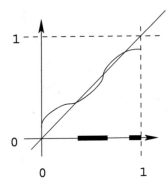

Proof Let C be the set $\{c \mid fc \leq c\}$ and c be an element of C. Then $p \leq c$ because p is a lower bound of C. Since the function f is increasing, we deduce that $fp \leq fc$. Also, $fc \leq c$ because c is an element of C, so by transitivity $fp \leq c$.

The element fp is less than all the elements in C, it is therefore also less than or equal to its greatest lower bound: $fp \leq p$.

Since the function f is increasing, $f(fp) \leq fp$, thus fp is an element of C, and since p is a lower bound of C, we deduce $p \leq fp$. By antisymmetry, $p = fp$.

Finally, by definition, all the fixed points of f belong to C, and they are therefore greater than p.   □

1.1.2 Inductive Definitions

We will now see how the fixed point theorems can be used to define sets and relations.

Definition 1.6 (Closure) Let E be a set, f a function from E^n to E and A a subset of E. The set A is *closed* under the function f if for all $x_1, \ldots, x_n$ in A such that f is defined in $x_1, \ldots, x_n$, $f\, x_1 \ldots x_n$ is also an element of A.

For example, the set of all the even numbers is closed under the function $n \mapsto n + 2$.

Definition 1.7 (Inductive definition) Let E be a set. An *inductive definition* over E is a family of partial functions f_1 from E^{n_1} to E, f_2 from E^{n_2} to E, ... This family defines a subset A of E: the least subset of E that is closed under the functions $f_1, f_2, \ldots$.

For example, the subset of $\mathbb{N}$ that contains all the even numbers is inductively defined by the number 0, that is, the function from $\mathbb{N}^0$ to $\mathbb{N}$ that returns the value 0, and the function from $\mathbb{N}$ to $\mathbb{N}$ defined by $n \mapsto n+2$. The subset of the even numbers is not the only subset of $\mathbb{N}$ that contains 0 and is closed under the function $n \mapsto n+2$ (the set $\mathbb{N}$, for instance, also satisfies these properties), but it is the smallest one.

The subset of $\{a, b, c\}^*$ containing all the words of the form $a^n b c^n$ is inductively defined by the word b and the function $m \mapsto amc$. In general, a context free grammar can always be specified as an inductive set. We will see that in logic, the set of theorems is defined as the subset of all the propositions that is inductively defined by the axioms and deduction rules.

The functions $f_1, f_2, \ldots$ are called *rules*. Instead of writing a rule as $x_1 \ldots x_n \mapsto t$, we will use the notation

$$\frac{x_1 \ldots x_n}{t}$$

For example, the set of even numbers is defined by the rules

$$\overline{0}$$

$$\frac{n}{n+2}$$

Let P be the set of even numbers. We will sometimes write the rules as follows:

$$\overline{0 \in P}$$

$$\frac{n \in P}{n+2 \in P}$$

To show that Definition 1.7 makes sense, we will show that there is always a smallest subset A that is closed under the functions $f_1, f_2, \ldots$.

Proposition 1.4 *Assume E is a set and $f_1, f_2, \ldots$ are rules over the set E. There exists a smallest subset A of E that is closed under the functions $f_1, f_2, \ldots$.*

Proof Let F be the function from $\wp(E)$ to $\wp(E)$ defined as follows.

$$FC = \{x \in E \mid \exists i \exists y_1 \ldots y_{n_i} \in C \; x = f_i \; y_1 \; \ldots \; y_{n_i}\}$$

A subset C of E is closed under the functions $f_1, f_2, \ldots$ if and only if $FC \subseteq C$.

The function F is trivially increasing: if $C \subseteq C'$, then $FC \subseteq FC'$. The set A is defined as the least fixed point of this function: the intersection of all the sets C such that $FC \subseteq C$, that is, the intersection of all the sets that are closed under the functions $f_1, f_2, \ldots$.

By the second fixed point theorem, this set is a fixed point of F, $FA = A$, and therefore $FA \subseteq A$. Hence, it is closed under the functions $f_1, f_2, \ldots$ And by definition, it is smaller than all the sets C such that $FC \subseteq C$. It is therefore the smallest set that is closed under these functions.   □

The first fixed point theorem gives us another characterisation of this set.

Proposition 1.5 *Assume E is a set and $f_1, f_2, \ldots$ are rules over the set E. The smallest subset A of E that is closed under the functions $f_1, f_2, \ldots$ is the set $\bigcup_k (F^k \emptyset)$ where the function F is defined by*

$$FC = \{x \in E \mid \exists i \exists y_1 \ldots y_{n_i} \in C \; x = f_i \; y_1 \; \ldots \; y_{n_i}\}$$

Proof We have seen that the function F is increasing. It is also continuous: if $C_0 \subseteq C_1 \subseteq C_2 \subseteq \cdots$, then $F(\bigcup_j C_j) = \bigcup_j (FC_j)$. Indeed, if an element x of E is in $F(\bigcup_j C_j)$, then there exists some number i and elements $y_1, \ldots, y_{n_i}$ of $\bigcup_j C_j$ such that $x = f_i \; y_1 \; \ldots \; y_{n_i}$. Each of these elements is in one of the C_j. Since the sequence C_j is increasing, they are all in C_k, which is the largest of these sets. Therefore, the element x belongs to FC_k and also to $\bigcup_j (FC_j)$. Conversely, if x is in $\bigcup_j (FC_j)$, then it belongs to some FC_k, and there is therefore a number i and elements $y_1, \ldots, y_{n_i}$ of C_k such that $x = f_i \; y_1 \; \ldots \; y_{n_i}$. The elements $y_1, \ldots, y_{n_i}$ are in $\bigcup_j C_j$ and therefore x is in $F(\bigcup_j C_j)$.

We have seen that the smallest subset A of E closed under the functions $f_1, f_2, \ldots$ is the least fixed point of the function F. By the first fixed point theorem, we have $A = \bigcup_k (F^k \emptyset)$. $\qquad\square$

1.1.3 Structural Induction

Inductive definitions suggest a method to write proofs. If a property is *hereditary*, that is, if each time it holds for $y_1, \ldots, y_{n_i}$, then it also holds for $f_i \; y_1 \; \ldots \; y_{n_i}$, then we can deduce that it holds for all the elements of A.

One way to show this, is to use the second fixed point theorem and to observe that the subset P of E containing all the elements that satisfy the property is closed under the functions f_i and thus it includes A. Another way is to use Proposition 1.5 and to show by induction on k that all the elements in $F^k \emptyset$ satisfy the property.

1.1.4 Derivations

An element x is in the set A if and only if it belongs to some set $F^k \emptyset$, that is, if there exists a function f_i such that $x = f_i \; y_1 \; \ldots \; y_{n_i}$ where $y_1, \ldots, y_{n_i}$ are in $F^{k-1} \emptyset$. This observation allows us to prove that an element x of E belongs to A if and only if there exists a tree whose nodes are labelled with elements of E and whose root is labelled with x, and such that whenever a node is labelled with an element y and its children are labelled with elements $z_1, \ldots, z_n$, there exists a rule f_i such that $y = f_i \; z_1 \; \ldots \; z_n$. Such a tree is called a *derivation* of x.

Definition 1.8 (Derivation) Let E be a set and $f_1, f_2, \ldots$ rules over the set E. A *derivation* in $f_1, f_2, \ldots$ is a tree where the nodes are labelled with elements of E such that if a node is labelled with an element y and its children are labelled with elements $z_1, \ldots, z_n$, then there is a rule f_i, such that $y = f_i \, z_1 \, \ldots \, z_n$.

If the root of the derivation is an element x of E, then this derivation is a *derivation of x*.

We can then define the set A as the set of elements of E for which there is a derivation.

We will use a specific notation for derivations. The root of the tree will be written at the bottom and the leaves at the top; moreover we will write a line over each node in the tree and write its children over the line.

For example, the following derivation shows that the number 8 is in the set of even numbers.

$$\frac{\dfrac{\dfrac{\dfrac{\dfrac{0}{2}}{4}}{6}}{8}}{}$$

If we call P the set of even numbers, we can write the derivation as follows

$$\frac{\dfrac{\dfrac{\dfrac{\dfrac{0 \in P}{2 \in P}}{4 \in P}}{6 \in P}}{8 \in P}}{}$$

Instead of labelling the nodes of a derivation with elements of E, we can also label them with rules.

Definition 1.9 (Derivation labelled with rules) Let E be a set and $f_1, f_2, \ldots$ rules over the set E. A *derivation labelled with rules* $f_1, f_2, \ldots$ is a tree whose nodes are labelled with $f_1, f_2, \ldots$ such that the number of children of a node labelled by f is the number of arguments of f.

By structural induction we can associate an element of E to each derivation labelled with rules: if the root of the derivation is labelled with the rule f_i and its immediate subtrees are associated to the elements $z_1, \ldots, z_n$, then we associate to the derivation the element $f_i \, z_1 \, \ldots \, z_n$. When an element is associated to a derivation, we say that the derivation is a *derivation of this element*.

We can then define the set A as the set of elements of E that have a derivation labelled with rules.

1.1.5 The Reflexive-Transitive Closure of a Relation

The reflexive-transitive closure of a relation is an example of inductive definition.

Definition 1.10 (Reflexive-transitive closure) Let R be a binary relation on a set E. The *reflexive-transitive closure* of the relation R is the relation R^* inductively defined by the rules

- $t \ R^* \ t$,
- if $t \ R \ t'$ and $t' \ R^* \ t''$, then $t \ R^* \ t''$.

If $t \ R^* \ t'$, a derivation of the pair (t, t') is a finite sequence $t_0, \dots, t_n$, such that $t_0 = t$, $t_n = t'$ and for all $i \le n - 1$, $t_i \ R \ t_{i+1}$.

If we see R as a directed graph, then derivations are paths in the graph and R^* is the relation that links two nodes when there is a path from one to the other in the graph.

1.2 Languages

1.2.1 Languages Without Variables

In the previous section we introduced inductive definitions; we will now use this technique to define the notion of a *language*. First we will give a general definition that applies to programming languages and logic languages alike. Later we will define the language of predicate logic.

The notion of language that we will define does not take into account superficial syntactic conventions, for instance, it does not matter whether we write $3 + 4$, $+(3, 4)$, or $3 \ 4 +$. This expression will be represented in an abstract way by a tree

Each node in the tree will be labelled with a symbol. The number of children of a node depends on the node's label—two children if the label is $+$, none if it is 3 or 4, ...

A language is thus a set of symbols, each with an associated *arity*, which is a natural number also called the *number of arguments* of the symbol. Symbols without arguments are called *constants*.

The set of *expressions* of the language is the set of trees inductively defined by the following rule.

- If f is a symbol of arity n and $t_1, \dots, t_n$ are expressions then $f(t_1, \dots, t_n)$, that is, the tree that has a root labelled with f and subtrees $t_1, \dots, t_n$, is an expression.

1.2.2 Variables

Suppose that we want to design a language of expressions, including for instance expressions such as $odd(3)$ or $odd(3) \Rightarrow even(3+1)$. We might also want to be able to express the fact that for all natural numbers, if a natural number is odd then its successor is even.

To build those expressions, natural languages such as English or French use indefinite pronouns (for example *all*, *any* and *some* in English), but replacing expressions by pronouns may produce ambiguities, in particular when several expressions are replaced in a sentence. For instance, the sentence "There is some natural number greater than any given natural number" might be understood as a property that holds for each natural number: for each natural number there is a greater one, which is true; but it could also mean that there exists a natural number that is greater than all natural numbers, which is false.

To avoid ambiguities, a more sophisticated mechanism is needed. We will introduce variables and specify their meaning and scope using quantifiers $\forall$, *for all*, or $\exists$, *there exists*, to bind variables. In this way we can distinguish the propositions $\forall x \exists y \ (y \geq x)$ and $\exists y \forall x \ (y \geq x)$.

A quantifier is a symbol that binds a variable in its argument. There are other examples of binders, for instance the symbols $\mapsto$, ∂/∂, $\int d$, $\sum$, $\prod$, ... We will generalise the definition of language given above, to take into account the fact that some symbols might bind variables.

The arity of a symbol f will no longer be a number n, instead, we will use a finite sequence of numbers $(k_1, \ldots, k_n)$ that will indicate that the symbol f binds k_1 variables in its first argument, k_2 variables in the second, ..., k_n variables in the nth argument.

In this way, when a language is given, that is, when we have a set of symbols with their arities, together with an infinite set of *variables*, we can define the set of expressions inductively as follows.

– Variables are expressions.
– If f is a symbol of arity $(k_1, \ldots, k_n)$, $t_1, \ldots, t_n$ are expressions and $x_1^1, \ldots, x_{k_1}^1$, $\ldots, x_1^n, \ldots, x_{k_n}^n$ are variables, then $f(x_1^1 \ldots x_{k_1}^1 t_1, \ldots, x_1^n \ldots x_{k_n}^n t_n)$ is an expression.

The notation $f(x_1^1 \ldots x_{k_1}^1 t_1, \ldots, x_1^n \ldots x_{k_n}^n t_n)$ denotes the tree

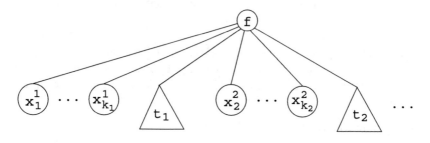

For example, the expression $\int_t^u v\, dx$ denotes the tree

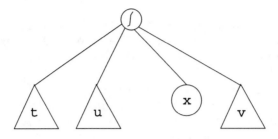

1.2.3 Many-Sorted Languages

In this book, we will sometimes use more general languages that are called *many-sorted languages*. For instance, using the constants 0 and 1, a binary symbol $+$, unary symbols *even* and *odd* and a binary symbol $\Rightarrow$ (none of these symbols binds any variable), we can build the expressions 1, $1 + 1$, $even(1 + 1)$ and $odd(1) \Rightarrow even(1 + 1)$. Unfortunately, we can also build the expressions $odd(even(1))$ and $1 \Rightarrow (1 + even(1))$. To exclude these expressions, we will distinguish two sorts of expression: *terms*, which denote natural numbers, and *propositions* which express properties of numbers. Thus, the symbol *even* takes an argument which should be a term, and builds a proposition. The symbol $\Rightarrow$ takes two propositions as arguments and builds a proposition.

We will therefore introduce a set $\{Term, Prop\}$ and call its elements *expression sorts*, and we will associate to the symbol *even* the arity $(Term, Prop)$. This indicates that in an expression of the form $even(t)$, the expression t must be of sort *Term*, and the whole expression $even(t)$ is of sort *Prop*.

More generally, we introduce a set S of sorts, and define the arity of a symbol f to be a finite sequence $(s_1, \ldots, s_n, s')$ of sorts. This arity indicates that the symbol f has n arguments, the first one of sort $s_1, \ldots,$ the nth one of sort s_n, and that the resulting expression is of sort s'.

When, in addition, there are bound variables, the arity of a symbol f is a finite sequence $((s_1^1, \ldots, s_{k_1}^1, s'^1), \ldots, (s_1^n, \ldots, s_{k_n}^n, s'^n), s'')$ indicating that the symbol f has n arguments, the first one of sort s'^1 and binding k_1 variables of sorts $s_1^1, \ldots, s_{k_1}^1, \ldots,$ and that the resulting expression is itself of sort s''.

Formally, expressions are defined as follows.

Definition 1.11 (Expressions in a language) Given a language $\mathcal{L}$, that is, a set of sorts and a set of symbols each with an associated arity, and a family of infinite, pairwise disjoint sets of *variables*, indexed by sorts, the set of expressions in $\mathcal{L}$ is inductively defined by the following rules.

– Variables of sort s are expressions of sort s.

- If f is a symbol of arity $((s_1^1, \ldots, s_{k_1}^1, s'^1), \ldots, (s_1^n, \ldots, s_{k_n}^n, s'^n), s''), x_1^1, \ldots, x_{k_1}^1,$
  $\ldots, x_1^n, \ldots, x_{k_n}^n$ are variables of sorts $s_1^1, \ldots, s_{k_1}^1, \ldots, s_1^n, \ldots, s_{k_n}^n$ and $t_1, \ldots, t_n$ are
  expressions of sorts $s'^1, \ldots, s'^n$ then $f(x_1^1 \ldots x_{k_1}^1 t_1, \ldots, x_1^n \ldots x_{k_n}^n t_n)$ is an expression of sort s''.

Definition 1.12 (Variables of an expression) The set of *variables* of an expression is defined by structural induction, as follows.

- $Var(x) = \{x\}$,
- $Var(f(x_1^1 \ldots x_{k_1}^1 t_1, \ldots, x_1^n \ldots x_{k_n}^n t_n))$
  $= Var(t_1) \cup \{x_1^1, \ldots, x_{k_1}^1\} \cup \cdots \cup Var(t_n) \cup \{x_n^n, \ldots, x_{k_n}^n\}$.

Definition 1.13 (Free variables) The set of *free variables* of an expression is defined by structural induction, as follows.

- $FV(x) = \{x\}$,
- $FV(f(x_1^1 \ldots x_{k_1}^1 t_1, \ldots, x_1^n \ldots x_{k_n}^n t_n))$
  $= (FV(t_1) \setminus \{x_1^1, \ldots, x_{k_1}^1\}) \cup \cdots \cup (FV(t_n) \setminus \{x_n^n, \ldots, x_{k_n}^n\})$.

For example, $Var(\forall x \ (x = x)) = \{x\}$, but $FV(\forall x \ (x = x)) = \emptyset$.
An expression without free variables is said to be *closed*.

Definition 1.14 (Height) The *height* of an expression is also defined by structural induction:

- $Height(x) = 0$,
- $Height(f(x_1^1 \ldots x_{k_1}^1 t_1, \ldots, x_1^n \ldots x_{k_n}^n t_n)) = 1 + \max(Height(t_1), \ldots, Height(t_n))$.

1.2.4 Substitution

The first operation that we need to define is substitution: indeed, the rôle of variables is not only to be bound but also to be substituted. For example, from the proposition $\forall x \ (odd(x) \Rightarrow even(x + 1))$, we might want to deduce the proposition $odd(3) \Rightarrow even(3 + 1)$, obtained by substituting the variable x by the expression 3.

Definition 1.15 (Substitution) A *substitution* is a mapping from variables to expressions, with a finite domain, such that each variable is associated to an expression of the same sort. In other words, a substitution is a finite set of pairs where the first element is a variable and the second an expression, such that each variable occurs at most once as first element in a pair. We can also define a substitution as an association list: $\theta = t_1/x_1, \ldots, t_n/x_n$.

When a substitution is applied to an expression, each occurrence of a variable $x_1, \ldots, x_n$ in the expression is replaced by $t_1, \ldots, t_n$, respectively.

Of course, this replacement only affects the free variables. For example, if we substitute the variable x by the expression 2 in the expression $x + 3$, we should obtain the expression $2 + 3$. However, if we substitute the variable x by the expression 2 in the expression $\forall x\ (x = x)$, we should obtain the expression $\forall x\ (x = x)$ instead of $\forall x\ (2 = 2)$.

A first attempt to describe the application of a substitution leads to the following definition:

Definition 1.16 (Application of a substitution—with capture) Let $\theta = t_1/x_1, \ldots,$ t_n/x_n be a substitution and t an expression. The expression $\langle\theta\rangle t$ is defined by induction as follows.

- $\langle\theta\rangle x_i = t_i$,
- $\langle\theta\rangle x = x$ if x is not in the domain of θ,
- $\langle\theta\rangle f(y_1^1 \ldots y_{k_1}^1\ u_1, \ldots, y_1^p \ldots y_{k_p}^p\ u_p)$
  $$= f(y_1^1 \ldots y_{k_1}^1\ \langle\theta_{|\mathcal{V}\setminus\{y_1^1,\ldots,y_{k_1}^1\}}\rangle u_1, \ldots, y_1^p \ldots y_{k_p}^p\ \langle\theta_{|\mathcal{V}\setminus\{y_1^p,\ldots,y_{k_p}^p\}}\rangle u_p)$$

where we use the notation $\theta_{|\mathcal{V}\setminus\{y_1,\ldots,y_k\}}$ for the restriction of the substitution θ to the set $\mathcal{V} \setminus \{y_1, \ldots, y_k\}$, that is, the substitution where we have omitted all the pairs where the first element is one of the variables $y_1, \ldots, y_k$.

This definition is problematic, because substitutions can *capture variables*. For example, the expression $\exists x\ (x + 1 = y)$ states that y is the successor of some number. If we substitute y by 4 in this expression, we obtain the expression $\exists x\ (x + 1 = 4)$, which indicates that 4 is the successor of some number. If we substitute y by z, we obtain the expression $\exists x\ (x + 1 = z)$, which again states that z is the successor of some number. But if we substitute y by x, we obtain the expression $\exists x\ (x + 1 = x)$ stating that there is some number which is its own successor, instead of the expected expression indicating that x is the successor of some number.

We can avoid this problem if we change the name of the bound variable: bound variables are dummies, their name does not matter. In other words, in the expression $\exists x\ (x + 1 = y)$, we can replace the bound variable x by any other variable, except of course y. Similarly, when we substitute in the expression u the variables $x_1, \ldots, x_n$ by expressions $t_1, \ldots, t_n$, we can change the names of the bound variables in u to avoid capture. It suffices to replace them by names that do not occur in $x_1, \ldots, x_n$, or in the variables of $t_1, \ldots, t_n$, or in the variables of u.

We start by defining, using the notion of substitution with capture defined above, an equivalence relation on expressions, by induction on their height. This relation is called *alphabetic equivalence* and it corresponds to bound-variable renaming.

Definition 1.17 (Alphabetic equivalence) The *alphabetic equivalence* relation, also called *alpha-equivalence*, is inductively defined by the rules

- $x \sim x$,
- $f(y_1^1 \ldots y_{k_1}^1\ t_1, \ldots, y_1^n \ldots y_{k_n}^n\ t_n) \sim f(y_1'^1 \ldots y_{k_1}'^1\ t_1', \ldots, y_1'^n \ldots y_{k_n}'^n\ t_n')$ if for all i, and for any sequence of fresh variables $z_1, \ldots, z_{k_i}$ (that is, variables that do not occur in t_i or t_i'), $\langle z_1/y_1^i, \ldots, z_{k_i}/y_{k_i}^i\rangle t_i \sim \langle z_1/y_1'^i, \ldots, z_{k_i}/y_{k_i}'^i\rangle t_i'$.

For example, the expressions $\forall x\ (x = x)$ and $\forall y\ (y = y)$ are α-equivalent.

In the rest of the book we will work with expressions *modulo α-equivalence*, that is, we will consider implicitly α-equivalence classes of expressions.

We can now define the operation of substitution by induction on the height of expressions.

Definition 1.18 (Application of a substitution) Let $\theta = t_1/x_1, \ldots, t_n/x_n$ be a substitution and t an expression. The expression θt is defined by induction on the height of t as follows.

- $\theta x_i = t_i$,
- $\theta x = x$ if x is not in the domain of θ,
- $\theta f(y_1^1 \ldots y_{k_1}^1 u_1, \ldots, y_1^p \ldots y_{k_p}^p u_p) = f(z_1^1 \ldots z_{k_1}^1 \theta \langle z_1^1/y_1^1, \ldots, z_{k_1}^1/y_{k_1}^1 \rangle u_1, \ldots,$
  $z_1^p \ldots z_{k_p}^p \theta \langle z_1^p/y_1^p, \ldots, z_{k_p}^p/y_{k_p}^p \rangle u_p)$ where $z_1^1, \ldots, z_{k_1}^1, \ldots, z_1^p, \ldots, z_{k_p}^p$ are variables that do not occur in $f(y_1^1 \ldots y_{k_1}^1 u_1, \ldots, y_1^p \ldots y_{k_p}^p u_p)$ or in θ.

For example, if we substitute the variable y by the expression $2 \times x$ in the expression $\exists x\ (x + 1 = y)$, we obtain the expression $\exists z\ (z + 1 = 2 \times x)$. The choice of variable z is arbitrary, we could have chosen v or w, and we would have obtained the same expression modulo α-equivalence.

Definition 1.19 (Composition of substitutions) The *composition* of the substitutions $\theta = t_1/x_1, \ldots, t_n/x_n$ and $\sigma = u_1/y_1, \ldots, u_p/y_p$ is the substitution

$$\theta \circ \sigma = \{\theta(\sigma z)/z \mid z \in \{x_1, \ldots, x_n, y_1, \ldots, y_p\}\}$$

We can prove, by induction on the height of t, that for any expression t

$$(\theta \circ \sigma)t = \theta(\sigma t)$$

1.2.5 Articulation

In the definitions given above, there were no restrictions on the number of symbols in a language. However, we should take into account that, *in fine*, expressions will be written using a finite alphabet. If each symbol of the language is represented by a letter in this alphabet, then the set of symbols of the language will be finite. However, it would be possible to represent a symbol by a word built out of several symbols from this finite alphabet, or more generally, a symbol could be represented by a labelled tree, where the labels are elements of a finite set. For instance, in Geometry, some symbols, such as π, are letters whereas others, such as "bisector", are words. The process could be iterated: we could represent the symbols of a language with trees labelled with trees which are in turn labelled with the elements of a finite set. This leads us to the following definition.

Definition 1.20 (Articulated set of trees)

- A set of trees is *simply articulated*, or *1-articulated*, if all the nodes of trees in this set are labelled with elements of a finite set.
- A set of trees is $(n + 1)$-*articulated*, if all the nodes of trees in this set are labelled with elements of an n-articulated set of trees.

A set of trees is *articulated* if it is n-articulated for some natural number n.

For example, the set of expressions without variables in a language consisting of a finite set of symbols is a simply articulated set. However, since the set of variables is infinite, the set of expressions of a language is at least doubly articulated: an infinite set of variables, such as $x, x', x'', x''', x'''', \ldots$ can be represented by a set of trees where nodes are labelled with symbols x or $'$.

If a language is articulated, its set of symbols is finite or countable. In some cases, languages with non-countable sets of symbols (thus non-articulated) are needed; we will see an example in Sect. 2.4. However, we must keep in mind that this notion of a language is more general the usual one, since expressions can no longer be written using a finite alphabet.

Let E be a set and $f_1, f_2, \ldots$ rules over the set E. The set of derivations using $f_1, f_2, \ldots$ is not always articulated. However, if E is an articulated set of trees, then the set of derivations using $f_1, f_2, \ldots$ is articulated. Similarly, if each rule $f_1, f_2, \ldots$ can be associated to an element of an articulated set, then the set of derivations labelled with rules $f_1, f_2, \ldots$ is articulated.

1.3 The Languages of Predicate Logic

The concept of language introduced in the previous section is very general. In this section we will focus in particular on the languages used in predicate logic. In these languages, most symbols do not bind any variable. The only exceptions are the quantifiers $\forall$ and $\exists$. Moreover, these languages include *terms*, to denote objects, and *propositions*, to express properties of these objects. Terms may be many-sorted. Thus, a language is defined by a non-empty set S of *term sorts*, a set $\mathcal{F}$ of *function symbols* that are used to build terms, and a set $\mathcal{P}$ of *predicate symbols* to build propositions.

The sorts of the language are the term sorts together with a distinguished sort *Prop* for propositions. Since function symbols do not bind variables, their arities have the form $(s_1, \ldots, s_n, s')$ where $s_1, \ldots, s_n$ and s' are term sorts. If a symbol f has arity $(s_1, \ldots, s_n, s')$ and $t_1, \ldots, t_n$ are terms of sorts $s_1, \ldots, s_n$, respectively, then the expression $f(t_1, \ldots, t_n)$ is a term of sort s'. Similarly, since predicate symbols do not bind variables, their arities have the form $(s_1, \ldots, s_n, Prop)$, where $s_1, \ldots, s_n$ are term sorts. Such an arity is written simply $(s_1, \ldots, s_n)$. If a symbol P has arity $(s_1, \ldots, s_n)$ and $t_1, \ldots, t_n$ are terms of sorts $s_1, \ldots, s_n$, respectively, then the expression $P(t_1, \ldots, t_n)$ is a proposition. In addition to these symbols, which are specific to each language, there is a set of symbols which is common to all the languages of predicate logic: $\top$ (read *true*), and $\bot$ (read *false*), with arity (*Prop*), $\neg$ (read *not*), with arity (*Prop, Prop*), $\wedge$ (read *and*), $\vee$ (read *or*), and $\Rightarrow$ (read *implies*), with arity (*Prop, Prop, Prop*) and finally, for each element of $\mathcal{S}$, two quantifiers $\forall_s$, *for all*, and $\exists_s$, *there exists*, with arity $((s, Prop), Prop)$. We do not need to introduce variables of sort *Prop* because none of the symbols can bind those variables.

Definition 1.21 (Language of predicate logic) A *language* $\mathcal{L}$ is a tuple $(\mathcal{S}, \mathcal{F}, \mathcal{P})$ where $\mathcal{S}$ is a non-empty set of *term sorts* and $\mathcal{F}$ and $\mathcal{P}$ are sets whose elements are called *function symbols* and *predicate symbols*, respectively. Each function symbol has an associated arity, which is an $(n + 1)$-tuple of elements of $\mathcal{S}$, and each predicate symbol has an arity which is an n-tuple of elements of $\mathcal{S}$.

Definition 1.22 (Term) Let $\mathcal{L} = (\mathcal{S}, \mathcal{F}, \mathcal{P})$ be a language and $(\mathcal{V}_s)_{s \in \mathcal{S}}$ a family of infinite, pairwise disjoint sets, indexed by term sorts, whose elements are called *variables*. The set of *terms* of sort s of the language $\mathcal{L}$, for a given family of sets of variables $(\mathcal{V}_s)_{s \in \mathcal{S}}$, is inductively defined as follows.

– Variables of sort s are terms of sort s.
– If f is a symbol of arity $(s_1, \ldots, s_n, s')$ and $t_1, \ldots, t_n$ are terms of sorts $s_1, \ldots, s_n$, then $f(t_1, \ldots, t_n)$ is a term of sort s'.

Definition 1.23 (Proposition) Let $\mathcal{L} = (\mathcal{S}, \mathcal{F}, \mathcal{P})$ be a language and $(\mathcal{V}_s)_{s \in \mathcal{S}}$ a family of infinite, pairwise disjoint sets, indexed by term sorts, whose elements are called *variables*. The set of *propositions* of the language $\mathcal{L}$, for a given family of sets of variables $(\mathcal{V}_s)_{s \in \mathcal{S}}$, is inductively defined as follows.

– If P is a predicate symbol of arity $(s_1, \ldots, s_n)$ and $t_1, \ldots, t_n$ are terms of sort $s_1, \ldots, s_n$, then the expression $P(t_1, \ldots, t_n)$ is a proposition.
– $\top$ and $\bot$ are propositions.
– If A is a proposition, then $\neg A$ is a proposition.
– If A and B are propositions, then $A \wedge B$, $A \vee B$ and $A \Rightarrow B$ are propositions.
– If A is a proposition and x is a variable of sort s, then $\forall_s x\ A$ and $\exists_s x\ A$ are propositions.

The notation $A \Leftrightarrow B$ will be used as an abbreviation for $(A \Rightarrow B) \wedge (B \Rightarrow A)$. A proposition of the form $P(t_1, \ldots, t_n)$ is called *atomic*.

If $\mathcal{S}$ is a singleton, the language has only one term sort and the arity of a function or predicate symbol can be simply specified by a number: the number of arguments of the symbol.

Exercise 1.2 Let $\mathcal{L}$ be a language with only one term sort and symbols $\mathbb{C}$, $\mathbb{N}$, 0, =, $\hat{}$, $\in$ and #, where the symbol $\hat{}$ denotes exponentiation and # cardinal.

1. Represent the proposition

> *Any complex number different from 0 has n nth roots.*

as a proposition in the language $\mathcal{L}$.

2. Which symbols are function symbols and which symbols are predicate symbols?
3. Specify the arity of each symbol.

1.4 Proofs

We would like to distinguish propositions that can be proved, such as $\exists x\ (x = 0 + 1)$, from propositions that cannot be proved, such as $\exists x\ (0 = x + 1)$.

We can distinguish them if we specify a set of rules and define inductively, using those rules, a subset of the set of propositions: the set of *theorems* or *provable propositions*.

Exercise 1.3 Consider the language with one term sort and function symbols 0 of arity zero, and S, *successor*, of arity 1, and a predicate symbol $\leq$ of arity 2. We have the following rules

$$\frac{\forall x\ A}{(t/x)A}$$

$$\frac{A \Rightarrow B \quad A}{B}$$

$$\frac{A \quad B}{A \wedge B}$$

$$\overline{\forall x \forall y \forall z\ ((x \leq y \wedge y \leq z) \Rightarrow x \leq z)}$$

$$\overline{\forall x\ (x \leq S(x))}$$

Show that the proposition

$$0 \leq S(S(0))$$

can be proved.

This kind of proof is usually called a *proof à la Frege and Hilbert*. It is difficult to write a proof in this way because the rules force us to use the same hypotheses for the whole proof. It is hard to translate a standard reasoning pattern: to prove $A \Rightarrow B$, assume A and prove B under this hypothesis. This observation led to the introduction of a notion of pair, consisting of a finite set of hypotheses and a conclusion. Such a pair is called a *sequent*.

Definition 1.24 (Sequent) A *sequent* is a pair $\Gamma \vdash A$, where Γ is a finite set of propositions and A is a proposition.

Definition 1.25 (Natural deduction rules)

$$\frac{}{\Gamma \vdash A} \text{ axiom } A \in \Gamma$$

$$\frac{}{\Gamma \vdash \top} \top\text{-intro}$$

$$\frac{\Gamma \vdash \bot}{\Gamma \vdash A} \bot\text{-elim}$$

$$\frac{\Gamma \vdash A \quad \Gamma \vdash B}{\Gamma \vdash A \wedge B} \wedge\text{-intro}$$

$$\frac{\Gamma \vdash A \wedge B}{\Gamma \vdash A} \wedge\text{-elim}$$

$$\frac{\Gamma \vdash A \wedge B}{\Gamma \vdash B} \wedge\text{-elim}$$

$$\frac{\Gamma \vdash A}{\Gamma \vdash A \vee B} \vee\text{-intro}$$

$$\frac{\Gamma \vdash B}{\Gamma \vdash A \vee B} \vee\text{-intro}$$

$$\frac{\Gamma \vdash A \vee B \quad \Gamma, A \vdash C \quad \Gamma, B \vdash C}{\Gamma \vdash C} \vee\text{-elim}$$

$$\frac{\Gamma, A \vdash B}{\Gamma \vdash A \Rightarrow B} \Rightarrow\text{-intro}$$

$$\frac{\Gamma \vdash A \Rightarrow B \quad \Gamma \vdash A}{\Gamma \vdash B} \Rightarrow\text{-elim}$$

$$\frac{\Gamma, A \vdash \bot}{\Gamma \vdash \neg A} \neg\text{-intro}$$

$$\frac{\Gamma \vdash A \quad \Gamma \vdash \neg A}{\Gamma \vdash \bot} \neg\text{-elim}$$

$$\frac{\Gamma \vdash A}{\Gamma \vdash \forall x \ A} \forall\text{-intro } x \text{ not free in } \Gamma$$

$$\frac{\Gamma \vdash \forall x \ A}{\Gamma \vdash (t/x)A} \forall\text{-elim}$$

$$\frac{\Gamma \vdash (t/x)A}{\Gamma \vdash \exists x \ A} \exists\text{-intro}$$

$$\frac{\Gamma \vdash \exists x \ A \quad \Gamma, A \vdash B}{\Gamma \vdash B} \ \exists\text{-elim } x \text{ not free in } \Gamma, B$$

$$\frac{}{\Gamma \vdash A \lor \neg A} \text{ excluded middle}$$

The rules ⊤-intro, ∧-intro, ∨-intro, ⇒-intro, ¬-intro, ∀-intro and ∃-intro are called *introduction rules* and the rules ⊥-elim, ∧-elim, ∨-elim, ⇒-elim, ¬-elim, ∀-elim and ∃-elim are *elimination rules*. Natural deduction rules are divided into four groups: introduction rules, elimination rules, the *axiom* rule and the rule of the *excluded middle*.

Definition 1.26 (Provable sequent) The set of *provable sequents* is inductively defined by the natural deduction rules.

Definition 1.27 (Proof) A *proof* of a sequent $\Gamma \vdash A$ is a derivation of this sequent, that is, a tree where nodes are labelled by sequents and where the root is labelled by $\Gamma \vdash A$, and such that if a node is labelled by a sequent $\Delta \vdash B$ and its children are labelled by sequents $\Sigma_1 \vdash C_1, \ldots, \Sigma_n \vdash C_n$ then there is a natural deduction rule that allows us to deduce $\Delta \vdash B$ from $\Sigma_1 \vdash C_1, \ldots, \Sigma_n \vdash C_n$.

Therefore, a sequent $\Gamma \vdash A$ is provable if there exists a proof of $\Gamma \vdash A$.

Exercise 1.4 Consider a language with three sorts of terms: *point*, *line* and *scalar*, two predicate symbols $=$ with arity *(scalar, scalar)* and $\in$ with arity *(point, line)* and two function symbols d, *distance*, with arity *(point, point, scalar)* and b, *bisector*, with arity *(point, point, line)*. Let Γ be the set containing the propositions

$$\forall x \forall y \forall z \ (x \in b(y, z) \Leftrightarrow d(x, y) = d(x, z))$$

$$\forall x \forall y \forall z \ ((x = y \land y = z) \Rightarrow x = z)$$

and A a proposition stating that if two bisectors of the triangle xyz intersect at a point w, then the three bisectors intersect at this point:

$$\forall w \forall x \forall y \forall z \ ((w \in b(x, y) \land w \in b(y, z)) \Rightarrow w \in b(x, z))$$

Write a proof of the sequent $\Gamma \vdash A$.

The following a property shows that it is possible to add useless hypotheses in a sequent.

Proposition 1.6 (Weakening) *If the sequent $\Gamma \vdash A$ is provable, then also the sequent $\Gamma, B \vdash A$ is provable.*

Proof By induction over the structure of a proof of $\Gamma \vdash A$.   □

Proposition 1.7 (Double negation) *The following propositions are equivalent.*

1. *The sequent $\Gamma \vdash A$ is provable.*
2. *The sequent $\Gamma, \neg A \vdash \bot$ is provable.*
3. *The sequent $\Gamma \vdash \neg\neg A$ is provable.*

Proof

- (1.) $\Rightarrow$ (2.)
  If the sequent $\Gamma \vdash A$ is provable, then, by Proposition 1.6, so is $\Gamma, \neg A \vdash A$. The sequent $\Gamma, \neg A \vdash \neg A$ is provable using rule *axiom* and thus the sequent $\Gamma, \neg A \vdash \bot$ can be derived using rule $\neg$-elim.
- (2.) $\Rightarrow$ (3.)
  If the sequent $\Gamma, \neg A \vdash \bot$ is provable, then the sequent $\Gamma \vdash \neg\neg A$ is provable with rule $\neg$-intro.
- (3.) $\Rightarrow$ (2.)
  If the sequent $\Gamma \vdash \neg\neg A$ is provable, then, by Proposition 1.6, so is $\Gamma, \neg A \vdash \neg\neg A$. The sequent $\Gamma, \neg A \vdash \neg A$ is provable using rule *axiom* and thus the sequent $\Gamma, \neg A \vdash \bot$ can be derived using rule $\neg$-elim.
- (2.) $\Rightarrow$ (1.)
  If the sequent $\Gamma, \neg A \vdash \bot$ has a proof π, then the sequent $\Gamma \vdash A$ has a proof

$$\cfrac{\cfrac{}{\Gamma \vdash A \vee \neg A}\ \text{excl. middle} \quad \cfrac{}{\Gamma, A \vdash A}\ \text{axiom} \quad \cfrac{\cfrac{\pi}{\Gamma, \neg A \vdash \bot}}{\Gamma, \neg A \vdash A}\ \bot\text{-elim}}{\Gamma \vdash A}\ \vee\text{-elim}$$

$\square$

Proposition 1.8 *The sequent $\vdash \neg\exists x \neg A \Rightarrow \forall x A$ is provable.*

Proof This sequent has a proof

$$\cfrac{\cfrac{\cfrac{}{\neg\exists x\neg A \vdash A \vee \neg A}\ \text{excl. middle} \quad \cfrac{}{\neg\exists x\neg A, A \vdash A}\ \text{axiom} \quad \cfrac{\cfrac{\cfrac{}{\neg\exists x\neg A, \neg A \vdash \neg\exists x\neg A}\ \text{axiom} \quad \cfrac{\cfrac{}{\neg\exists x\neg A, \neg A \vdash \neg A}\ \text{axiom}}{\neg\exists x\neg A, \neg A \vdash \exists x\neg A}\ \exists\text{-intro}}{\neg\exists x\neg A, \neg A \vdash \bot}\ \neg\text{-elim}}{\neg\exists x\neg A, \neg A \vdash A}\ \bot\text{-elim}}{\cfrac{\cfrac{\neg\exists x\neg A \vdash A}{\neg\exists x\neg A \vdash \forall x A}\ \forall\text{-intro}}{\vdash \neg\exists x\neg A \Rightarrow \forall x A}\ \Rightarrow\text{-intro}}}{}\ \vee\text{-elim}$$

$\square$

Definition 1.28 (Theory) A *theory* is a finite or infinite set of closed propositions; the elements of a theory are called *axioms*.

If a theory $\mathcal{T}$ is finite, we say that a proposition A is a *theorem in this theory*, or that the proposition *can be proved in this theory*, if the sequent $\mathcal{T} \vdash A$ is provable. However, in the general case the pair $\mathcal{T} \vdash A$ is not a sequent. We need to give a more general definition.

Definition 1.29 (Theorem)   A proposition A is a *theorem in the theory* $\mathcal{T}$, or *a provable proposition in this theory*, if there exists a finite subset Γ of $\mathcal{T}$ such that the sequent $\Gamma \vdash A$ is provable.

Definition 1.30 (Consistency, contradiction)   A theory $\mathcal{T}$ is *consistent* if there exists some proposition that is not provable in $\mathcal{T}$. Otherwise it is *contradictory*.

Proposition 1.9 *A theory is contradictory if and only if the proposition $\perp$ can be proved in this theory.*

Proof If a theory is contradictory all propositions are provable, in particular the proposition $\perp$. Conversely, if the proposition $\perp$ can be proved in a given theory, then there exists a finite subset Γ of $\mathcal{T}$ such that the sequent $\Gamma \vdash \perp$ has a proof π. Let A be an arbitrary proposition. The sequent $\Gamma \vdash A$ has a proof

$$\cfrac{\cfrac{\pi}{\Gamma \vdash \perp}}{\Gamma \vdash A} \perp\text{-elim}$$

and therefore the proposition A is provable in the theory $\mathcal{T}$. $\square$

Proposition 1.10 *A theory $\mathcal{T}$ is contradictory if and only if there exists a proposition A such that both A and $\neg A$ are provable in this theory.*

Proof If the theory is contradictory, all propositions are provable, therefore the propositions $\top$ and $\neg\top$ are provable.

Conversely, if the propositions A and $\neg A$ are provable in the theory, there are two finite subsets Γ and Γ' such that the sequents $\Gamma \vdash A$ and $\Gamma' \vdash \neg A$ are provable. By Proposition 1.6, the sequents $\Gamma, \Gamma' \vdash A$ and $\Gamma, \Gamma' \vdash \neg A$ have proofs π_1 and π_2. Therefore, the sequent $\Gamma, \Gamma' \vdash \perp$ has a proof

$$\cfrac{\cfrac{\pi_2}{\Gamma, \Gamma' \vdash \neg A} \quad \cfrac{\pi_1}{\Gamma, \Gamma' \vdash A}}{\Gamma, \Gamma' \vdash \perp} \neg\text{-elim}$$

Thus, the proposition $\perp$ is provable in the theory $\mathcal{T}$ and, by Proposition 1.9, the theory $\mathcal{T}$ is contradictory. $\square$

Exercise 1.5   Show that if the sequent $\Gamma \vdash A \Leftrightarrow A'$ is provable and x is not free in Γ then so are the sequents $\Gamma \vdash (A \wedge B) \Leftrightarrow (A' \wedge B)$, $\Gamma \vdash (B \wedge A) \Leftrightarrow (B \wedge A')$, $\Gamma \vdash (A \vee B) \Leftrightarrow (A' \vee B)$, $\Gamma \vdash (B \vee A) \Leftrightarrow (B \vee A')$, $\Gamma \vdash (A \Rightarrow B) \Leftrightarrow (A' \Rightarrow B)$, $\Gamma \vdash (B \Rightarrow A) \Leftrightarrow (B \Rightarrow A')$, $\Gamma \vdash (\neg A) \Leftrightarrow (\neg A')$, $\Gamma \vdash (\forall x\, A) \Leftrightarrow (\forall x\, A')$ and $\Gamma \vdash (\exists x\, A) \Leftrightarrow (\exists x\, A')$.

Exercise 1.6   A many-sorted theory can be *relativised*, that is, transformed into a theory with only one sort of terms. For this, to each function symbol f of arity $(s_1, \ldots, s_n, s')$ we associate a function symbol f' of arity n, and to each predicate symbol P of arity $(s_1, \ldots, s_n)$ we associate a predicate symbol P' of arity n. For each sort s, we introduce a unary predicate symbol S_s. Then, terms and propositions can be translated as follows.

- $|x| = x$,
- $|f(t_1, \ldots, t_n)| = f'(|t_1|, \ldots, |t_n|)$,
- $|P(t_1, \ldots, t_n)| = P'(|t_1|, \ldots, |t_n|)$,
- $|\top| = \top$,
- $|\bot| = \bot$,
- $|\neg A| = \neg|A|$,
- $|A \wedge B| = |A| \wedge |B|, |A \vee B| = |A| \vee |B|, |A \Rightarrow B| = |A| \Rightarrow |B|$,
- $|\forall_s x\ A| = \forall x\ (S_s(x) \Rightarrow |A|), |\exists_s x\ A| = \exists x\ (S_s(x) \wedge |A|)$.

A theory is translated by translating each axiom and adding an axiom

$$\exists x\ S_s(x)$$

for each sort s and an axiom

$$\forall x_1 \ldots \forall x_n\ ((S_{s_1}(x_1) \wedge \cdots \wedge S_{s_n}(x_n)) \Rightarrow (S_{s'}(f'(x_1, \ldots, x_n))))$$

for each function symbol f of arity $(s_1, \ldots, s_n, s')$.

Let T' be the theory consisting of an axiom $S_s(x)$ for each variable of sort s. Show that if the term t has sort s, then the proposition $S_s(|t|)$ is provable in the theory $|T|, T'$.

Show that if the proposition A is provable in the theory T, then the proposition $|A|$ is provable in the theory $|T|, T'$.

Show that if the closed proposition A is provable in the theory T, then the proposition $|A|$ is provable in the theory $|T|$.

1.5 Examples of Theories

Definition 1.31 (Equality axioms) Consider a language with predicates $=_s$ of sort (s, s) for some sorts s. The *axioms of equality* for this language are the following.

For each sort s for which there is an equality symbol, we have the identity axiom

$$\forall_s x\ (x =_s x)$$

For each function symbol f of arity $(s_1, \ldots, s_n, s')$ such that the sort s' has an equality symbol and for each natural number i such that the sort s_i has an equality symbol, we have the axiom

$$\forall x_1 \ldots \forall x_i \forall x_i' \ldots \forall x_n\ (x_i =_{s_i} x_i' \Rightarrow f(x_1, \ldots, x_i, \ldots, x_n) =_{s'} f(x_1, \ldots, x_i', \ldots, x_n))$$

For each predicate symbol P of arity $(s_1, \ldots, s_n)$ and each natural number i such that the sort s_i has an equality symbol, we have the axiom

$$\forall x_1 \ldots \forall x_i \forall x_i' \forall x_n\ (x_i =_{s_i} x_i' \Rightarrow (P(x_1, \ldots, x_i, \ldots, x_n) \Rightarrow P(x_1, \ldots, x_i', \ldots, x_n)))$$

Exercise 1.7 Give a proof for each of the following propositions in the theory of equality.

$$\forall_s x \forall_s y \forall_s z \ (x =_s y \Rightarrow (y =_s z \Rightarrow x =_s z))$$

$$\forall_s x \forall_s y \ (x =_s y \Rightarrow y =_s x)$$

Definition 1.32 (The theory of classes) Consider a language with two term sorts: ι for objects and κ for classes of objects, and with an arbitrary number of function symbols of arity $(\iota, \ldots, \iota, \iota)$ and predicate symbols of arity $(\iota, \ldots, \iota)$, as well as a predicate symbol ϵ of arity (ι, κ).

The *theory of classes* for this language includes an axiom

$$\forall x_1 \ldots \forall x_n \exists c \forall y \ (y \in c \Leftrightarrow A)$$

for each proposition A that does not contain the symbol ϵ and whose free variables are included in $x_1, \ldots, x_n, y$. This set of axioms is known as the *comprehension schema*.

Definition 1.33 (Arithmetic) The language of arithmetic includes two term sorts ι and κ, a constant 0 of sort ι, function symbols S, *successor*, of arity (ι, ι), $+$ and $\times$ of arity (ι, ι, ι) and predicate symbols ϵ of arity (ι, κ) and $=$ of arity (ι, ι). In addition to the equality axioms and the comprehension schema, we have the axioms for successor

$$\forall x \forall y \ (S(x) = S(y) \Rightarrow x = y)$$

$$\forall x \ \neg(0 = S(x))$$

the induction axiom

$$\forall c \ (0 \in c \Rightarrow \forall x \ (x \in c \Rightarrow S(x) \in c) \Rightarrow \forall y \ y \in c)$$

and the axioms for addition and multiplication

$$\forall y \ (0 + y = y)$$

$$\forall x \forall y \ (S(x) + y = S(x + y))$$

$$\forall y \ (0 \times y = 0)$$

$$\forall x \forall y \ (S(x) \times y = (x \times y) + y)$$

Exercise 1.8 (Induction schema) This exercise relies on Exercise 1.5, which should be done prior to this one.

Show that, for each proposition A in the language of arithmetic that does not contain the symbol ϵ and whose free variables are included in $x_1, \ldots, x_n, y$, the proposition

$$\forall x_1 \ldots \forall x_n \left((0/y)A \Rightarrow \forall m \left((m/y)A \Rightarrow (S(m)/y)A\right) \Rightarrow \forall n \, (n/y)A\right)$$

is provable in the theory of arithmetic.

Definition 1.34 (Naive set theory) The language of the naive theory of sets has one sort and a binary predicate symbol $\in$. It contains an axiom of the form

$$\forall x_1 \ldots \forall x_n \exists a \forall y \, (y \in a \Leftrightarrow A)$$

for each proposition A with free variables in $x_1, \ldots, x_n, y$.

Exercise 1.9 (Russell's paradox) Show that the sequent

$$\forall y \, (y \in a \Leftrightarrow \neg y \in y) \vdash \bot$$

is provable and then deduce that the naive theory of sets is contradictory. Why is it that this paradox does not apply to the theory of classes?

Definition 1.35 (The theory of binary classes) Consider a language with two term sorts ι for objects and σ for binary classes, with an arbitrary number of function symbols of arity $(\iota, \ldots, \iota, \iota)$ and predicate symbols of arity $(\iota, \ldots, \iota)$, as well as a predicate symbol ϵ_2 with arity (ι, ι, σ).

The theory of binary classes includes an axiom of the form

$$\forall x_1 \ldots \forall x_n \exists r \forall y \forall z \, (y, z \, \epsilon_2 \, r \Leftrightarrow A)$$

for each proposition A that does not contain the symbol ϵ_2 and whose free variables are in $x_1, \ldots, x_n, y, z$. This set of axioms is usually called *binary comprehension schema*.

Definition 1.36 (ZF: Zermelo-Fraenkel set theory) The language of Zermelo-Fraenkel set theory has two term sorts ι and σ, a predicate symbol ϵ_2 of arity (ι, ι, σ), a predicate symbol $=$ of arity (ι, ι) and a predicate symbol $\in$ of arity (ι, ι) (to represent that a set is a member of another set). In addition to the equality axioms and the binary comprehension schema, Zermelo-Fraenkel set theory has the following axioms.

The *axiom of extensionality* postulates that two sets are equal if they have the same elements,

$$\forall x \forall y \, ((\forall z \, (z \in x \Leftrightarrow z \in y)) \Rightarrow x = y)$$

The *axiom of union* postulates that if we have a set x with elements $v_0, v_1, \ldots$, then we can build the union of the sets $v_0, v_1, \ldots$

$$\forall x \exists z \forall w \, (w \in z \Leftrightarrow (\exists v \, (w \in v \land v \in x)))$$

The *axiom of the power set* postulates that if we have a set x we can build a set where the elements are all the subsets of x

$$\forall x \exists z \forall w \ (w \in z \Leftrightarrow (\forall v \ (v \in w \Rightarrow v \in x)))$$

The *axiom of infinity* postulates that we can build an infinite set. Let *Empty* be the proposition $\forall y \ (\neg(y \in x))$. We denote by *Empty*$[t]$ the proposition (t/x)*Empty*. Let *Succ* be the proposition $\forall z \ (z \in y \Leftrightarrow (z \in x \lor z = x))$. We denote by *Succ*$[t, u]$ the proposition $(t/x, u/y)$*Succ*. Intuitively, this means that u is the set $t \cup \{t\}$. The axiom of infinity is

$$\exists I \ (\forall x \ (Empty[x] \Rightarrow x \in I) \land \forall x \forall y \ ((x \in I \land Succ[x, y]) \Rightarrow y \in I))$$

The *axiom of replacement* postulates that if we have a set a and a functional binary class r, we can build the set of the objects associated to an element of a by the binary class r. Let *functional* be the proposition $\forall y \forall z \forall z' \ ((y, z \ \epsilon_2 \ r \land y, z' \ \epsilon_2 \ r) \Rightarrow z = z')$. We denote by *functional*$[t]$ the proposition (t/r)*functional*. The axiom of replacement is

$$\forall r \ (functional[r] \Rightarrow \forall a \exists b \forall z \ (z \in b \Leftrightarrow \exists y \ (y \in a \land y, z \ \epsilon_2 \ r)))$$

Exercise 1.10 (Replacement Schema) This exercise relies on Exercise 1.5, which should be done prior to this one.

Let A be a proposition that does not contain the symbol ϵ_2 and with free variables in $x_1, \ldots, x_n, y, z$. We denote by $A[t, u]$ the proposition $(t/y, u/z)A$. Show that the proposition

$$\forall x_1 \ldots \forall x_m \ ((\forall y \forall z \forall z' \ ((A[y, z] \land A[y, z']) \Rightarrow z = z'))$$
$$\Rightarrow \forall a \exists b \forall z \ (z \in b \Leftrightarrow \exists y \ (y \in a \land A[y, z])))$$

is provable in *ZF*.

Exercise 1.11 (Separation Schema) This exercise relies on Exercises 1.5 and 1.10, which should be done prior to this one.

Let A be a proposition that does not contain the symbol ϵ_2 and with free variables in $x_1, \ldots, x_n, y$. We denote by $A[t]$ the proposition $(t/y)A$. Show that the proposition

$$\forall x_1 \ldots \forall x_n \forall a \exists b \forall y \ (y \in b \Leftrightarrow (y \in a \land A[y]))$$

is provable in *ZF*.

Exercise 1.12 (Theorem of the empty set) This exercise relies on Exercise 1.11, which should be done prior to this one.

Show that the proposition

$$\exists b \ Empty[b]$$

is provable in *ZF*.

Exercise 1.13 (Theorem of pairing) This exercise relies on Exercise 1.10, which should be done prior to this one.

Let *One* be the proposition $\forall y\ (y \in x \Leftrightarrow Empty[y])$. We denote by *One*[*t*] the proposition $(t/x)One$. Intuitively, this means that $t = \{\emptyset\}$. Let *Two* be the proposition $\forall y\ (y \in x \Leftrightarrow (Empty[y] \vee One[y]))$. We denote by *Two*[*t*] the proposition $(t/x)Two$. Intuitively, this means that $t = \{\emptyset, \{\emptyset\}\}$.

Show that the propositions $\exists x\ Empty[x]$, $\exists x\ One[x]$, $\exists x\ Two[x]$ and $\forall x\ \neg(Empty[x] \wedge One[x])$ are provable in *ZF*.

Show that the proposition

$$\forall x \forall y \exists z \forall w\ (w \in z \Leftrightarrow (w = x \vee w = y))$$

is provable in *ZF*.

Exercise 1.14 (Pairing) This exercise relies on Exercise 1.13, which should be done prior to this one.

In set theory, the ordered pair (a, b) is a set containing the elements $\{a\}$ and $\{a, b\}$. Write a proposition, using only the symbols $=$ and $\in$, to state that the pair consisting of the elements x and y is equal to z. Write a proposition to state that the ordered pair consisting of the elements x and y is an element of z.

Exercise 1.15 (Union of two sets) This exercise relies on Exercise 1.13, which should be done prior to this one.

Show that the proposition

$$\forall x \forall y \exists z \forall w\ (w \in z \Leftrightarrow (w \in x \vee w \in y))$$

is provable in *ZF*.

Exercise 1.16 This exercise relies on Exercises 1.12 and 1.15, which should be done prior to this one.

Show that the following propositions are provable.

$$\exists x\ Empty[x]$$

$$\forall x \exists y\ Succ[x, y]$$

$$\forall x \forall y\ ((Empty[x] \wedge Empty[y]) \Rightarrow x = y)$$

$$\forall x \forall y \forall y'\ ((Succ[x, y] \wedge Succ[x, y']) \Rightarrow y = y')$$

$$\forall x \forall y\ \neg(Succ[x, y] \wedge Empty[y])$$

Exercise 1.17 (Von Neumann's natural numbers) This exercise relies on Exercises 1.11 and 1.16, which should be done prior to this one.

In set theory, the natural numbers are defined by the following sets $0 = \emptyset$, $1 = \{0\}$, $2 = \{0, 1\}$, $3 = \{0, 1, 2\}$, …. Thus, a set is a natural number if it belongs to all the sets that contain 0 and are closed under successor. Write a proposition N with a free variable x and using only the symbols $=$ and $\in$ to state that x is a natural numbers. We denote by $N[t]$ the proposition $(t/x)N$. Note that all the natural numbers belong to the set I whose existence is postulated in the axiom of infinity. Prove the proposition

$$\exists \mathbb{N}\ (x \in \mathbb{N} \Leftrightarrow N[x])$$

Write a proposition specifying the induction principle: if a set contains 0 and is closed under successor, then it contains all the natural numbers. Show that this proposition is provable in ZF.

Exercise 1.18 This exercise relies on Exercises 1.11, 1.13, 1.14, 1.16 and 1.17, which should be done prior to this one.

Let *succ* be the functional binary class defined by comprehension as follows: $x, y \in_2 succ \Leftrightarrow Succ[x, y]$. The axiom of infinity postulates the existence of a set containing 0 and closed under the functional binary class *succ*. In this exercise we will show that as a consequence of this axiom, if a is an arbitrary set and r an arbitrary functional binary class, then there exists a set containing a and closed under r. That is, we aim at proving the proposition

$$\forall a \forall r\ (functional[r] \Rightarrow \exists E\ (a \in E \wedge \forall y \forall y'\ ((y \in E \wedge y, y' \in_2 r) \Rightarrow y' \in E)))$$

To do this, we assume *functional[r]* and try to prove the proposition $\exists E\ (a \in E \wedge \forall y \forall y'\ ((y \in E \wedge y, y' \in_2 r) \Rightarrow y' \in E)))$.

Let A be the proposition

$$n \in \mathbb{N} \wedge \forall g\ (((\forall p\ (Empty[p] \Rightarrow (p, a) \in g))$$
$$\wedge \forall p \forall p' \forall y \forall y'\ ((p \in n \wedge (p, y) \in g \wedge Succ[p, p'] \wedge y, y' \in_2 r) \Rightarrow (p', y') \in g))$$
$$\Rightarrow (n, x) \in g)$$

We denote by $A[t, u]$ the proposition $(t/n, u/x)A$

1. Prove the propositions

$$\forall n\ (Empty[n] \Rightarrow A[n, a])$$

$$\forall n \forall n' \forall x \forall x'\ ((A[n, x] \wedge Succ[n, n'] \wedge x, x' \in_2 r) \Rightarrow A[n', x'])$$

2. We now want to prove the proposition

$$\forall n \forall x \forall y\ ((A[n, x] \wedge A[n, y]) \Rightarrow x = y)$$

First, we will assume

$$\forall p \forall x \forall y\ ((p \in n \wedge A[p, x] \wedge A[p, y]) \Rightarrow x = y)$$

and prove

$$\forall x \forall y \ ((A[n, x] \wedge A[n, y]) \Rightarrow x = y)$$

Let r' be the binary class defined by comprehension as follows:

$$p, c \in_2 r' \Leftrightarrow \exists y \ (c = (p, y) \wedge ((Empty[p] \wedge y = a)$$
$$\vee \ \exists m \exists w \ (m \in n \wedge A[m, w] \wedge Succ[m, p] \wedge w, y \in_2 r)))$$

Show that the binary class r' is functional. Let G be the image of successor of n under the binary class r', which can be built using the replacement axiom.
    Prove the proposition $\forall p \forall x \ ((p, x) \in G \Rightarrow A[p, x])$.
    Prove the propositions

$$\forall p \ (Empty[p] \Rightarrow (p, a) \in G)$$

$$\forall p \forall p' \forall x \forall x' \ ((p \in n \wedge (p, x) \in G \wedge Succ[p, p'] \wedge x, x' \in_2 r) \Rightarrow (p', x') \in G))$$

Deduce the proposition

$$\forall x \ (A[n, x] \Rightarrow (n, x) \in G)$$

Prove the proposition

$$\forall n \forall x \forall y \ (((n, x) \in G \wedge (n, y) \in G) \Rightarrow x = y)$$

Prove the proposition

$$\forall n \forall x \forall y \ ((A[n, x] \wedge A[n, y]) \Rightarrow x = y)$$

Let C be the subset of $\mathbb{N}$ containing all n such that $\forall p \forall x \forall y \ ((p \in n \wedge A[p, x] \wedge A[p, y]) \Rightarrow x = y)$. Show that the set C contains 0 and is closed under successor. Show that it contains all the natural numbers. Then deduce

$$\forall n \forall x \forall y \ ((A[n, x] \wedge A[n, y]) \Rightarrow x = y)$$

3. Let s be the binary class defined by comprehension using the proposition A. Show that the binary class s is functional. Let E be the image of $\mathbb{N}$ under s, built using the axiom of replacement. Prove the propositions

$$a \in E$$

$$\forall y \forall y' \ ((y \in E \wedge y, y' \in_2 r) \Rightarrow y' \in E)$$

1.6 Variations on the Principle of the Excluded Middle

We defined the principle of the excluded middle using the rule

$$\frac{}{\Gamma \vdash A \vee \neg A}\ \text{excluded middle}$$

but there are many alternative definitions.

1.6.1 Double Negation

As a first alternative, we could replace the rule shown above by the rule

$$\frac{\Gamma \vdash \neg\neg A}{\Gamma \vdash A}\ \text{double negation}$$

which defines an equivalent system.

Proposition 1.11 *The sequents that can be proved in natural deduction and in the system where the rule of the* excluded middle *is replaced by the* double negation *rule are exactly the same.*

Proof We need to show that if the sequent $\Gamma \vdash \neg\neg A$ is provable in natural deduction, then the sequent $\Gamma \vdash A$ is provable as well. This is a consequence of Proposition 1.7.

   We also need to show that all sequents of the form $\Gamma \vdash A \vee \neg A$ are provable in the system in which the rule of the *excluded middle* is replaced by the *double negation* rule. The following derivation proves the sequent $\Gamma \vdash A \vee \neg A$.

$$\frac{\dfrac{\dfrac{\Gamma, \neg(A \vee \neg A), A \vdash \neg(A \vee \neg A)\ \text{axiom} \qquad \dfrac{\dfrac{\Gamma, \neg(A \vee \neg A), A \vdash A\ \text{axiom}}{\Gamma, \neg(A \vee \neg A), A \vdash A \vee \neg A}\ \vee\text{-intro}}{}}{\dfrac{\Gamma, \neg(A \vee \neg A), A \vdash \bot}{\Gamma, \neg(A \vee \neg A) \vdash \neg A}\ \neg\text{-intro}}\ \neg\text{-elim} \qquad \Gamma, \neg(A \vee \neg A) \vdash \neg(A \vee \neg A)\ \text{axiom}}{\dfrac{\dfrac{\Gamma, \neg(A \vee \neg A) \vdash A \vee \neg A}{\Gamma, \neg(A \vee \neg A) \vdash \bot}\ \vee\text{-intro}}{\dfrac{\Gamma \vdash \neg\neg(A \vee \neg A)}{\Gamma \vdash A \vee \neg A}\ \text{double negation}}\ \neg\text{-intro}}$$

$\square$

1.6.2 Multi-conclusion Sequents

It may seem surprising that if we change the form of the sequents and consider sequents with several conclusions then the principle of the excluded middle can be expressed without introducing a new rule.

This can be explained by analysing the proof given above. If the context Γ is empty and the proposition A is just a 0-ary predicate symbol, it boils down to proving the sequent $\vdash A \vee \neg A$. Using the rule $\vee$-intro, we are left with the sequent $\vdash A$ or the sequent $\vdash \neg A$; neither of them is provable. The rule $\vee$-intro replaces the conclusion $A \vee \neg A$ of the sequent to be proved by either the conclusion A or the conclusion $\neg A$, and in doing so it destroys the proposition $A \vee \neg A$. The *double negation* rule and the $\neg$-intro rule allow us to save a copy of this proposition, by memorising it in the hypothesis $\neg(A \vee \neg A)$. We can then use this hypothesis as many times as we want, by moving it to the conclusion of the sequent using the rules $\neg$-elim and *axiom*. In the proof given above, we use the proposition twice, in order to use twice the rule $\vee$-intro and obtain first $\neg A$ and then A. The conclusion $\neg A$ becomes the hypothesis A and since we have A both as an assumption and a conclusion, we can use the rule *axiom*.

Another alternative would be to leave the proposition $A \vee \neg A$ in the conclusion of the sequent, but of course this will require a syntax for sequents where not only multiple hypotheses but also multiple conclusions are permitted. We will also need a rule to duplicate conclusions

$$\frac{\Gamma \vdash A, A, \Delta}{\Gamma \vdash A, \Delta} \text{ contraction}$$

In addition, sequents should be defined as pairs of finite multiset instead of pairs of finite sets.

Intuitively, a proposition in the conclusions of a sequent plays the same rôle as its negation in the hypotheses of the sequent. Thus, the comma separating two hypotheses in a sequent can be thought of as an *and* whereas the one separating the conclusions behaves like an *or*.

The proof given above can be rewritten as follows.

$$\cfrac{\cfrac{\cfrac{\cfrac{\overline{\Gamma, A \vdash \bot, A} \text{ axiom}}{\Gamma, A \vdash \bot, A \vee \neg A} \text{ $\vee$-intro}}{\Gamma \vdash \neg A, A \vee \neg A} \text{ $\neg$-intro}}{\Gamma \vdash A \vee \neg A, A \vee \neg A} \text{ $\vee$-intro}}{\Gamma \vdash A \vee \neg A} \text{ contraction}$$

This leads us to an alternative definition of natural deduction.

Definition 1.37 (Rules of system D')

$$\frac{}{\Gamma \vdash A, \Delta} \text{ axiom } A \in \Gamma$$

$$\frac{\Gamma \vdash A, A, \Delta}{\Gamma \vdash A, \Delta} \text{ contraction}$$

$$\frac{}{\Gamma \vdash \top, \Delta} \text{ $\top$-intro}$$

$$\frac{\Gamma \vdash \bot, \Delta}{\Gamma \vdash A, \Delta} \bot\text{-elim}$$

$$\frac{\Gamma \vdash A, \Delta \quad \Gamma \vdash B, \Delta}{\Gamma \vdash A \wedge B, \Delta} \wedge\text{-intro}$$

$$\frac{\Gamma \vdash A \wedge B, \Delta}{\Gamma \vdash A, \Delta} \wedge\text{-elim}$$

$$\frac{\Gamma \vdash A \wedge B, \Delta}{\Gamma \vdash B, \Delta} \wedge\text{-elim}$$

$$\frac{\Gamma \vdash A, \Delta}{\Gamma \vdash A \vee B, \Delta} \vee\text{-intro}$$

$$\frac{\Gamma \vdash B, \Delta}{\Gamma \vdash A \vee B, \Delta} \vee\text{-intro}$$

$$\frac{\Gamma \vdash A \vee B, \Delta \quad \Gamma, A \vdash C, \Delta \quad \Gamma, B \vdash C, \Delta}{\Gamma \vdash C, \Delta} \vee\text{-elim}$$

$$\frac{\Gamma, A \vdash B, \Delta}{\Gamma \vdash A \Rightarrow B, \Delta} \Rightarrow\text{-intro}$$

$$\frac{\Gamma \vdash A \Rightarrow B, \Delta \quad \Gamma \vdash A, \Delta}{\Gamma \vdash B, \Delta} \Rightarrow\text{-elim}$$

$$\frac{\Gamma, A \vdash \bot, \Delta}{\Gamma \vdash \neg A, \Delta} \neg\text{-intro}$$

$$\frac{\Gamma \vdash A, \Delta \quad \Gamma \vdash \neg A, \Delta}{\Gamma \vdash \bot, \Delta} \neg\text{-elim}$$

$$\frac{\Gamma \vdash A, \Delta}{\Gamma \vdash \forall x \, A, \Delta} \forall\text{-intro } x \text{ not free in } \Gamma, \Delta$$

$$\frac{\Gamma \vdash \forall x \, A, \Delta}{\Gamma \vdash (t/x)A, \Delta} \forall\text{-elim}$$

$$\frac{\Gamma \vdash (t/x)A, \Delta}{\Gamma \vdash \exists x \, A, \Delta} \exists\text{-intro}$$

$$\frac{\Gamma \vdash \exists x \, A, \Delta \quad \Gamma, A \vdash B, \Delta}{\Gamma \vdash B, \Delta} \exists\text{-elim } x \text{ not free in } \Gamma, \Delta, B$$

Proposition 1.12 *A sequent $\Gamma \vdash A$ is provable in natural deduction if and only if it is provable in the system D'.*

Proof If there is a proof for the sequent $\Gamma \vdash A$ in natural deduction, we can prove by induction over the structure of this proof that the sequent is provable in the system D'. All the natural deduction rules are also rules in system D', except for the rule of the *excluded middle*, but we have already seen that sequents of the form $\Gamma \vdash A \vee \neg A$ are provable in system D'.

To prove the converse, thanks to Proposition 1.7 it is sufficient to show that if the sequent $\Gamma \vdash A$ is provable in the system D', then the sequent $\Gamma, \neg A \vdash \bot$ is provable in natural deduction. More generally, we can prove that if the sequent $\Gamma \vdash \Delta$ is provable in the system D', then the sequent $\Gamma, \neg \Delta \vdash \bot$ is provable in natural deduction, where $\neg \Delta$ is the set containing the negations of all the propositions in Δ. This can be shown by induction over the structure of the proof of $\Gamma \vdash \Delta$ in system D'. If the proof has the form

$$\frac{\dfrac{\pi}{\Gamma \vdash A, A, \Delta'}}{\Gamma \vdash A, \Delta'} \text{ contraction}$$

then the sets $\Gamma, \neg A, \neg A, \neg \Delta$ and $\Gamma, \neg A, \neg \Delta$ are identical, and by induction the sequent $\Gamma, \neg A, \neg \Delta \vdash \bot$ is provable in natural deduction. If the proof has the form

$$\frac{\dfrac{\pi_1}{\Gamma_1 \vdash A_1, \Delta'} \quad \ldots \quad \dfrac{\pi_n}{\Gamma_n \vdash A_n, \Delta'}}{\Gamma \vdash B, \Delta'} r$$

where r is a rule in the system D' different from *contraction*, then by induction the sequents $\Gamma_1, \neg A_1, \neg \Delta' \vdash \bot, \ldots, \Gamma_n, \neg A_n, \neg \Delta' \vdash \bot$ are provable in natural deduction. The sequents $\Gamma_1, \neg \Delta' \vdash A_1, \ldots, \Gamma_n, \neg \Delta' \vdash A_n$ are also provable, as a consequence of Proposition 1.7. Using the natural deduction rule corresponding to r in D', we can then build a natural deduction proof for the sequent $\Gamma, \neg \Delta' \vdash B$ and using the Proposition 1.7 again, we obtain a proof of the sequent $\Gamma, \neg B, \neg \Delta' \vdash \bot$.   □

The following property of system D' is analogous to Proposition 1.6.

Proposition 1.13 (Weakening) *If the sequent $\Gamma \vdash \Delta$ is provable in the system D' then the sequents $\Gamma, A \vdash \Delta$ and $\Gamma \vdash A, \Delta$ are also provable.*

Proof By induction over the structure of the proof of $\Gamma \vdash \Delta$.   □

When a notion of truth is defined, as we have done in this chapter, one cannot avoid wondering whether the tools used in the definition are "legitimate". On one hand, it is not possible to start from scratch and assume that we know nothing. If we do not have a language, a basic set of concepts, and an idea of truth, how could we give a definition? On the other hand, if we already have a working notion of mathematical truth, the definition is trivial: the proposition "Every vector space has a basis" is true if every vector space has a basis.

In this chapter, we have given a definition that can be seen as a middle ground between the two extreme approaches mentioned above: the proposition "Every vector space has a basis" is true if there is a proof π of this proposition.

To present this definition, we have relied on certain mathematical notions, such as the notion of a natural number, finite set, or tree. However, a proof is built out of a finite number of symbols and the fact that a sequence of symbols is, or is not, a proof of a proposition can be easily verified: it is sufficient to check that each step in the proof consists of the application of a natural deduction rule. The proposition "The sequence of symbols π is a proof of the proposition 'Every vector space has a basis'" uses only finite objects and verifiable relations between these objects. This kind of proposition is said to be *combinatorial*. The notion of truth that is needed in order to understand the definitions given in this chapter is simply the elementary notion of truth of combinatorial propositions.

Chapter 2
Models

After defining the concept of proof in the previous chapter, we will now study in this chapter some properties of proofs. In particular, we will introduce tools that will allow us to prove *independence results* of the form: the proposition A is not provable in the theory $\mathcal{T}$.

To define the notion of proof we had to restrict ourselves to combinatorial propositions, but to study properties of proofs we will not need to impose any restriction. Any mathematical tool can be used to show independence results.

2.1 The Notion of a Model

Definition 2.1 (Model) Let $\mathcal{L} = (\mathcal{S}, \mathcal{F}, \mathcal{P})$ be a language. A *model* of this language is a structure $\mathcal{M} = ((\mathcal{M}_s)_{s \in \mathcal{S}}, \mathcal{B}, \mathcal{B}^+, (\hat{f})_{f \in \mathcal{F}}, (\hat{P})_{P \in \mathcal{P}}, \hat{\top}, \hat{\bot}, \hat{\neg}, \hat{\wedge}, \hat{\vee}, \hat{\Rightarrow}, \hat{\forall}, \hat{\exists})$ consisting of

- a non-empty set $\mathcal{M}_s$ for each sort s in $\mathcal{S}$,
- a non-empty set $\mathcal{B}$, and a subset $\mathcal{B}^+$ of $\mathcal{B}$,
- a function $\hat{f}$ from $\mathcal{M}_{s_1} \times \cdots \times \mathcal{M}_{s_n}$ to $\mathcal{M}_{s'}$ for each function symbol $f \in \mathcal{F}$ of arity $(s_1, \ldots, s_n, s')$,
- a function $\hat{P}$ from $\mathcal{M}_{s_1} \times \cdots \times \mathcal{M}_{s_n}$ to $\mathcal{B}$ for each predicate symbol $P \in \mathcal{P}$ of arity $(s_1, \ldots, s_n)$,
- two distinguished elements $\hat{\top}$ and $\hat{\bot}$ of $\mathcal{B}$, and
- a function $\hat{\neg}$ from $\mathcal{B}$ to $\mathcal{B}$, three functions $\hat{\wedge}$, $\hat{\vee}$ and $\hat{\Rightarrow}$ from $\mathcal{B} \times \mathcal{B}$ to $\mathcal{B}$ and two functions $\hat{\forall}$ and $\hat{\exists}$ from $\wp^+(\mathcal{B})$ to $\mathcal{B}$ where $\wp^+(\mathcal{B})$ is the set of all non-empty subsets of $\mathcal{B}$.

Let $\mathcal{L} = (\mathcal{S}, \mathcal{F}, \mathcal{P})$ be a language and $\mathcal{M}$ a model of this language. We will define a function $[\![\ ]\!]$ associating to each term t of sort s an element $[\![t]\!]$ of $\mathcal{M}_s$, and to each proposition A an element $[\![A]\!]$ of $\mathcal{B}$. In addition, this function will be a morphism, that is, $[\![f(t_1, \ldots, t_n)]\!] = \hat{f}([\![t_1]\!], \ldots, [\![t_n]\!])$, $[\![P(t_1, \ldots, t_n)]\!] =$

G. Dowek, *Proofs and Algorithms*, Undergraduate Topics in Computer Science, DOI 10.1007/978-0-85729-121-9_2, © Springer-Verlag London Limited 2011

$\hat{P}(\llbracket t_1 \rrbracket, \ldots, \llbracket t_n \rrbracket)$, $\llbracket A \wedge B \rrbracket = \hat{\wedge}(\llbracket A \rrbracket, \llbracket B \rrbracket), \ldots$ It is well known that a morphism between vector spaces is fully defined by the image of a basis. Similarly, a morphism between a language and a model is fully defined by the image of the variables. Therefore, we have the following definition.

Definition 2.2 (Valuation) Let $\mathcal{L} = (\mathcal{S}, \mathcal{F}, \mathcal{P})$ be a language, $\mathcal{M}$ a model of this language and $(\mathcal{V}_s)_{s \in \mathcal{S}}$ a family of sets of variables. A *valuation* is a function, with a finite domain, that maps the variables $x_1, \ldots, x_n$ of sorts $s_1, \ldots, s_n$ to elements $a_1, \ldots, a_n$ of $\mathcal{M}_{s_1}, \ldots, \mathcal{M}_{s_n}$.

The valuation that associates the element a_1 to the variable $x_1, \ldots, a_n$ to the variable x_n will be written $x_1 = a_1, \ldots, x_n = a_n$. Let ϕ be a valuation, x a variable and a an element of $\mathcal{M}$, we denote by $(\phi, x = a)$ the valuation that coincides with ϕ everywhere except on x where it has the value a.

A valuation can be extended into a morphism $\llbracket \ \rrbracket_\phi$ between terms and propositions of the language $\mathcal{L}$ with free variables in the domain of ϕ, and the model $\mathcal{M}$. The extension is defined as follows: $\llbracket x \rrbracket_\phi$ is $\phi(x)$, $\llbracket f(t_1, \ldots, t_n) \rrbracket_\phi$ is $\hat{f}(\llbracket t_1 \rrbracket_\phi, \ldots, \llbracket t_n \rrbracket_\phi), \ldots$ The definition is more complicated for bound variables and quantifiers. Indeed, the free variables of the proposition A are the free variables of $\forall x\ A$ and possibly x. To define $\llbracket \forall x\ A \rrbracket_\phi$ we must first consider all the values $\llbracket A \rrbracket_{\phi, x=a}$ obtained by associating x to an arbitrary element a of $\mathcal{M}_s$; we obtain in this way a non-empty subset of $\mathcal{B}$. We then apply the function $\hat{\forall}$ (which is a function from the set of all non-empty subsets of $\mathcal{B}$ to $\mathcal{B}$) to this set.

Definition 2.3 (Denotation) Let $\mathcal{L} = (\mathcal{S}, \mathcal{F}, \mathcal{P})$ be a language, $\mathcal{M}$ a model of this language, $(\mathcal{V}_s)_{s \in \mathcal{S}}$ a family of sets of variables, ϕ a valuation and t a term with free variables in the domain of ϕ. The *denotation* of the term t in the model $\mathcal{M}$ under the valuation ϕ is the element $\llbracket t \rrbracket_\phi$ of $\mathcal{M}_s$ defined by induction over the structure of t as follows.

- $\llbracket x \rrbracket_\phi = \phi(x)$,
- $\llbracket f(t_1, \ldots, t_n) \rrbracket_\phi = \hat{f}(\llbracket t_1 \rrbracket_\phi, \ldots, \llbracket t_n \rrbracket_\phi)$.

Let A be a proposition with free variables in the domain of ϕ. The *denotation* of the proposition A in the model $\mathcal{M}$ under the valuation ϕ is an element $\llbracket A \rrbracket_\phi$ of $\mathcal{B}$ defined by induction over the structure of A as follows.

- $\llbracket P(t_1, \ldots, t_n) \rrbracket_\phi = \hat{P}(\llbracket t_1 \rrbracket_\phi, \ldots, \llbracket t_n \rrbracket_\phi)$,
- $\llbracket \top \rrbracket_\phi = \hat{\top}$,
- $\llbracket \bot \rrbracket_\phi = \hat{\bot}$,
- $\llbracket \neg A \rrbracket_\phi = \hat{\neg}(\llbracket A \rrbracket_\phi)$,
- $\llbracket A \wedge B \rrbracket_\phi = \hat{\wedge}(\llbracket A \rrbracket_\phi, \llbracket B \rrbracket_\phi)$,
- $\llbracket A \vee B \rrbracket_\phi = \hat{\vee}(\llbracket A \rrbracket_\phi, \llbracket B \rrbracket_\phi)$,
- $\llbracket A \Rightarrow B \rrbracket_\phi = \hat{\Rightarrow}(\llbracket A \rrbracket_\phi, \llbracket B \rrbracket_\phi)$,
- $\llbracket \forall x\ A \rrbracket_\phi = \hat{\forall}(\{\llbracket A \rrbracket_{\phi, x=a} \mid a \in \mathcal{M}_s\})$,
- $\llbracket \exists x\ A \rrbracket_\phi = \hat{\exists}(\{\llbracket A \rrbracket_{\phi, x=a} \mid a \in \mathcal{M}_s\})$.

Proposition 2.1 (Substitution)

$$[(u/x)t]_\phi = [t]_{\phi, x = [u]_\phi}$$

$$[(u/x)A]_\phi = [A]_{\phi, x = [u]_\phi}$$

Proof By induction over the structure of t and the structure of A.   □

Definition 2.4 (Validity) Let $\mathcal{L} = (\mathcal{S}, \mathcal{F}, \mathcal{P})$ be a language, $\mathcal{M}$ a model of this language, and $(\mathcal{V}_s)_{s \in \mathcal{S}}$ a family of sets of variables. A closed proposition is *valid* in the model $\mathcal{M}$ if $[A]_\emptyset$ is in the set $\mathcal{B}^+$. In this case we will also say that $\mathcal{M}$ is a *model* of A.

A proposition A with free variables $x_1, \ldots, x_n$ is *valid* in the model $\mathcal{M}$ if the closed proposition $\forall x_1 \ldots \forall x_n \, A$ is valid, that is, if for every valuation ϕ whose domain includes the variables $x_1, \ldots, x_n$, $[A]_\phi$ belongs to the set $\mathcal{B}^+$.

A sequent $A_1, \ldots, A_n \vdash B_1, \ldots, B_p$ is *valid* in the model $\mathcal{M}$ if the proposition $(A_1 \wedge \cdots \wedge A_n) \Rightarrow (B_1 \vee \cdots \vee B_p)$ is valid.

A theory $\mathcal{T}$ is *valid* in a model if all of its axioms are valid.

Definition 2.5 (Two-valued model) Let $\mathcal{L} = (\mathcal{S}, \mathcal{F}, \mathcal{P})$ be a language. A *two-valued* model of $\mathcal{L}$ is a model such that $\mathcal{B} = \{0, 1\}$, $\mathcal{B}^+ = \{1\}$, $\hat{\top} = 1$, $\hat{\bot} = 0$ and $\hat{\neg}$, $\hat{\wedge}$, $\hat{\vee}$, $\hat{\Rightarrow}$ $\hat{\forall}$ and $\hat{\exists}$ are the functions

$\hat{\neg}$	0	1
	1	0

$\hat{\wedge}$	0	1
0	0	0
1	0	1

$\hat{\vee}$	0	1
0	0	1
1	1	1

$\hat{\Rightarrow}$	0	1
0	1	1
1	0	1

$\hat{\forall}$	$\{0\}$	$\{0, 1\}$	$\{1\}$
	0	0	1

$\hat{\exists}$	$\{0\}$	$\{0, 1\}$	$\{1\}$
	0	1	1

All the models that we will consider in the rest of the book will be two-valued.

Exercise 2.1 Consider a language with one term sort, consisting of a binary function symbol $+$ and a binary predicate $=$. Let $\mathcal{M}_1$ be the model consisting of the set $\mathbb{N}$, addition on $\mathbb{N}$ and the characteristic function of equality in $\mathbb{N}$, that is, the function $\hat{=}$ from $\mathbb{N}^2$ to $\{0, 1\}$ such that $\hat{=}(n, p) = 1$ if $n = p$ and $\hat{=}(n, p) = 0$ otherwise. Is the proposition $\forall x \forall y \exists z \, (x + z = y)$ valid in this model?

Same question for the model $\mathcal{M}_2$ consisting of the set $\mathbb{Z}$, addition and the characteristic function of equality in $\mathbb{Z}$.

Is the proposition $\forall x \forall y \, (x + y = y + x)$ valid in $\mathcal{M}_1$? And in $\mathcal{M}_2$? Give an example of a model in which this proposition is not valid.

2.2 The Soundness Theorem

One of the motivations for the study of models is that validity in a model is an invariant of provability: provable sequents are valid in all models. Thus, if a proposition is provable in a theory, then it is valid in all the models of the theory. This suggests a method to show that a proposition is not provable in a given theory: it is sufficient to show that there is a model of the theory in which the proposition is not valid. The second formulation of the soundness theorem given below states this principle.

Proposition 2.2 *If a sequent* $A_1, \ldots, A_n \vdash B_1, \ldots, B_p$ *is provable in natural deduction, then it is valid in all models.*

Proof By induction over the structure of proofs.   □

The soundness theorem is a consequence of this proposition, and can be formulated in three different (equivalent) ways.

Theorem 2.1 (Soundness) *Let* T *be a theory and* A *a proposition.*

1. *If* A *is provable in* T, *then* A *is valid in all the models of* T.
2. *If there exists a model of* T *that is not a model of* A, *then* A *is not provable in* T.
3. *If* T *has a model, then* T *is consistent.*

Proof Let $\mathcal{M}$ be a model of the theory T and let A be a proposition that is provable in T. There exists a finite subset $H_1, \ldots, H_n$ of T such that the sequent $H_1, \ldots, H_n \vdash A$ is provable. By Proposition 2.2, this sequent is valid in $\mathcal{M}$, that is, the proposition $(H_1 \wedge \cdots \wedge H_n) \Rightarrow A$ is valid in this model. The propositions $H_1, \ldots, H_n$ are valid in $\mathcal{M}$, therefore, also A is valid in $\mathcal{M}$. This proves the first claim. The second claim is a trivial consequence of the first. The third is a consequence of the second taking $A = \bot$.   □

Exercise 2.2 Consider the theory consisting of the axiom $P(c) \vee Q(c)$. Show that the proposition $P(c)$ is not provable in this theory. Show that the proposition $\neg P(c)$ is not provable either. What can be said of proposition $Q(c)$?

We can use the soundness theorem to prove that the axiom of infinity is not provable from the other axioms in *ZF*.

Definition 2.6 (The set of hereditarily finite sets) Let V_n be a sequence of sets defined by induction: $V_0 = \emptyset$ and $V_{i+1} = \wp(V_i)$. Let $V_\omega = \bigcup_i V_i$.

Proposition 2.3 *Let* $\mathcal{M} = (\mathcal{M}_\iota, \mathcal{M}_\sigma, \hat{\epsilon}_2, \hat{=}, \hat{\in})$ *be the model where* $\mathcal{M}_\iota = V_\omega$, $\mathcal{M}_\sigma = \wp(\mathcal{M}_\iota \times \mathcal{M}_\iota)$, $\hat{\epsilon}_2$ *is the function from* $\mathcal{M}_\iota \times \mathcal{M}_\iota \times \mathcal{M}_\sigma$ *to* $\{0, 1\}$ *such that* $\hat{\epsilon}_2(a, b, c) = 1$ *if* (a, b) *is in* c *and* $\hat{\epsilon}_2(a, b, c) = 0$ *otherwise,* $\hat{=}$ *is the function from* $\mathcal{M}_\iota \times \mathcal{M}_\iota$ *to* $\{0, 1\}$ *such that* $\hat{=}(a, b) = 1$ *if* $a = b$ *and* $\hat{=}(a, b) = 0$ *otherwise,* $\hat{\in}$ *the* *function from $\mathcal{M}_\iota \times \mathcal{M}_\iota$ to $\{0, 1\}$ such that $\hat{\in}(a, b) = 1$ if a is in b and $\hat{\in}(a, b) = 0$ otherwise.*

Then $\mathcal{M}$ is a model of each of the axioms of ZF except the axiom of infinity.

Proof We prove the case corresponding to the axiom of union. First, note that the union of a family of subsets of V_j is also a subset of V_j, and the union of a family of elements of V_{j+1} is an element of V_{j+1}. We will show that, if c is an element of V_ω, the union $\bigcup_{b \in c} b$ of the elements of c is also in V_ω. Since $c \in V_\omega$, by definition of V_ω there exists a natural number i different from zero such that $c \in V_i$. If $i = 1$, $c = \emptyset$ and the union of the elements of c is also the empty set, therefore it is an element of V_ω. Otherwise, there exists some natural number j such that $i = j + 2$. Since $c \in V_{j+2}$, $c \subseteq V_{j+1}$ and the elements of c are in V_{j+1}. Therefore, the union of the elements of c is also in V_{j+1}, hence in V_ω. Thus,

$$\llbracket \forall w \ (w \in z \Leftrightarrow (\exists v \ (w \in v \wedge v \in x))) \rrbracket_{x=c, z=\bigcup_{b \in c} b} = 1$$

and therefore

$$\llbracket \forall x \exists z \forall w \ (w \in z \Leftrightarrow (\exists v \ (w \in v \wedge v \in x))) \rrbracket = 1$$

We can prove in the same way that the axiom of extensionality, the axiom of the power set and the axiom of replacement are valid in this model.

The axioms of equality and the comprehension schema are trivially valid in this model.

Finally, we show by contradiction that the axiom of infinity is not valid in this model. First, note that we can prove by induction on i that all the elements of V_i are finite sets. As a consequence, all the elements of V_ω are finite sets.

Assume the axiom of infinity is valid in V_ω, then there is a set a in V_ω that contains the empty set and if it contains the set b it contains also the set $b \cup \{b\}$. Therefore, this set contains all the elements in the sequence defined by induction as follows: $e_0 = \emptyset, e_1 = \{e_0\}, e_2 = \{e_0, e_1\}, e_3 = \{e_0, e_1, e_2\}, \ldots, e_{i+1} = e_i \cup \{e_i\}, \ldots$. Since these elements are all different, the set a is infinite (contradiction). $\quad\square$

Proposition 2.4 *The axiom of infinity cannot be proved from the other axioms in ZF.*

Proof All the axioms in ZF, except the axiom of infinity, are valid in the model $\mathcal{M}$ defined in Proposition 2.3. $\quad\square$

2.3 The Completeness Theorem

The soundness theorem tells us that if a proposition A is provable in a theory $\mathcal{T}$ then it is valid in all the models of the theory. The completeness theorem, first proved in 1930 by K. Gödel (although it should not be confused with Gödel's famous theorem), is the converse of the soundness theorem.

2.3.1 Three Formulations of the Completeness Theorem

Similarly to the soundness theorem, the completeness theorem can be formulated in three different (but equivalent) ways.

Theorem 2.2 (Completeness) *Let T be a theory and A a proposition.*

1. *If A is valid in all the models of T then A is provable in T.*
2. *If A is not provable in T, then there exists a model of T which is not a model of A.*
3. *If T is consistent then T has a model.*

The first two formulations are trivially equivalent. The third one is a consequence of the second, taking $A = \bot$. We will show that (2) is a consequence of (3). Consider a theory T and a proposition A not provable in this theory. By Proposition 1.7, the proposition $\bot$ is not provable in the theory $T, \neg A$. Therefore by (3) the theory $T, \neg A$ has a model. This model is a model of T but not a model of A.

2.3.2 Proving the Completeness Theorem

We will prove the third formulation of the completeness theorem, restricting ourselves to the case of a finite or countable language.

Let $\mathcal{L} = (\mathcal{S}, \mathcal{F}, \mathcal{P})$ be such a language and T a consistent theory in this language. We will build a model for this theory. The idea is to define the domain $\mathcal{M}_s$ as a set of closed terms of sort s, the function $\hat{f}$ as the function that associates to the closed terms $t_1, \ldots, t_n$ the term $f(t_1, \ldots, t_n)$ and $\hat{P}$ as the function that associates $t_1, \ldots, t_n$ to 1 if the proposition $P(t_1, \ldots, t_n)$ is provable and 0 if it is not provable.

There is a problem though: even if we assume that the theory T is consistent, this structure is not necessarily a model of the theory. For instance, if the theory T consists of the axiom $P(c) \vee Q(c)$, neither the proposition $P(c)$ nor the proposition $Q(c)$ is provable—see Exercise 2.2. Thus, according to the construction above, we have to define $\hat{P}(c) = 0$ and $\hat{Q}(c) = 0$, which means that the proposition $P(c) \vee Q(c)$ is not valid in this model.

To make sure that this construction works, first we need to complete the theory: if a proposition A is undetermined, that is, neither A nor $\neg A$ is provable, we must choose to add either the axiom A or the axiom $\neg A$. In our example, if we add the axiom $P(c)$ then when we build the model we will have $\hat{P}(c) = 1$ and thus the proposition $P(c) \vee Q(c)$ is valid in the model. If we decide to add the axiom $\neg P(c)$ instead, then the proposition $Q(c)$ becomes provable, and when we build the model we have $\hat{Q}(c) = 1$, thus the proposition $P(c) \vee Q(c)$ is again valid.

However, it is not sufficient to complete the theory. For example, consider the theory $\neg P(c), \exists x\, P(x)$. In this case, according to the construction described above, we have to define $\mathcal{M} = \{c\}$ and $\hat{P}(c) = 0$. Therefore the proposition $\exists x\, P(x)$ is not valid in this model. The problem here is that no closed term can be used as a witness of the fact that there is an object satisfying the property P. To solve this problem, we need to add a constant d and an axiom $P(d)$ before building the model. This constant d is called *Henkin's witness* for the proposition $\exists x\, P(x)$.

To prove the completeness theorem we need to show first the following property.

Proposition 2.5 *Let $\mathcal{L} = (\mathcal{S}, \mathcal{F}, \mathcal{P})$ be a language and $\mathcal{T}$ a consistent theory in this language. There exists a language $\mathcal{L}'$ such that $\mathcal{L} \subseteq \mathcal{L}'$, and a theory $\mathcal{U}$ in the language $\mathcal{L}'$, such that $\mathcal{T} \subseteq \mathcal{U}$ and the following properties hold.*

1. *The theory $\mathcal{U}$ is consistent.*
2. *For any closed proposition A in the language $\mathcal{L}'$, either the proposition A or the proposition $\neg A$ is provable in $\mathcal{U}$.*
3. *If the proposition $\exists x\, A$ is provable in $\mathcal{U}$, there exists a constant c such that $(c/x)A$ is provable in $\mathcal{U}$.*

To prove this proposition we proceed as in the proof of the theorem of the incomplete basis: we inspect all the propositions, one by one, in order to select some of the them. When inspecting a proposition A, we check whether A or $\neg A$ is provable from the axioms in $\mathcal{T}$ and the propositions already retained. If A is provable, we select it. If $\neg A$ is provable, we select it. If neither A nor $\neg A$ is provable, we choose A to be retained (this is an arbitrary choice). Moreover, if A has the form $\exists x\, B$, then we also retain the proposition $(c/x)B$ where c is a new constant to be added to the language.

Proof Let $\mathcal{H} = \{c_i^s\}$ be a countable set containing an infinite number of constants $c_0^s, c_1^s, c_2^s, \ldots$ for each sort s. Let $\mathcal{L}'$ be the language $(\mathcal{S}, \mathcal{F} \uplus \mathcal{H}, \mathcal{P})$.

The language $\mathcal{L}'$ and the sets $\mathcal{V}_s$ are countable, therefore the set of propositions in this language is countable. Let $A_0, A_1, A_2, \ldots$ be the elements in this set. We define a family of theories $\mathcal{U}_n$ as follows. We start by defining $\mathcal{U}_0 = \mathcal{T}$. If A_n is provable in the theory $\mathcal{U}_n$, we define $B = A_n$; if $\neg A_n$ is provable in the theory $\mathcal{U}_n$, we define $B = \neg A_n$ and if neither of them is provable in the theory $\mathcal{U}_n$, then we arbitrarily define $B = A_n$. If B does not have the form $\exists x\, C$, then we define $\mathcal{U}_{n+1} = \mathcal{U}_n \cup \{B\}$; if B has the form $\exists x\, C$, we define $\mathcal{U}_{n+1} = \mathcal{U}_n \cup \{B, (c_i^s/x)C\}$, where s is the sort of x and i is the least natural number such that the constant c_i^s is neither in $\mathcal{U}_n$ nor in B. Such a constant exists because each $\mathcal{U}_i$ contains only a finite number of constants from $\mathcal{H}$. Finally, we define $\mathcal{U} = \bigcup_i \mathcal{U}_i$.

We can show by induction on i that all the theories $\mathcal{U}_i$ are consistent. As a consequence the theory $\mathcal{U}$ is also consistent. Indeed, if we assume that a proof for $\bot$ exists in $\mathcal{U}$ we obtain a contradiction: If $\bot$ is provable, then there is a finite subset $B_1, \ldots, B_n$ of $\mathcal{U}$ such that the sequent $B_1, \ldots, B_n \vdash \bot$ is provable. Each proposition B_j belongs to one of the sets $\mathcal{U}_{i_j}$ and they all belong to $\mathcal{U}_k$ where k is the greatest of the i_j. This means that the theory $\mathcal{U}_k$ is contradictory (a contradiction).

Let A be an arbitrary closed proposition. There exists an index i such that $A_i = A$ and either A or $\neg A$ is an element of $\mathcal{U}_{i+1}$. Hence, the theory $\mathcal{U}$ contains the axiom A or the axiom $\neg A$ and one of these propositions is provable.

Finally, if the proposition $\exists x\ A$ is provable in $\mathcal{U}$, then there exists an index i such that $A_i = \exists x\ A$. Since the theory $\mathcal{U}_i$ is consistent and the proposition A_i is provable, the proposition $\neg A_i$ is not provable. Therefore, $\mathcal{U}_{i+1} = \mathcal{U}_i \cup \{\exists x\ A, (c/x)A\}$ for some constant c. This means that the theory $\mathcal{U}$ contains the axiom $(c/x)A$ and this proposition is provable.   □

Proposition 2.6 *Let $\mathcal{U}$ be a theory satisfying the following properties*:

1. *The theory $\mathcal{U}$ is consistent.*
2. *For any closed proposition A, either A or $\neg A$ is provable in $\mathcal{U}$.*
3. *If the proposition $\exists x\ A$ is provable in $\mathcal{U}$, there exists a closed term t such that the proposition $(t/x)A$ is also provable in $\mathcal{U}$.*

Then

- *The proposition $\neg A$ is provable in $\mathcal{U}$ if and only if the proposition A is not provable in $\mathcal{U}$.*
- *The proposition $A \wedge B$ is provable in $\mathcal{U}$ if and only if the proposition A is provable in $\mathcal{U}$ and the proposition B is provable in $\mathcal{U}$.*
- *The proposition $A \vee B$ is provable in $\mathcal{U}$ if and only if the proposition A is provable in $\mathcal{U}$ or the proposition B is provable in $\mathcal{U}$.*
- *The proposition $A \Rightarrow B$ is provable in $\mathcal{U}$ if and only if the proposition A is provable in $\mathcal{U}$, then so is the proposition B.*
- *The proposition $\forall x\ A$ is provable in $\mathcal{U}$ if and only if for all closed term t, the proposition $(t/x)A$ is provable in $\mathcal{U}$.*
- *The proposition $\exists x\ A$ is provable in $\mathcal{U}$ if and only if there exists a closed term t such that the proposition $(t/x)A$ is provable in $\mathcal{U}$.*

Proof

- If the proposition A is provable in $\mathcal{U}$ then the proposition $\neg A$ is not, because the theory $\mathcal{U}$ is consistent. Conversely, the second condition implies that if the proposition $\neg A$ is not provable in $\mathcal{U}$, then the proposition A is provable in $\mathcal{U}$.
- If the propositions A and B are provable in $\mathcal{U}$ then the proposition $A \wedge B$ is also provable, using the $\wedge$-intro rule. Conversely, if the proposition $A \wedge B$ is provable in $\mathcal{U}$, then the propositions A and B are also provable, using the $\wedge$-elim rule.
- If the proposition A or the proposition B is provable in $\mathcal{U}$ then so is the proposition $A \vee B$, using the $\vee$-intro rule. Conversely, if the proposition $A \vee B$ is provable in $\mathcal{U}$, then, the second condition implies that the proposition A or the proposition $\neg A$ is provable in $\mathcal{U}$. In the first case, the proposition A is provable in $\mathcal{U}$, and in the second, since the proposition $A \vee B$ and $\neg A$ are provable, the proposition B is also provable in $\mathcal{U}$ using the rules *axiom*, $\neg$-elim, $\bot$-elim and $\vee$-elim.
- Assume that if the proposition A is provable in $\mathcal{U}$ then the proposition B is provable in $\mathcal{U}$. The second condition implies that either the proposition A or the proposition $\neg A$ is provable in $\mathcal{U}$. In the first case, the proposition B is provable in $\mathcal{U}$ and therefore the proposition $A \Rightarrow B$ is provable using the $\Rightarrow$-intro rule. In the second case, the proposition $\neg A$ is provable and therefore the proposition $A \Rightarrow B$

is provable using the rules $\Rightarrow$-intro, $\perp$-elim and $\neg$-elim. Conversely, if $A \Rightarrow B$ is provable in $\mathcal{U}$, then, if A is provable in $\mathcal{U}$ then B is provable in $\mathcal{U}$ using the $\Rightarrow$-elim rule.

- Assume that for every closed term t the proposition $(t/x)A$ is provable in $\mathcal{U}$. If the proposition $\exists x \ \neg A$ is provable in $\mathcal{U}$, then, according to the third condition, there exists a closed term t such that $\neg(t/x)A$ is provable. But then the theory $\mathcal{U}$ would be contradictory, against our assumptions. Therefore the proposition $\exists x \ \neg A$ is not provable in $\mathcal{U}$ and $\neg \exists x \ \neg A$ is. The proposition $\forall x \ A$ is thus provable, by Proposition 1.8. Conversely, if the proposition $\forall x \ A$ is provable in the theory $\mathcal{U}$, all the propositions $(t/x)A$ are provable using the $\forall$-elim rule.

- If there exists a closed term t such that the proposition $(t/x)A$ is provable in $\mathcal{U}$ then the proposition $\exists x \ A$ is provable using the $\exists$-intro rule. Conversely, if the proposition $\exists x \ A$ is provable in $\mathcal{U}$ then, according to the third condition, there exists a closed term t such that $(t/x)A$ is provable in $\mathcal{U}$.

□

We are finally in a position to prove the completeness theorem.

Proof Let $\mathcal{T}$ be a consistent theory and $\mathcal{U}$ the theory built in Proposition 2.5. We define the domain $\mathcal{M}_s$ to be the set of closed terms of sort s in the language $\mathcal{L}'$, the function $\hat{f}$ to be the function associating to the closed terms $t_1, \ldots, t_n$ the term $f(t_1, \ldots, t_n)$ and the function $\hat{P}$ to be the function associating to $t_1, \ldots, t_n$ the number 1 if the proposition $P(t_1, \ldots, t_n)$ is provable in $\mathcal{U}$ and 0 otherwise.

Let A be a closed proposition. We show by induction over the structure of the proposition A that A is provable in $\mathcal{U}$ if and only if A is valid in this model. If A is an atomic proposition, the equivalence follows directly from the definition of the functions $\hat{P}$. If A is a proposition of the form $B \wedge C$, then the proposition A is provable in $\mathcal{U}$ if and only if the propositions B and C are provable—Proposition 2.6—if and only if the propositions B and C are valid in $\mathcal{M}$—inductive hypothesis—if and only if the proposition A is valid in $\mathcal{M}$. The other cases are similar. □

In this proof we have only considered finite or countable languages. The completeness theorem applies also to non-countable languages and the proof follows the same lines. Only the proof of Proposition 2.5 differs. First, we need to add a set of constants for each sort, which must have the same cardinal as the language. Second, instead of enumerating the propositions, we need to well-order them using the axiom of choice. Finally, the family of sets $(\mathcal{U}_i)_i$ will no longer be indexed by the natural numbers, we will need a greater ordinal.

2.3.3 Models of Equality—Normal Models

Definition 2.7 (Normal model) Let $\mathcal{L}$ be a language containing predicates $=_s$ of sort (s, s) for some sorts s, and $\mathcal{T}$ be a theory containing at least the axioms of equality for these sorts. A *normal model* of the theory T is a model in which the functions $\hat{=}_s$ over $\mathcal{M}_s$ are defined by $\hat{=}_s(x, y) = 1$ if $x = y$ and $\hat{=}_s(x, y) = 0$ otherwise.

Proposition 2.7 (Completeness of normal models) *Let T be a theory containing at least the axioms of equality. If T is consistent then it has a normal model.*

Proof Since the theory is consistent, it has a model $\mathcal{M}$. For every sort s for which there is an equality predicate in the language, let R_s be the relation containing the pairs of elements a and b such that $\hat{=}(a, b) = 1$. This is an equivalence relation. We define $\mathcal{M}'_s = \mathcal{M}_s / R_s$. Since the model $\mathcal{M}$ is a model of the equality axioms, the functions $\hat{f}$ and $\hat{P}$ can be defined on the quotient. In this way we can define a normal model $\mathcal{M}'$ that satisfies the same propositions as $\mathcal{M}$. It is therefore a model of T.   □

2.3.4 Proofs of Relative Consistency

The completeness theorem can be used to build proofs of *relative consistency*. The model V_ω defined in Sect. 2.2 is a model of the theory ZF^f, that is, the theory consisting of the axioms of ZF except that the axiom of infinity is replaced by its negation. It is possible to formalise the construction of this model in ZF. In other words, the proposition "There exists a model of ZF^f" is provable in ZF. The soundness theorem allows us to deduce then that the proposition "The theory ZF^f is consistent" is provable in ZF.

This kind of result is not standard, it is in fact an exception. If instead of the elementary theory ZF^f we consider a more interesting theory, such as ZFC or $ZF\neg C$, which are obtained by adding to the axioms of ZF the axiom of choice or its negation, respectively, then as a consequence of Gödel's second incompleteness theorem—which is out of the scope of this book, but shows that under general conditions the consistency of a theory cannot be proved in the same theory—we know that it is impossible to prove in ZF the consistency of ZF, and *a fortiori* that of ZFC or $ZF\neg C$.

Nevertheless, it is possible to prove in ZF relative consistency theorems. For instance, K. Gödel proved that if the theory ZF is consistent, then so is the theory ZFC, and A. Fraenkel and A. Mostowski proved that if the theory ZF is consistent then so is the theory $ZF\neg C$.

In other words, to prove the consistency of the theories ZFC and $ZF\neg C$, we add the axiom "The theory ZF is consistent" to the usual mathematical theories formalised in ZF. Then, these proofs will use the completeness theorem to deduce from the consistency of ZF the existence of a model of ZF and finally use this model to build a model of ZFC or $ZF\neg C$.

Exercise 2.3 In this exercise, inspired by the proof of relative consistency of $ZF\neg C$ proposed by Fraenkel and Mostowski, we will show that if ZF is consistent then

ZF^+ is consistent, where ZF^+ is the theory obtained by adding to ZF the axiom $\exists x \ (x \in x)$. In other words, if ZF is consistent then the proposition $\neg\exists x \ (x \in x)$ is not provable.

1. Show that the following propositions are equivalent.
    (a) If ZF is consistent then ZF^+ is consistent.
    (b) If ZF has a model then ZF^+ has a model.
    (c) If ZF has a normal model then ZF^+ has a normal model.
    Our aim is to prove the proposition (c). Let $\mathcal{M} = (M, \mathcal{C}, \hat{\epsilon}_2, \hat{\epsilon})$ be a normal model of ZF.

2. Show that there exists an element 0 in $\mathcal{M}$ such that none of the elements a of $\mathcal{M}$ satisfies $a \ \hat{\epsilon} \ 0$. Show that there exists an element 1 in $\mathcal{M}$ such that for every element a in $\mathcal{M}$, we have $a \ \hat{\epsilon} \ 1$ if and only if $a = 0$.
    Let f be the bijection from $\mathcal{M}$ to $\mathcal{M}$ defined by $f(0) = 1$, $f(1) = 0$ and $f(a) = a$ if a is different from 0 and 1. Let $\mathcal{M}'$ be the model $(M, \mathcal{C}, \hat{\epsilon}_2, \hat{\epsilon}')$ where $\hat{\epsilon}'$ is the relation such that $a \ \hat{\epsilon}' \ b$ if and only if $a \ \hat{\epsilon} \ f(b)$. The goal is to prove that $\mathcal{M}'$ is a normal model of ZF^+.

3. Show that there exists a proposition *Zero* such that $[\![Zero]\!]^{\mathcal{M}}_{x=a} = 1$ if and only if $a = 0$. Show that there exists a proposition *One* such that $[\![One]\!]^{\mathcal{M}}_{x=a} = 1$ if and only if $a = 1$. Show that there exists a proposition F such that $[\![F]\!]^{\mathcal{M}}_{x=a, y=b} = 1$ if and only if $b = f(a)$. Show that there exists a proposition E such that $[\![E]\!]^{\mathcal{M}}_{x=a, y=b} = 1$ if and only if $a \ \hat{\epsilon}' \ b$. Show that $\mathcal{M}'$ is a model of the binary comprehension schema.

4. Show that the axiom of extensionality is valid in $\mathcal{M}'$.

5. Let a be an element of $\mathcal{M}$. Define $a_1 = f(a)$. Show that there exists an element a_2 of $\mathcal{M}$ such that $x \ \hat{\epsilon} \ a_2$ if and only if there exists some y such that $x = f(y)$ and $y \ \hat{\epsilon} \ a_1$. Show that there exists an element a_3 of $\mathcal{M}$ such that $x \ \hat{\epsilon} \ a_3$ if and only if there exists some z such that $x \ \hat{\epsilon} \ z$ and $z \ \hat{\epsilon} \ a_2$. Let $a_4 = f^{-1}(a_3)$. Show that $x \ \hat{\epsilon}' \ a_4$ if and only if there exists some y such that $x \ \hat{\epsilon}' \ y$ and $y \ \hat{\epsilon}' \ a$. Show that the axiom of union is valid in $\mathcal{M}'$.

6. Let a be an element of $\mathcal{M}$. Define $a_1 = f(a)$. Show that there exists an element a_2 of $\mathcal{M}$ such that $x \ \hat{\epsilon} \ a_2$ if and only if for every z, $z \ \hat{\epsilon} \ x$ implies $z \ \hat{\epsilon} \ a_1$. Show that there exists an element a_3 of $\mathcal{M}$ such that $x \ \hat{\epsilon} \ a_3$ if and only if $f(x) \ \hat{\epsilon} \ a_2$. Let $a_4 = f^{-1}(a_3)$. Show that $x \ \hat{\epsilon}' \ a_4$ if and only if for every z, $z \ \hat{\epsilon}' \ x$ implies $z \ \hat{\epsilon}' \ a$. Show that the axiom of the power set is valid in $\mathcal{M}'$.

7. Let a be an element of $\mathcal{M}$ and r an element of $\mathcal{C}$ that is a functional binary class (more precisely, if $a, b \ \hat{\epsilon}_2 \ r$ and $a, b' \ \hat{\epsilon}_2 \ r$ then $b = b'$). Define $a_1 = f(a)$. Show that there exists an element a_2 of $\mathcal{M}$ such that $x \ \hat{\epsilon} \ a_2$ if and only if there exists some y such that $y \ \hat{\epsilon} \ a_1$ and $y, x \ \hat{\epsilon}_2 \ r$. Let $a_3 = f^{-1}(a_2)$. Show that $x \ \hat{\epsilon}' \ a_3$ if and only if there exists some y such that $y \ \hat{\epsilon}' \ a$ and $y, x \ \hat{\epsilon}_2 \ r$. Show that the axiom of replacement is valid in $\mathcal{M}'$.

8. In this question we will assume that the following result is true (it was proved in Exercise 1.18): *If a is an element of $\mathcal{M}$ and r an element of $\mathcal{C}$ that is a functional binary class, then there exists an element E of $\mathcal{M}$ such that $a \ \hat{\epsilon} \ E$ and if $x \ \hat{\epsilon} \ E$ and $x, x' \ \hat{\epsilon}_2 \ r$ then $x' \ \hat{\epsilon} \ E$.*
    Show that there is no object a such that $a \ \hat{\epsilon}' \ 1$.

Let a be an element of $\mathcal{M}$. Let $S(a)$ be the element of $\mathcal{M}$ such that $x \; \hat{\in} \; S(a)$ if and only if $x \; \hat{\in} \; a$ or $x = a$ and let $S'(a)$ be the element of $\mathcal{M}$ such that $x \; \hat{\in}' \; S'(a)$ if and only if $x \; \hat{\in}' \; a$ or $x = a$. Show that if a is neither 0 nor 1, then $S'(a) = S(a)$. What is the object $S'(0)$? And the object $S'(1)$? Show that the binary class r such that $a, b \; \hat{\in}_2 \; r$ if $b = S'(a)$ is in $\mathcal{C}$ and is functional.

Show that there exists a set I' that contains 1 and such that if $a \; \hat{\in} \; I'$ then $S'(a) \; \hat{\in} \; I'$.

Show that the axiom of infinity is valid in $\mathcal{M}'$.

9. Show that $0 \; \hat{\in}' \; 0$. Show that the proposition $\exists x \; (x \in x)$ is valid in $\mathcal{M}'$.

2.3.5   Conservativity

Definition 2.8 (Extension) Let $\mathcal{L}$ and $\mathcal{L}'$ be two languages such that $\mathcal{L} \subseteq \mathcal{L}'$. Let $\mathcal{T}$ be a theory in the language $\mathcal{L}$ and $\mathcal{T}'$ a theory in $\mathcal{L}'$. The theory $\mathcal{T}'$ is an *extension* of $\mathcal{T}$ if every proposition that is provable in $\mathcal{T}$ is also provable in $\mathcal{T}'$.

Definition 2.9 (Conservative extension) Let $\mathcal{L}$ and $\mathcal{L}'$ be two languages such that $\mathcal{L} \subseteq \mathcal{L}'$. Let $\mathcal{T}$ be a theory in the language $\mathcal{L}$ and $\mathcal{T}'$ a theory in $\mathcal{L}'$. Assume that $\mathcal{T}'$ is an extension of $\mathcal{T}$. The theory $\mathcal{T}'$ is a *conservative* extension of $\mathcal{T}$ if every proposition in $\mathcal{L}$ provable in $\mathcal{T}'$ is also provable in $\mathcal{T}$.

For example, if the language $\mathcal{L}$ contains a constant c and a predicate symbol P, and if the theory $\mathcal{T}$ consists of the axiom $P(c)$, then, by adding a constant d and the axiom $P(d)$ we obtain a conservative extension: although the proposition $P(d)$ is provable in $\mathcal{T}'$ but not in $\mathcal{T}$, we will see that all the propositions of the language $\mathcal{L}$— note that $P(d)$ is not one of them—that are provable in $\mathcal{T}'$ are also provable in $\mathcal{T}$.

Note that if the language $\mathcal{L}$ contains a constant c and a predicate symbol P, and if the theory $\mathcal{T}$ is empty, then by adding a constant d and the axiom $P(d)$ we obtain an extension which is not conservative. Indeed , the proposition $\exists x \; P(x)$, which is well formed in $\mathcal{T}$, is provable in $\mathcal{T}'$ but not in $\mathcal{T}$.

Although in a small example such as the one above it is possible to show that an extension is conservative by showing that proofs in $\mathcal{T}'$ can be translated into proofs in $\mathcal{T}$, in the general case the situation is more complicated. The completeness theorem is a useful tool to prove that a theory is a conservative extension of another one.

Definition 2.10 (Extension of a model) Let $\mathcal{L}$ and $\mathcal{L}'$ be two languages such that $\mathcal{L} \subseteq \mathcal{L}'$. Let $\mathcal{M}$ be a model of $\mathcal{L}$ and $\mathcal{M}'$ a model of $\mathcal{L}'$. The model $\mathcal{M}'$ is an *extension* of $\mathcal{M}$ if for every sort s of $\mathcal{L}$ we have $\mathcal{M}_s = \mathcal{M}'_s$ and for every function or predicate symbol f of $\mathcal{L}$ we have $\hat{f}^{\mathcal{M}} = \hat{f}^{\mathcal{M}'}$.

Proposition 2.8 *Let $\mathcal{L}$ be a language and $\mathcal{T}$ a theory in this language. Let $\mathcal{L}'$ be a language such that $\mathcal{L} \subseteq \mathcal{L}'$ and let $\mathcal{T}'$ be a theory in $\mathcal{L}'$ such that $\mathcal{T} \subseteq \mathcal{T}'$. If for* *every model $\mathcal{M}$ of T there exists an extension $\mathcal{M}'$ of $\mathcal{M}$ that is a model of T', then T' is a conservative extension of T.*

Proof Let A be a proposition in the language $\mathcal{L}$. Assume that A is provable in T'. Let $\mathcal{M}$ be an arbitrary model of T. There exists a model $\mathcal{M}'$ of T' that is an extension of $\mathcal{M}$. Since $\mathcal{M}'$ is a model of T', the proposition A is valid in $\mathcal{M}'$, therefore its denotation in $\mathcal{M}'$ is 1. Since $\mathcal{M}'$ is an extension of $\mathcal{M}$ the denotation of A in $\mathcal{M}$ is also 1. The proposition A is therefore valid in $\mathcal{M}$. Since the proposition A is valid in all the models of T, it is provable in T. □

For example, if $\mathcal{L}$ contains c and P and the theory T consists of the axiom $P(c)$, then by adding a constant d and the axiom $P(d)$ we obtain a conservative extension. Indeed, any model $\mathcal{M}$ of T can be extended into a model of T' by defining $\hat{d} = \hat{c}$.

Exercise 2.4 In Exercise 1.6, we showed that the propositions A and theories T of a many-sorted language can be relativised to propositions $|A|$ and theories $|T|$ in a single-sorted language. Then, if the closed proposition A is provable in T, the proposition $|A|$ is provable in $|T|$.

Show that the converse also holds: if $|A|$ is provable in $|T|$ then A is provable in T.

When formulating arithmetic or set theory, we can avoid introducing classes, and thus the sorts κ and σ and the symbols ϵ and ϵ_2, if we replace each axiom that uses classes by an axiom schema, that is, an infinite set of axioms. For example, the axiom of induction can be replaced by the induction schema, defined as the set of axioms

$$\forall x_1 \ldots \forall x_n \ ((0/y)A \Rightarrow \forall m \ ((m/y)A \Rightarrow (S(m)/y)A) \Rightarrow \forall n \ (n/y)A)$$

for each proposition A, where $x_1, \ldots, x_n$ are the free variables of A that are different from y. For example, for the proposition $y + 0 = y$ we have the axiom

$$0 + 0 = 0 \Rightarrow \forall m \ (m + 0 = m \Rightarrow S(m) + 0 = S(m)) \Rightarrow \forall n \ (n + 0 = n)$$

We obtain in this way the theory defined below.

Definition 2.11 The language of arithmetic contains a constant 0, a unary function symbol S, two binary function symbols $+$ and $\times$ and a binary predicate symbol $=$. In addition to the axioms of equality, we have the axioms

$$\forall x \forall y \ (S(x) = S(y) \Rightarrow x = y)$$

$$\forall x \ \neg(0 = S(x))$$

$$\forall x_1 \ldots \forall x_n \ ((0/y)A \Rightarrow \forall m \ ((m/y)A \Rightarrow (S(m)/y)A) \Rightarrow \forall n \ (n/y)A)$$

$$\forall y \ (0 + y = y)$$

$$\forall x \forall y \ (S(x) + y = S(x + y))$$

$$\forall y \ (0 \times y = 0)$$

$$\forall x \forall y \ (S(x) \times y = (x \times y) + y)$$

We can now show that the single-sorted theory of classes is a conservative extension of this theory. More generally, for any theory that contains an axiom schema, there is an alternative definition in the theory of classes where the schema is simply replaced by one axiom. We will show this result only for the case of arithmetic, to avoid having to formalise the notion of an axiom schema in the general case.

Proposition 2.9 *The formulation of the theory of arithmetic given in Definition* 1.33 *is a conservative extension of the one given in Definition* 2.11.

Proof Each instance of the induction schema can be proved in the theory given in Definition 1.33. Therefore, this theory is an extension of the one presented in Definition 2.11. To show that the extension is conservative, we show that every model of the theory given in Definition 2.11 can be extended to a model of the theory in Definition 1.33.

Let $(\mathcal{M}, \hat{0}, \hat{S}, \hat{+}, \hat{\times}, \hat{=})$ be a model of the theory given in Definition 2.11. A subset E of $\mathcal{M}$ is *definable in arithmetic* if there exists a proposition A in the language of the theory given in Definition 2.11, with free variables in $x_1, \ldots, x_n, y$, and elements $a_1, \ldots, a_n$ in $\mathcal{M}$, such that b is in E if and only if

$$[\![A]\!]_{x_1=a_1,\ldots,x_n=a_n,y=b} = 1$$

Let $\overline{\wp}(\mathcal{M})$ be the set of all the definable subsets of $\mathcal{M}$. We extend the model $\mathcal{M}$, by defining $\mathcal{M}_\kappa = \overline{\wp}(\mathcal{M})$ and $\hat{\epsilon}(b, E) = 1$ if b is an element of E and 0 otherwise.

The resulting structure is a model of the comprehencion schema. We now prove that it is a model of the axiom of induction.

$$\forall c \ (0 \in c \Rightarrow \forall m \ (m \in c \Rightarrow S(m) \in c) \Rightarrow \forall n \ n \in c)$$

For this, we consider an arbitrary element E of $\mathcal{M}_\kappa$ and show that

$$[\![(0 \in c \Rightarrow \forall m \ (m \in c \Rightarrow S(m) \in c) \Rightarrow \forall n \ n \in c)]\!]_{c=E} = 1$$

The set E is definable; let A and $a_1, \ldots, a_n$ be a proposition and elements of $\mathcal{M}$, respectively, defining E. Then $\mathcal{M}$ is a model of the instance of the induction schema corresponding to A, and therefore

$$[\![(0/y)A \Rightarrow \forall m \ ((m/y)A \Rightarrow (S(m)/y)A) \Rightarrow \forall n \ (n/y)A]\!]_{x_1=a_1,\ldots,x_n=a_n} = 1$$

Since the denotations of the propositions $t \in c$ and $(t/y)A$ are exactly the same in a valuation where $\phi c = E, \phi x_1 = a_1, \ldots, \phi x_n = a_n$, we deduce that

$$[\![(0 \in c \Rightarrow \forall m \ (m \in c \Rightarrow S(m) \in c) \Rightarrow \forall n \ n \in c)]\!]_{c=E} = 1 \qquad \square$$

Exercise 2.5 Give a formulation of the theory *ZF* with an axiom schema. Show that the theory defined using binary classes is a conservative extension of this theory.

Using the axiom of the power set given in Definition 1.36

$$\forall x \exists z \forall w \ (w \in z \Leftrightarrow (\forall v \ (v \in w \Rightarrow v \in x)))$$

we can show that if A is a set, then there exists a set containing all the subsets of A. However, we do not have a notation (such as $\wp(A)$) for this set.

We could introduce a function symbol $\wp$ and an axiom

$$\forall x \forall w \ (w \in \wp(x) \Leftrightarrow (\forall v \ (v \in w \Rightarrow v \in x)))$$

and show that the theory obtained is a conservative extension of the theory of sets previously defined.

Theorem 2.3 (Skolem) *Let T be a theory and A a proposition of the form $\forall x_1 \ldots \forall x_n \exists y \ B$, provable in T. Then the theory obtained by adding a function symbol f and the axiom $\forall x_1 \ldots \forall x_n \ (f(x_1, \ldots, x_n)/y)B$ is a conservative extension of T.*

Proof Let $\mathcal{M}$ be a model of T. We show that it can be extended into a model of this axiom. Let $a_1, \ldots, a_n$ be arbitrary elements of $\mathcal{M}$. There exists an element b of $\mathcal{M}$ such that

$$[\![B]\!]_{x_1=a_1,\ldots,x_n=a_n,y=b} = 1$$

Therefore, we can define $\hat{f}$ to be the function that associates to each n-tuple $a_1, \ldots, a_n$ such an element b. □

2.4 Other Applications of the Notion of Model

In this chapter, we have shown that the concept of model can be used to prove several properties of proofs, for example properties of independence, consistency, relative consistency, conservativity. However, in mathematics and in computer science, the concept of model is not just a tool to study proofs: it has multiple applications. We finish the chapter by giving some examples where models and languages are used for various different purposes.

2.4.1 Algebraic Structures

It is not particularly interesting to write proofs in the theory consisting of the equality axioms and the axioms

$$\forall x \forall y \forall z \ ((x+y)+z = x+(y+z))$$

$$\forall x\ (x + 0 = x \land 0 + x = x)$$

$$\forall x \exists y\ (x + y = 0 \land y + x = 0)$$

However, normal models of this theory are interesting in their own right: they are the groups. We can derive results in group theory by proving properties of the models of this theory. Let us give an example.

Theorem 2.4 (Löwenheim-Skolem) *Let $\mathcal{L} = (\mathcal{S}, \mathcal{F}, \mathcal{P})$ be a finite or countable language, $\mathcal{T}$ a theory in this language and κ an arbitrary, infinite set. If the theory $\mathcal{T}$ has a finite model, it has a model of the same cardinality as κ.*

Proof This theorem is a simple consequence of the completeness theorem for an arbitrary cardinality.

Consider the language $(\mathcal{S}, \mathcal{F} \uplus \kappa, \mathcal{P} \uplus \{=\})$ obtained by adding to our initial language a symbol $=$ and a constant for each element of κ, and the theory $\mathcal{T}'$ obtained by adding to $\mathcal{T}$ the axioms of equality and the axioms $\neg a = b$ for each pair (a, b) of distinct elements in κ. Let $\mathcal{M}$ be an infinite model of the theory $\mathcal{T}$.

It is not difficult to show that any finite subset of $\mathcal{T}'$ is consistent: a finite subset of $\mathcal{T}'$ will only use a finite number of constants from κ; we can extend the model $\mathcal{M}$, associating to those constants different elements of $\mathcal{M}$ (this is always possible because $\mathcal{M}$ is infinite), and to the other constants in κ an arbitrary element.

We deduce that the theory $\mathcal{T}'$ is consistent. Indeed, assume it is not consistent, then there is a finite subset Γ of $\mathcal{T}'$, such that the sequent $\Gamma \vdash \bot$ is provable. This contradicts our assumption that all finite subsets of $\mathcal{T}'$ are consistent.

Let $\mathcal{M}'$ be the normal model of $\mathcal{T}'$ that we built in the proof of the completeness theorem. This model has at least as many elements as κ because the elements of κ are associated to different elements here. We can then show that since κ is infinite, there are as many closed terms in the language $(\mathcal{S}, \mathcal{F} \uplus \kappa, \mathcal{P} \uplus \{=\})$ as elements in κ and therefore the model has at most the number of elements of κ. It has therefore exactly the same cardinality as κ. $\qquad\Box$

From this result we can derive the following corollary.

Proposition 2.10 *There are groups of every infinite cardinality. Every infinite set can be endowed with a group structure.*

Note that this theorem does not mention the concept of model. It is a well-known result in group theory, obtained as a corollary of a result in logic.

Another interesting consequence of the theorem of Löwenheim-Skolem is the existence of non-countable normal models of arithmetic, and more generally, of any theory that admits $\mathbb{N}$ as a model. This result might seem surprising, since at first sight all normal models of arithmetic seem to have the same cardinal as $\mathbb{N}$. Indeed, consider a normal model $\mathcal{M}$ of arithmetic, and the function F from $\mathbb{N}$ to $\mathcal{M}$ associating $\hat{S}^n(\hat{0})$ to n.

The image I of this function contains $\hat{0}$, is closed under $\hat{S}$ and $\mathcal{M}$ is a model of the axiom of induction. It seems then that all the elements of $\mathcal{M}$ should be in I, and therefore $\mathcal{M}$ should be countable. Where is the mistake?

The mistake stems from our assumption that if $\mathcal{M}$ is a model of the axiom of induction, every set I containing $\hat{0}$ and closed under $\hat{S}$ must contain all the set $\mathcal{M}$. This is only true if I is in the set $\mathcal{M}_\kappa$. But the comprehension schema requires $\mathcal{M}_\kappa$ to contain all the subsets of $\mathcal{M}$ that are definable by a proposition A, and that is not the case for the set I. In other words, amongst the subsets of $\mathbb{N}$ (and the power set of $\mathbb{N}$ is uncountable), the comprehension schema says that there is a small number—countable—of sets that are definable, and the axiom of induction says that if one of these sets contains 0 and is closed under successor, then it contains all the natural numbers. There is therefore a significant degree of freedom.

Definition 2.12 (Standard model) A *standard* model of the theory of classes is a model such that $\mathcal{M}_\kappa = \wp(\mathcal{M}_\iota)$.

Exercise 2.6 Show that all the standard models of arithmetic have the same cardinal as $\mathbb{N}$.

In the same way we can show that although the fields that are totally ordered, Archimedean and complete are isomorphic to $\mathbb{R}$, there are non standard models of this theory that are countable.

The notion of standard model is essential in the applications of model theory to algebra. However, it is not really useful to study proofs, since the theorem of Löwenheim-Skolem tells us that all the theories that can be defined in a finite or countable language have non-standard models.

2.4.2 Definability

Models can also be used to define the notion of *definable* set, or more generally, definable relation.

Definition 2.13 Let $\mathcal{M}$ be a set and $R_1, \ldots, R_n$ relations over this set. We will say that a relation S over $\mathcal{M}$ is *definable* in the structure $(\mathcal{M}, R_1, \ldots, R_n)$ if there exists a proposition A in the language that consists of the symbols $P_1, \ldots, P_n$ and with free variables $x_1, \ldots, x_p$, such that the elements $a_1, \ldots, a_p$ are in the relation S if and only if

$$[\![A]\!]_{x_1 = a_1, \ldots, x_n = a_n} = 1$$

in the model $(\mathcal{M}, R_1, \ldots, R_n)$.

If R_1 and R_2 are two binary relations, their intersection is definable from R_1 and R_2 using the proposition $P_1(x, y) \wedge P_2(x, y)$. In general, if two relations of the same arity are definable, so is their intersection. The set of definable relations is therefore closed under intersection. It is also closed under union and complement. However, the set of definable relations contains more elements than the inductively defined set containing $R_1, \ldots, R_n$ and closed under intersection, union and complement. Indeed, since in a proposition the same variable can be used several times, and variables can be permuted, it is possible to define for instance the set of objects that relate to themselves, $P(x, x)$, or the inverse of a relation, $P(y, x)$. Moreover, the use of quantifiers opens up a wealth of possibilities, since we can, for instance, define the composition of two relations $\exists z \ (P_1(x, z) \wedge P_2(z, y))$.

However, not all relations are definable. We can for instance prove that the reflexive-transitive closure of a relation is not definable using the relation itself.

In database theory, definable relations correspond to definable queries.

Part II
Algorithms

Chapter 3
Computable Functions

In this chapter we will study algorithms that take n natural numbers $p_1, \ldots, p_n$ as input and compute a natural number q. Each of these algorithms can be associated to a function from $\mathbb{N}^n$ to $\mathbb{N}$ that maps the integers $p_1, \ldots, p_n$ to q. Functions that can be associated to an algorithm are said to be *computable*. The notion of a computable function, simpler and more abstract than the notion of an algorithm, turns out to be an important concept when studying the limits of computability. In Chap. 4 we will introduce a more operational approach to computation, but first in this chapter we will study computable functions.

3.1 Computable Functions

Let F_n be the set of partial functions from $\mathbb{N}^n$ to $\mathbb{N}$ and F the union of all the sets F_n.

Definition 3.1 (Computable functions) The set of *computable functions* is the subset of F inductively defined as the smallest set containing

- the projection functions

$$x_1, \ldots, x_n \mapsto x_i$$

- the zero functions

$$x_1, \ldots, x_n \mapsto 0$$

- the successor function

$$x \mapsto x + 1$$

and closed under

- composition, that is, the operation that associates to the functions h from $\mathbb{N}^m$ to $\mathbb{N}$ and $g_1, \ldots, g_m$ from $\mathbb{N}^n$ to $\mathbb{N}$ the function from $\mathbb{N}^n$ to $\mathbb{N}$

$$x_1, \ldots, x_n \mapsto h(g_1(x_1, \ldots, x_n), \ldots, g_m(x_1, \ldots, x_n))$$

G. Dowek, *Proofs and Algorithms*, Undergraduate Topics in Computer Science, DOI 10.1007/978-0-85729-121-9_3, © Springer-Verlag London Limited 2011

- recursive definitions, that is, the operation that associates to g from $\mathbb{N}^{n-1}$ to $\mathbb{N}$ and h from $\mathbb{N}^{n+1}$ to $\mathbb{N}$ the function f from $\mathbb{N}^n$ to $\mathbb{N}$ defined by

$$f(x_1, \ldots, x_{n-1}, 0) = g(x_1, \ldots, x_{n-1})$$
$$f(x_1, \ldots, x_{n-1}, y+1) = h(x_1, \ldots, x_{n-1}, y, f(x_1, \ldots, x_{n-1}, y))$$

- and minimisation, that is, the operation that associates to g from $\mathbb{N}^{n+1}$ to $\mathbb{N}$ the function f from $\mathbb{N}^n$ to $\mathbb{N}$ such that $f(x_1, \ldots, x_n)$ is the least natural number y such that $g(x_1, \ldots, x_n, y) = 0$.

We need to define more precisely the sets of numbers for which these functions are defined. The projections, the zero functions and the successor function are total. The function $x_1, \ldots, x_n \mapsto h(g_1(x_1, \ldots, x_n), \ldots, g_m(x_1, \ldots, x_n))$ is defined for $p_1, \ldots, p_n$ if the functions $g_1, \ldots, g_m$ are defined for $p_1, \ldots, p_n$ and the function h is defined for $g_1(p_1, \ldots, p_n), \ldots, g_m(p_1, \ldots, p_n)$. A function f that is recursively defined using the functions g and h is defined for $p_1, \ldots, p_{n-1}, 0$ if g is defined for $p_1, \ldots, p_{n-1}$, and it is defined for $p_1, \ldots, p_{n-1}, q+1$ if it is defined for $p_1, \ldots, p_{n-1}, q$ and in addition h is defined for $p_1, \ldots, p_{n-1}, q$, $f(p_1, \ldots, p_{n-1}, q)$. The function f defined as the minimisation of a function g is defined for $p_1, \ldots, p_n$ if there exists a natural number q such that g is defined and does not return 0 for $p_1, \ldots, p_n, r$, for any r strictly less than q, and it returns 0 for $p_1, \ldots, p_n, q$.

It is because of this last rule that the set of functions defined above includes partial functions. The first three rules define total functions and the two that follow preserve totality. However, minimisation transforms the total function $x, y \mapsto x$ into a partial function, which returns the value 0 for 0, and is undefined for any other natural number. Indeed, if p is a natural number different from 0 then there is no q such that $(x, y \mapsto x)(p, q) = 0$.

We will see in Sect. 3.4.2 and in Chap. 4 that when a function f is undefined for a natural number p, its corresponding program is non-terminating. Indeed, if the function f is defined by minimisation of the function g, then to compute f we have to compute the values of g at $(p, 0)$, $(p, 1)$, $(p, 2)$, ... until we find a zero, if there is one. If there is no zero, the computation will continue forever.

Proposition 3.1 (The predecessor function) *The* predecessor *function, defined by* $f(n+1) = n$ *and* $f(0) = 0$, *is computable.*

Proof It is a recursively defined function.   □

Proposition 3.2 (The four arithmetic operations) *Addition, multiplication, the "subtraction" operation defined by* $n \dot{-} p = n - p$ *if* $n \geq p$ *and* $n \dot{-} p = 0$ *otherwise, the quotient and remainder of Euclidean division, are all computable functions.*

Proof The functions $+$, $\dot{-}$ and $\times$ can be defined using recursion. The quotient of a division can be computed using minimisation, and the remainder can be computed using quotient, multiplication and subtraction.   □

Proposition 3.3 (The function $\chi_\leq$) *The characteristic function of the ordering relation* $\chi_\leq$, *defined by* $\chi_\leq(x, y) = 1$ *if* $x \leq y$ *and* $\chi_\leq(x, y) = 0$ *otherwise, is computable.*

Proof $\chi_\leq(x, y) = 1 \dot- (x \dot- y)$. $\qquad\square$

Proposition 3.4 (Test) *Let* f, g *and* h *be three computable functions, and* i *the function defined by* $i(x_1, \ldots, x_n) = g(x_1, \ldots, x_n)$ *if* $f(x_1, \ldots, x_n) = 0$ *and* $i(x_1, \ldots, x_n) = h(x_1, \ldots, x_n)$ *otherwise. The function* i, *defined for all the numbers that are in the domains of definition of the three functions* f, g *and* h, *is computable.*

Proof The function that maps the three natural numbers p, q, r to q if $p = 0$ and to r otherwise can be defined recursively as follows:

$$k(0, q, r) = q$$
$$k(p + 1, q, r) = r$$

and the function i can be defined by composition using f, g, h and k. $\qquad\square$

Definition 3.2 (Decidable and semi-decidable sets) A subset A of $\mathbb{N}$ is *decidable* if its characteristic function is computable, that is, if there exists a computable function f such that $f(x) = 1$ if $x \in A$ and $f(x) = 0$ otherwise.

It is *semi-decidable* if there exists a computable function f such that $f(x) = 1$ if $x \in A$ and f is undefined for x otherwise.

Exercise 3.1 Show that any decidable set is also semi-decidable.

Definition 3.3 (Primitive recursive functions) The set of *primitive recursive* functions is inductively defined as the smallest set of functions that contains the projections, the zero functions and the successor function, and is closed under composition and recursive definitions.

Exercise 3.2 *Ackermann*'s function is defined as follows: $A_0(x) = 2^x$ and $A_{n+1}(x) = \underbrace{A_n \circ \cdots \circ A_n}_{x \text{ times}}(1)$. Alternatively, it can be defined as

$$A_0(x) = 2^x$$
$$A_{n+1}(0) = 1$$
$$A_{n+1}(x + 1) = A_n(A_{n+1}(x))$$

1. Show that, for any i and any x, $A_i(x) \geq x + 1$.
2. Show that, for any i, the function $x \mapsto A_i(x)$ is strictly increasing.
3. Show that, for any x, the function $i \mapsto A_i(x)$ is increasing.
4. Show that, for any x, $A_0(x) \geq 2x$ and, if $x \geq 2$, then $A_0(x) \geq x + 2$. Show that, for any i and any x, $A_i(x) \geq 2x$ and, if $x \geq 2$, then $A_i(x) \geq x + 2$.

5. Show that, if $x \geq 2$, then $A_{i+1}(x+2) \geq A_i(A_i(x+2))$. Show that, if $x \geq 4$, then $A_{i+1}(x) \geq A_i(A_i(x))$.

6. We will say that a function f of arity n is *dominated* by a unary function g if for any $x_1, \ldots, x_n$, $f(x_1, \ldots, x_n) \leq g(\max(x_1, \ldots, x_n, 4))$.
   Show that the projections, the zero functions and the successor function are all dominated by the function A_0, that is, by the function $x \mapsto 2^x$.

7. Let $g_1, \ldots, g_m$ and h be functions dominated by the functions $A_{i_1}, \ldots, A_{i_m}$ and A_j, respectively. Let k be the greatest of the numbers $i_1, \ldots, i_m$ and j. Show that the composition of h and $g_1, \ldots, g_m$ is dominated by A_{k+1}.

8. Let g and h be two functions dominated by A_i and A_j, and let k be the greatest of i and j. Let f be the function recursively defined using g and h. Show that $f(x_1, \ldots, x_{n-1}, y) \leq A_{k+1}(y + \max(x_1, \ldots, x_{n-1}, 4))$. Show that $f(x_1, \ldots, x_{n-1}, y) \leq A_{k+1}(2 \max(x_1, \ldots, x_{n-1}, y, 4))$. Show that $f(x_1, \ldots, x_{n-1}, y) \leq A_{k+1}(A_{k+1}(\max(x_1, \ldots, x_{n-1}, y, 4)))$.
   Show that f is dominated by A_{k+2}.

9. Show that, for any primitive recursive function, there exists a natural number i such that f is dominated by A_i.

10. Show that the function $i \mapsto A_i(i)$ is not primitive recursive.

11. Show that Ackermann's function is not primitive recursive.

3.2 Computability over Lists and Trees

3.2.1 Computability over Lists

The computable functions introduced in Definition 3.1 work on natural numbers. We will now extend this definition to lists of numbers as follows. First, we associate to each list l a natural number $\lceil l \rceil$ (the list's *index*). Then, we say that a function that maps a list l to the list $F(l)$ is *computable* if the function that maps l's index to $F(l)$'s index, which is a function over the natural numbers, is computable.

To associate indices (i.e., numbers) to lists we use the following function.

Definition 3.4 The function ; is defined by

$$p; q = (p+q)(p+q+1)/2 + p + 1$$

Proposition 3.5 *The function ; is a bijection from $\mathbb{N}^2$ to $\mathbb{N}^*$.*

Proof Let n be a natural number different from 0. Let k be the greatest natural number such that $k(k+1)/2 \leq n-1$ and $p = n - 1 - k(k+1)/2$. Since k is the greatest such number, we deduce that $n - 1 < (k+1)(k+2)/2$ and therefore $p < (k+1)(k+2)/2 - k(k+1)/2 = k+1$, and $p \leq k$. Define $q = k - p$, then

$$n = k(k+1)/2 + p + 1 = (p+q)(p+q+1)/2 + p + 1 = p; q$$

Thus, the function ; is surjective.

Assume $p; q = p'; q'$, and let k be the greatest natural number such that $k(k + 1)/2 \leq (p; q) - 1$. Then $k(k+1)/2 \leq (p; q) - 1 = (p+q)(p+q+1)/2 + p < (p+q)(p+q+1)/2 + p + q + 1 = (p+q+1)(p+q+2)/2$, and therefore $k < p+q+1$, that is, $k \leq p+q$. In addition, $(p+q)(p+q+1)/2 \leq (p+q)(p+q+1)/2 + p = (p; q) - 1 < (k+1)(k+2)/2$ and therefore $p + q < k + 1$, that is, $p + q \leq k$. We deduce $p + q = k$. Similarly, $p' + q' = k$ and therefore $p' + q' = p + q$. Since $(p+q)(p+q+1)/2 + p + 1 = (p'+q')(p'+q'+1)/2 + p' + 1$, we deduce that $p = p'$ and therefore $q = q'$. Thus, the function ; is injective. $\square$

Definition 3.5 The function *hd*, *head*, maps 0 to 0 and each natural number n different from 0 to the unique natural number p such that there exists some q satisfying $n = p; q$. The function *tl*, *tail*, maps 0 to 0 and each natural number n different from 0 to the unique natural number q such that there exists some p satisfying $n = p; q$.

Proposition 3.6 *The functions* ;, *hd and tl are computable.*

Proof The function ; is defined using arithmetic operations and the other functions are defined using arithmetic operations, the characteristic function of the ordering relation, and minimisation. They are therefore computable functions. $\square$

Proposition 3.7 *If* $n \neq 0$, *then* $hd(n) < n$ *and* $tl(n) < n$.

Proof $p; q > p$ and $p; q > q$. $\square$

Definition 3.6 (Indexing lists of natural numbers) We can associate an *index* to each list l of natural numbers as follows:

$$\ulcorner p_1, \ldots, p_n \urcorner = p_1; (p_2; (\ldots; (p_n; 0) \ldots))$$

Proposition 3.8 *The function sub that takes two natural numbers* p *and* n *as input and returns the index associated to the list obtained by deleting the* n *first elements from the list with index* p, *if this list has at least* n *elements, or the index of the empty list otherwise, is computable.*

Proof This function is defined by

$$sub(p, 0) = p$$
$$sub(p, n + 1) = tl(sub(p, n))$$ $\square$

Proposition 3.9 *The function length that associates to a natural number* p *the length of the list with index* p *is computable.*

Proof The length of a list p is the least natural number n such that $sub(p, n) = 0$. $\square$

Proposition 3.10 *The function nth that associates to two natural numbers* n *and* p *the* nth *element of the list with index* p, *if this element exists, and the number* 0 *otherwise, is computable.*

Proof This function is defined by nth $(p, n) = hd(sub(p, n))$.   □

The induction schema used in Definition 3.1 might seem restrictive at first sight, because to define the value of h for $y + 1$ we can only use the value of h for y (instead of all the values of h for z such that $z < y + 1$). For instance, it is not obvious that the well-known Fibonacci function, usually defined by well-founded induction as $f(0) = f(1) = 1$ and $f(n + 2) = f(n) + f(n + 1)$, is computable.

However, it is not difficult to prove that if a function f is defined by well-founded induction, then the function F that associates x to $\ulcorner f(0), f(1), \ldots, f(x) \urcorner$ can be defined by standard induction, and therefore F, and also f, are computable.

3.2.2 Computability over Trees

It is also useful to extend the notion of computability to expressions in a language, or more generally, to trees. In this way we can define computations over programs, propositions, and proofs, amongst others.

To extend the notion of computable function, we will start by defining a mapping between trees and natural numbers. Each tree will be associated to a natural number—its *index*—and we will say that a function F that associates to a tree t another tree $F(t)$ is *computable* if the function that associates to t's index $F(t)$'s index (a function over natural numbers) is computable.

Definition 3.7 (Indexing trees) Let E be a set with an associated injective function over $\mathbb{N}$, such that each element f of E is associated to its *index* $\ulcorner f \urcorner$. Given a tree t with nodes labelled by elements of E, we define its index $\ulcorner t \urcorner$ by structural induction, as follows

$$\ulcorner f(t_1, \ldots, t_n) \urcorner = \ulcorner f \urcorner; (\ulcorner t_1 \urcorner; (\ulcorner t_2 \urcorner; \ldots (\ulcorner t_n \urcorner; 0) \ldots))$$

We have thus a mechanism to index the trees that are labelled by elements of a finite set E: it suffices to associate a natural number to each element of E, and it can be shown that the set of computable functions does not depend on the function used to associate indices to the elements of E.

However, the set E is often infinite, and may itself be a set of trees. For instance, we have seen that proofs are trees labelled by sequents, which are trees labelled by propositions, which in turn are trees labelled by variables, function symbols and predicate symbols, which again are trees labelled by the elements of a finite set. The set of proofs is therefore an articulated set of trees.

If we associate an arbitrary natural number to each element of this finite set, Definition 3.7 allows us to index first all the variables, function symbols and predicate symbols, then all the propositions, sequents and finally proofs.

The same methodology applies to any set of articulated trees. It is possible to show that the set of computable functions does not depend on the function used to associate numbers (i.e., indices) to the initial, finite set.

Proposition 3.11 *The functions that associate to the index p of the tree a the label of its root and the number of subtrees of the root node, respectively, as well as the function that associates to p and i the index of the ith immediate subtree of a, are all computable.*

Proof If p is the index of the tree a, the root label is $hd(p)$ and the number of children of the root node is $length(tl(p))$. The index of the ith immediate subtree is nth $(tl(p), i)$.   □

Proposition 3.12 *That function that associates to the natural number p the index $\ulcorner S^p(0) \urcorner$ of the tree $S^p(0)$ is computable. The function that associates to the index $\ulcorner S^p(0) \urcorner$ of the tree $S^p(0)$ the natural number p, and to all natural numbers that are not of the form $\ulcorner S^p(0) \urcorner$ the number 0 is computable.*

Proof The first function is defined by induction, the second by well-founded induction.   □

3.2.3 Derivations

Definition 3.8 (Effective rules) Let E be an articulated set of trees and let $f_1, f_2, \ldots$ be rules over the set E. The set of rules $f_1, f_2, \ldots$ is *effective* if the set G of indices of lists $b, a_1, \ldots, a_n$ such that there exists a rule f_i satisfying $b = f_i a_1 \cdots a_n$ is decidable, that is, if the union of the graphs of the functions $f_1, f_2, \ldots$ is a decidable set.

Proposition 3.13 *Let E be an articulated set of trees and $f_1, f_2, \ldots$ a set of effective rules. Then, the set of derivations using $f_1, f_2, \ldots$ is decidable.*

Proof We show that there exists a computable function g that takes a list of trees as argument and returns 1 if all the trees are derivations and 0 otherwise. First, note that the function that associates to a list of trees the list of their roots is computable. Indeed, it can be defined by well-founded induction using computable functions. Let l be a list of trees. If l is an empty list, we define $g(l) = 1$. Otherwise, let $a = hd(l)$ be the first tree in the list, and $l' = tl(l)$ be the list containing the remaining trees in the list. Let $r = hd(a)$ be the root of a, $l'' = tl(a)$ the list of the immediate subtrees of a and s the list of the roots of the trees in l''. Then, if $r; s$ is in G, $g(l') = 1$ and $g(l'') = 1$ we define $g(l) = 1$, otherwise we define $g(l) = 0$. The function g is thus defined by well-founded induction, using computable functions, since by Proposition 3.7 the indices associated to the lists l' and l'' are natural numbers strictly less than l's index. It is therefore a computable function.   □

Note that the set A inductively defined by the rules $f_1, f_2, \ldots$ is not always decidable. It is semi-decidable in general. Let x be an element of E, we can enumerate all the trees and check each one of them to see whether it is a derivation with root x or not. If x is an element of A, we will eventually find the corresponding derivation, otherwise the process of enumeration will continue forever.

Proposition 3.14 (Inductively defined sets of trees) *Let E be an articulated set of trees and $f_1, f_2, \ldots$ an effective set of rules over the set E. Then, the subset A of E inductively defined by these rules is semi-decidable.*

Proof Let $g(x, y)$ be the computable function such that $g(x, y) = 1$ if x is the index associated to a derivation of an element of E and the root of x is y, and $g(x, y) = 0$ otherwise. The function h such that $h(y)$ is the least natural number x such that $1 \overset{.}{-} g(x, y) = 0$ composed with the constant function 1 is a semi-decision algorithm for A. If y is in A then $h(y) = 1$, otherwise h is not defined for y. $\square$

3.3 Eliminating Recursion

There is an alternative definition of the set of computable functions, which, although less natural than Definition 3.1, will be useful in the next chapters of the book.

Definition 3.9 The set $\mathcal{C}$ is inductively defined as the smallest set that contains

- the projection functions,
- the zero functions (i.e., constant functions that always return 0),
- the successor function,
- addition,
- multiplication and
- the characteristic function of the ordering relation $\chi_{\leq}$, defined by $\chi_{\leq}(x, y) = 1$ if $x \leq y$ and $\chi_{\leq}(x, y) = 0$ otherwise,

and closed under

- composition and
- minimisation.

This definition is similar to Definition 3.1, but note that we have replaced the recursive closure by three basic functions: addition, multiplication and $\chi_{\leq}$. Our goal now is to prove that these two definitions are equivalent, that is, we want to prove that a function is in the set $\mathcal{C}$ if and only if it is computable. In order to do this, we need to prove that the set $\mathcal{C}$ is closed under recursive definitions; in other words, we need to prove that if g and h are functions in $\mathcal{C}$ and f is recursively defined using g and h, then f is in $\mathcal{C}$.

The function defined recursively from g and h returns the value r for $x_1, \ldots, x_{n-1}, y$ if there exists a finite sequence $s_0, \ldots, s_y$ such that $s_0 = g(x_1, \ldots, x_{n-1})$, for all i strictly less than y, $s_{i+1} = h(x_1, \ldots, x_{n-1}, i, s_i)$, and $s_y = r$. We will represent the finite sequence $s_0, \ldots, s_y$ by a natural number. As a first attempt, we could try to represent it by the natural number s_0; $(\ldots; (s_y; 0)\ldots)$, since it is easy to show that the functions $;$, hd and tl are in the set C. However, since we do not have recursive definitions yet, we cannot show that the function nth is in the set C. Instead, we will use another representation of finite sequences, which is based on the use of a function known as *Gödel's function β*.

Definition 3.10 Gödel's function β is defined by

$$\beta(k, l, i) = l \bmod (k(i + 1) + 1)$$

where $x \bmod y$ is the remainder of the Euclidean division of x by y.

Proposition 3.15 *For any finite sequence $s_0, \ldots, s_y$, there are two natural numbers k, l such that for any i less than y, $s_i = \beta(k, l, i)$.*

Proof Let m be a natural number strictly greater than $y + 1, s_0, \ldots, s_y$. It is easy to check that the numbers $e_i = m!(i + 1) + 1$ for i less than y are pairwise coprimes: if e_i and e_j have a prime common divisor c, then c divides also their difference $m!(i - j)$, and is therefore less than m, it divides $m!(i + 1)$ and therefore it cannot divide $e_i = m!(i + 1) + 1$. We use now a well-known result in number theory, the *theorem of the Chinese remainders*: if $e_0, \ldots, e_y$ is a sequence of pairwise coprime numbers and $s_0, \ldots, s_y$ a sequence of arbitrary natural numbers, there exists a natural number z such that for all i, $s_i \equiv z[\bmod e_i]$. Thus, using this theorem we deduce that there exists a number z such that $s_i \equiv z[\bmod e_i]$. We take $k = m!$ and $l = z$. Then, $s_i \equiv l[\bmod e_i]$ and since s_i is less than m which is in turn less than k and therefore less than $k(i + 1) + 1$, s_i is the remainder of the Euclidean division of l by $k(i + 1) + 1$, that is, $s_i = \beta(k, l, i)$. $\square$

The fact that a function recursively defined using g and h produces the value r for $x_1, \ldots, x_{n-1}, y$ is now expressed by the fact that there exist two numbers k and l such that $\beta(k, l, 0) = g(x_1, \ldots, x_{n-1})$, for all i strictly less than y, $\beta(k, l, i + 1) = h(x_1, \ldots, x_{n-1}, i, \beta(k, l, i))$ and $\beta(k, l, y) = r$.

Instead of stating that for all i strictly less than y, $\beta(k, l, i + 1) = h(x_1, \ldots, x_{n-1}, i, \beta(k, l, i))$, we can equivalently state that the least zero of the function f_1 that associates 1 to $x_1, \ldots, x_{n-1}, y, k, l, i$ if $i < y$ and $\beta(k, l, i + 1) = h(x_1, \ldots, x_{n-1}, i, \beta(k, l, i))$ and 0 otherwise, is y. Nevertheless, it is not easy to show that the function f_1 is in C, since this function must be defined and take the value 0 for y whether h is defined for $x_1, \ldots, x_{n-1}, y, \beta(k, l, y)$ or not. To avoid this problem, we will prove a more general theorem: if the function f is computable, then the function f^* is in C, where the function f^* is defined as follows.

Definition 3.11 Let f be a function with n arguments. We denote by f^* the function with $n + 1$ arguments defined by $f^*(0, x_1, \ldots, x_n) = 0$ and $f^*(w, x_1, \ldots, x_n) = f(x_1, \ldots, x_n)$ if $w \neq 0$.

Proposition 3.16 *The set C contains the subtraction function $\dot{-}$, the quotient and remainder of the Euclidean division, and the functions $\chi_{\mathbb{N}^*}$, $\chi_<$ and $\chi_=$, which are,* *respectively, the characteristic functions of the set* $\mathbb{N}^*$ *and the relations* $<$ *and* $=$, *the function* β *and the functions* $;,$ *hd and tl.*

Proof Subtraction, quotient and remainder can be defined using addition, multiplication, minimisation and the characteristic function of the ordering relation. The functions $\chi_{\mathbb{N}^*}$, $\chi_<$ and $\chi_=$ can be defined using subtraction. The function β can be defined using addition, multiplication and the remainder function. The function $;$ is defined using addition, multiplication and quotient. Finally, the functions *hd* and *tl* can be defined using addition, multiplication, quotient and minimisation. $\square$

Proposition 3.17 *If f is a function defined by recursion using two functions g and h such that g^* and h^* are in $\mathcal{C}$, then f^* is in $\mathcal{C}$.*

Proof The function f^* satisfies the properties

$$f^*(w, x_1, \ldots, x_{n-1}, 0) = g^*(w, x_1, \ldots, x_{n-1})$$
$$f^*(w, x_1, \ldots, x_{n-1}, y+1) = h^*(w, x_1, \ldots, x_{n-1}, y, f^*(w, x_1, \ldots, x_{n-1}, y))$$

and it is therefore the function recursively defined from g^* and h^*.

Let f_1 be the function from $\mathcal{C}$ that associates the number $\chi_<(i, y) \times \chi_=(h^*(w \times \chi_<(i, y), x_1, \ldots, x_{n-1}, i, \beta(k, l, i)), \beta(k, l, i+1))$ to $w, x_1, \ldots, x_{n-1}, y, k, l$ and i. If $i \geq y$ then f^* is defined and it is equal to 0 for $w, x_1, \ldots, x_{n-1}, y, k, l, i$ and if $i < y$ then

$$f_1(w, x_1, \ldots, x_{n-1}, y, k, l) = \chi_=(h^*(w, x_1, \ldots, x_{n-1}, i, \beta(k, l, i)), \beta(k, l, i+1))$$

Let f_2 be the function from $\mathcal{C}$ that maps $w, x_1, \ldots, x_{n-1}, y, k$ and l to the least natural number i such that $f_1(w, x_1, \ldots, x_{n-1}, y, k, l, i) = 0$. The natural number $f_2(w, x_1, \ldots, x_{n-1}, y, k, l)$ is equal to y if and only if for all i strictly less than y, h^* is defined for $w, x_1, \ldots, x_{n-1}, i, \beta(k, l, i)$ and $h^*(w, x_1, \ldots, x_{n-1}, i, \beta(k, l, i)) = \beta(k, l, i+1)$.

As a consequence, we deduce that there exists a function f_3 in $\mathcal{C}$ that maps $w, x_1, \ldots, x_{n-1}, y, k, l$ and r to 0 if and only if the function g^* is defined for $w, x_1, \ldots, x_{n-1}$ and returns the value $\beta(k, l, 0)$, for all i strictly less than y, the function h^* is defined for $w, x_1, \ldots, x_{n-1}, i, \beta(k, l, i)$ and returns the value $\beta(k, l, i+1)$ and $\beta(k, l, y) = r$.

Let f_4 be the function from $\mathcal{C}$ that maps $w, x_1, \ldots, x_{n-1}, y$ to the smallest j such that $f_3(w, x_1, \ldots, x_{n-1}, y, hd(hd(j)), tl(hd(j)), tl(j)) = 0$ and f_5 the function from $\mathcal{C}$ that maps $w, x_1, \ldots, x_{n-1}, y$ to $tl(f_4(w, x_1, \ldots, x_{n-1}, y))$. By Proposition 3.15, the function f_5 associates the value r to $x_1, \ldots, x_{n-1}, y$ if and only if there exists a sequence s such that $s_0 = g^*(w, x_1, \ldots, x_{n-1})$, for all i strictly less than y, $s_{i+1} = h^*(w, x_1, \ldots, x_{n-1}, i, s_i)$ and $s_y = r$. Thus, the function f_5 turns out to be the function f^*, and therefore is in the set $\mathcal{C}$. $\square$

Proposition 3.18 *A function is in the set $\mathcal{C}$ if and only if it is computable.*

Proof By Definition 3.1 and Propositions 3.2 and 3.3, the set of computable functions is closed under all the rules in the inductive definition of $\mathcal{C}$, and therefore it contains all the functions in the set $\mathcal{C}$.

To prove the other direction, we start by showing, by induction on the construction of f, that if f is a computable function then f^* is in $\mathcal{C}$. If f is a projection, a zero function or the successor function, then $f^*(w, x_1, \ldots, x_n) = \chi_{\mathbb{N}^*}(w) \times f(x_1, \ldots, x_n)$ and thus the function f^* belongs to $\mathcal{C}$. If f is defined as the composition of the functions h and $g_1, \ldots, g_m$, then, by induction hypothesis, the functions $h^*, g_1^*, \ldots, g_m^*$ are in $\mathcal{C}$ and $f^*(w, x_1, \ldots, x_n) = h^*(w, g_1^*(w, x_1, \ldots, x_n), \ldots, g_m^*(w, x_1, \ldots, x_n))$. The function f^* is the composition of a projection, $g_1^*, \ldots, g_m^*$ and h^*, therefore it is also in $\mathcal{C}$. If f is recursively defined from the functions g and h, then, by induction hypothesis, the functions g^* and h^* are in the set $\mathcal{C}$ and by Proposition 3.17, so is the function f^*. If f is defined by minimisation of a function g, then the function g^* is in $\mathcal{C}$ by induction hypothesis, and f^* is the function that maps $w, x_1, \ldots, x_n$ to the smallest i such that $g^*(w, x_1, \ldots, x_n, i) = 0$; this is therefore the function defined by minimisation of g^* and thus it is in $\mathcal{C}$.

Since the function f^* is in $\mathcal{C}$, so is the function that maps $x_1, \ldots, x_n$ to the natural number $f^*(1, x_1, \ldots, x_n)$, which is in fact the function f. $\qquad\square$

3.4 Programs

The set of computable functions is inductively defined, therefore for each computable function there is at least one derivation. These derivations are trees, usually called *programs*.

The nodes in these trees are labelled by symbols that correspond to the eight rules in Definition 3.9: π_i^n, where i and n are natural numbers and $1 \leq i \leq n$, in the case of a projection rule, Z^n for a rule corresponding to a zero function, $Succ$ for the successor rule, $+$ for the addition rule, $\times$ for the multiplication rule, $\chi_\leq$ for the rule corresponding to the characteristic function of the ordering relation, o_m^n for the composition rule, and μ^n for minimisation.

Programs are therefore trees where nodes are labelled by the symbols π_i^n, Z^n, $Succ$, $+$, $\times$, $\chi_\leq$, o_m^n and μ^n, which are in turn trees labelled by elements of a finite set.

Of course, if we use an alternative definition of computable functions, we get a different definition of program: using Definition 3.1, programs are trees with nodes labelled by the symbols π_i^n, Z^n, $Succ$, o_m^n, μ^n and Rec^n for recursive definitions.

Definition 3.12 (Termination, value) A program is *terminating* for the inputs $p_1, \ldots, p_n$ if the function f computed by the program is defined for $p_1, \ldots, p_n$. We say that a program *returns the value q* for $p_1, \ldots, p_n$ if in addition $f(p_1, \ldots, p_n) = q$.

Exercise 3.3 Which is the function computed by the program $o_1^1(Succ, Succ)$?

Exercise 3.4 Which is the function computed by the program $\mu^1(\pi_1^2)$?

3.4.1 Undecidability of the Halting Problem

Theorem 3.1 (Undecidability of the halting problem) *The set of pairs of natural numbers (p, q) such that p is the index associated to a program that is terminating for the input q is undecidable.*

Proof By contradiction. Suppose that there exists a program t such that t applied to two natural numbers p and q always terminates and returns the result 1 if p is the index of a terminating program for the input q, and the result 0 otherwise. Recall that the program $b = \mu^1(\pi_1^2)$ is terminating when applied to the number 0 and non-terminating when applied to a natural number different from 0. Now consider the program $u = \circ_1^1(b, \circ_2^1(t, \pi_1^1, \pi_1^1))$. Each time we apply the program u to a number p, we apply first the program $\circ_2^1(t, \pi_1^1, \pi_1^1)$ to this number. We obtain the result 1 if p is the index of a program that is terminating on the input p and the result 0 otherwise. Therefore, the program u applied to the natural number p does not terminate if p is the number of a program that is terminating on the input p, and terminates otherwise.

Let m be the natural number $\ulcorner u \urcorner$. The program u does not terminate on the input m if m is the number of a program that terminates on m, and it terminates otherwise. In other words, the program u applied to m is not terminating if the program u is terminating when applied to m, and it terminates otherwise. The program u applied to m does not terminate if and only if it terminates—a contradiction. $\qquad\square$

3.4.2 The Interpreter

There exists nevertheless a computable function G^n that behaves as an *interpreter*, that is, takes as arguments the number associated to a program u of arity n and natural numbers $p_1, \ldots, p_n$ and returns the value of the computable function represented by the program u for the inputs $p_1, \ldots, p_n$, if this value exists. Showing the existence of this interpreter will allow us to generalise the theorem of undecidability of the halting problem. This will lead us to a description of a computation as a sequence of small steps, that is, a view of computation as a process that unfolds over time (we will come back to this idea in Chap. 4).

To define the function G^n, we need a language that can express programs and their inputs (i.e., natural numbers). We will extend the language of programs to include the symbols 0 and S in order to represent the natural numbers (note that these are different from the symbols Z^n and $Succ$ used in the language of programs). We will write $\underline{p}$ as an abbreviation for the term $S(S(\ldots(S(0))\ldots))$ where the symbol S occurs p times, representing the natural number p. We will then introduce a family of symbols App^n to build terms of the form $App^n(u, \underline{p_1}, \ldots, \underline{p_n})$ which will represent the application of the program u to the natural numbers $\underline{p_1}, \ldots, \underline{p_n}$.

The problem now is to define a computable function F that associates to the index of a term $App^n(u, \underline{p_1}, \ldots, \underline{p_n})$, the index of the term $\underline{q}$ representing the natural number q, which is the value of the computable function denoted by the program u for the inputs $p_1, \ldots, p_n$, assuming this value exists. The term q is called the *value* of the term $App^n(u, \underline{p_1}, \ldots, \underline{p_n})$. Once we have defined the function F, we can simply define the function G^n, using Proposition 3.12, as the function that associates to the index of the term u and the natural numbers $p_1, \ldots, p_n$ the natural number q such that $\ulcorner q \urcorner = F(\ulcorner App^n(u, \underline{p_1}, \ldots, \underline{p_n}) \urcorner)$, if q exists.

If the program u has the form $o_m^n(w, v_1, \ldots, v_m)$, we will first compute the values $q_1, \ldots, q_m$ of the programs $v_1, \ldots, v_m$ for $p_1, \ldots, p_n$, and then compute the value of the program w for $q_1, \ldots, q_m$. In order to achieve this, we first build the term $App^m(w, App^n(v_1, \underline{p_1}, \ldots, \underline{p_n}), \ldots, App^n(v_m, \underline{p_1}, \ldots, \underline{p_n}))$, then compute the values of the terms $App^n(v_i, \underline{p_1}, \ldots, \underline{p_n})$ obtaining $\underline{q_1}, \ldots, \underline{q_m}$, and finally we compute the value of the term $App^m(w, \underline{q_1}, \ldots, \underline{q_m})$. However, to proceed in this way we need to be able to apply the symbol App^m not only to terms representing natural numbers but also to other terms containing the symbol App^n which are not yet evaluated. Thus, to compute the value of such a term, we need to start by computing the values of its arguments.

To compute the result of a program that uses minimisation, we will also need to introduce a family of symbols M^n and a symbol Ifz. The value of the term $M^{n+1}(u, \underline{p_1}, \ldots, \underline{p_n}, q)$ is the least natural number r greater than or equal to q such that $f(p_1, \ldots, p_n, r) = 0$ where f is the function computed by the program u. The value of the term $Ifz(p, v, w)$ is the value of the term v if $p = 0$ and the value of the term w otherwise.

We start by defining a function F_1 that associates to the index of each term of the form $App^n(u, \underline{p_1}, \ldots, \underline{p_n})$, $M^{n+1}(u, v_1, \ldots, v_n, w)$ or $Ifz(\underline{p}, v, w)$, the index of a term that denotes an intermediate state in the computation.

Definition 3.13 (A step of computation at the root) The computable function F_1 is defined by cases:

- if t is the index of a term of the form $App^n(u, \underline{p_1}, \ldots, \underline{p_n})$, then
  - if u is of the form π_i^n, then $F_1(t) = \ulcorner p_i \urcorner$,
  - if u is of the form Z^n, then $F_1(t) = \ulcorner 0 \urcorner$,
  - if $u = Succ$, then $F_1(t) = \ulcorner S(p_1) \urcorner$, that is, $\ulcorner S \urcorner; (\ulcorner p_1 \urcorner; 0)$, or, equivalently, $\ulcorner S \urcorner; (hd(tl(tl(t))); 0)$,
  - if $u = +$, then $F_1(t) = \ulcorner p_1 + p_2 \urcorner$,
  - if $u = \times$, then $F_1(t) = \ulcorner p_1 \times p_2 \urcorner$,
  - if $u = \chi_\le$, then $F_1(t) = \ulcorner \chi_\le(p_1, p_2) \urcorner$,
  - if u is of the form $o_m^n(w, v_1, \ldots, v_m)$, then

  $$F_1(t) = \ulcorner App^m(w, App^n(v_1, \underline{p_1}, \ldots, \underline{p_n}), \ldots, App^n(v_m, \underline{p_1}, \ldots, \underline{p_n})) \urcorner$$

  - if u is of the form $\mu^n(v)$, then

  $$F_1(t) = \ulcorner M^{n+1}(v, \underline{p_1}, \ldots, \underline{p_n}, \underline{0}) \urcorner$$

- if t is the index of a term of the form $M^{n+1}(u, v_1, \ldots, v_n, w)$, then

  $$F_1(t) = \ulcorner Ifz(App^{n+1}(u, v_1, \ldots, v_n, w), w, M^{n+1}(u, v_1, \ldots, v_n, S(w))) \urcorner$$

- if t is the index of a term of the form $Ifz(\underline{p}, v, w)$, then $F_1(t) = \ulcorner v \urcorner$, if $p = 0$ and $F_1(t) = \ulcorner w \urcorner$ otherwise,
- otherwise, we define $F_1(t) = 0$.

The function F_1 performs a step of computation from a term of the form $App^n(u, v_1, \ldots, v_n)$ where the terms $v_1, \ldots, v_n$ are natural numbers $\underline{p_1}, \ldots, \underline{p_n}$. If instead these are terms that need to be computed, then the function F_2 defined below performs a step of computation on those terms.

Definition 3.14 (A step of computation) The computable function F_2 is defined by well-founded induction:

- if t is the index of a term of the form $App^n(u, v_1, \ldots, v_n)$, then if the terms $v_1, \ldots, v_n$ are of the form $\underline{p_1}, \ldots, \underline{p_n}$, we define $F_2(t) = F_1(t)$, otherwise, let v_i be the first term that is not of the form $\underline{p}$ and v' the term with index $F_2(\ulcorner v_i \urcorner)$, we define
$$F_2(t) = \ulcorner App^n(u, v_1, \ldots, v_{i-1}, v', v_{i+1}, \ldots, v_n) \urcorner$$
- if t is the index of a term of the form $M^{n+1}(u, v_1, \ldots, v_n, w)$, we define $F_2(t) = F_1(t)$,
- if t is the index of a term of the form $Ifz(u, v, w)$, then if the term u is of the form $\underline{p}$, we define $F_2(t) = F_1(t)$, otherwise let u' be the term with index $F_2(\ulcorner u \urcorner)$, we define $F_2(t) = \ulcorner Ifz(u', v, w)) \urcorner$,
- otherwise, we define $F_2(t) = 0$.

Now in order to define an interpreter F it is sufficient to iterate the function F_2 on the term t until we obtain a term of the form $\underline{q}$. For this, we will define a function F_3 to iterate the function F_2 p times, a function F_4 that will check whether $F_3(t, p)$ is of the form $\underline{q}$ or not, a function F_5 to count the number of steps that are needed to obtain such a term, and finally the function F.

Definition 3.15 (The interpreter) Let F_3 be the computable function such that $F_3(t, p) = F_2^p(t)$. This function is defined by

$$F_3(t, 0) = t$$
$$F_3(t, p + 1) = F_2(F_3(t, p))$$

Let F_4 be the computable function such that $F_4(t, n) = 0$ if $F_3(t, n)$ is the index of a term of the form $\underline{q}$, otherwise $F_4(t, n) = 1$. This function can be defined by composition, using F_3 and the function that returns 0 for all the indices of terms of the form $\underline{q}$ and 1 for any other input. Let F_5 be the computable function such that $F_5(t)$ is the number of steps that are needed to compute t. $F_5(t)$ can be defined by minimisation: it is the least natural number p such that $F_4(t, p) = 0$. Let F be the computable function defined by $F(t) = F_3(t, F_5(t))$. Finally, G^n is computable function that associates to t and $p_1, \ldots, p_n$ the natural number q such that $\ulcorner q \urcorner = F(\ulcorner App^n(t, \underline{p_1}, \ldots, \underline{p_n}) \urcorner)$.

If $F_3(t, n)$ never returns the index of a term representing a natural number, in other words, if the iterations of F_2 continue forever, then F_5 and F are undefined for t: the interpreter does not terminate if the program to be interpreted is non-terminating.

Proposition 3.19 *Let f be a computable function, u the index of a program that represents this function and $p_1, \ldots, p_n$ natural numbers. The function f is defined for $p_1, \ldots, p_n$ if and only if the function F is defined for $\ulcorner App^n(u, \underline{p_1}, \ldots, \underline{p_n}) \urcorner$, and if these two functions are defined, then $F(\ulcorner App^n(u, \underline{p_1}, \ldots, \underline{p_n}) \urcorner) = \ulcorner f(p_1, \ldots, p_n) \urcorner$.*

Proof By induction on the construction of f.   □

Proposition 3.20 *Let f be a computable function, u the index of a program representing this function and $p_1, \ldots, p_n$ natural numbers. The function f is defined for $p_1, \ldots, p_n$ if and only if the function G^n is defined for $u, p_1, \ldots, p_n$ and if these two functions are defined then $G^n(u, p_1, \ldots, p_n) = f(p_1, \ldots, p_n)$.*

Proof Consequence of Proposition 3.19.   □

Exercise 3.5 Show that the function F_3 is primitive recursive.

Exercise 3.6 Define an interpreter for the programs written in the language generated by the symbols π_i^n, Z^n, $Succ$, o_m^n, μ^n and Rec^n, corresponding to Definition 3.1.

As a corollary of the existence of this interpreter, we obtain a generalisation of the theorem of undecidability of the halting problem.

Proposition 3.21 *Let A be a decidable subset of the set of terminating programs. There exists a computable, total function that is not represented by any program in A.*

Proof Let H be the computable function defined as follows: if n is the index of a unary program in A and p is a natural number then $H(n, p) = G^1(n, p)$, otherwise $H(n, p) = 0$.

The function H is computable; it is an interpreter for unary programs in A and it is total.

Let H' be the function such that $H'(p) = H(p, p) + 1$. If A contains a term t representing the function H', then $H(\ulcorner t \urcorner, p) = H'(p) = H(p, p) + 1$ for all p, but then for $p = \ulcorner t \urcorner$ we obtain $H(\ulcorner t \urcorner, \ulcorner t \urcorner) = H(\ulcorner t \urcorner, \ulcorner t \urcorner) + 1$, which is a contradiction.   □

This result shows that a programming language in which all programs are terminating is necessarily incomplete: it cannot express its own interpreter. For instance, the imperative language consisting of variable declarations, assignment, sequence and `for` loops is not complete.

Using this result we could also give an alternative proof of the undecidability of the halting problem: Assume that the set containing all the terminating programs is decidable, then by the previous result we deduce that there exists a total function that is not in this set (contradiction).

We could also prove that there exists a computable total function that is not primitive recursive, since the set of programs that can be represented in the language π_i^n, Z^n, $Succ$, o_m^n, Rec^n is decidable.

Chapter 4
Computation as a Sequence of Small Steps

The interpreter defined in Sect. 3.4.2 suggests a new approach to the definition of computation, where programs are expressions in a language $\mathcal{L}$. Given a program t and arguments $p_1, \ldots, p_n$, we can build a term, that is an expression in a language $\mathcal{L}'$ that extends the language $\mathcal{L}$; then, the execution of the program is defined by a computable total function from terms in $\mathcal{L}'$ to terms in $\mathcal{L}'$. This function describes a small step of computation, but we can iterate it until we obtain a natural number, i.e., the result of the computation, or otherwise continue iterating forever if the program t is non-terminating for the arguments $p_1, \ldots, p_n$.

Thus, the notion of termination given in Definition 3.12 corresponds to the one familiar to programmers: a program that does not terminate is a program that continues computing forever.

The languages $\mathcal{L}$ and $\mathcal{L}'$ and the function that describes a small step of computation can be seen as the definition of a programming language, and a partial function f is said to be *representable* in this language if there exists a program t such that the term built out of the program t and the natural numbers $p_1, \ldots, p_n$ computes a natural number $f(p_1, \ldots, p_n)$ when the function f is defined for $p_1, \ldots, p_n$ and does not terminate otherwise. It is easy to show that all the partial functions that can be represented in such a language are computable.

Some programming languages, for instance the one defined in Sect. 3.4.2, can express all computable functions; these languages are said to be *Turing complete*.

Traditional programming languages such as Java, Caml, C, ... are Turing complete, and so are a number of programming languages developed by researchers to study programming language properties. These languages do not have the same applications as traditional programming languages: it is more difficult to express algorithms in them because they have only a minimal number of primitive constructions, but this makes them simpler to study. By simplifying the language in which algorithms are expressed, one can better reason about algorithms, in particular if the goal is to establish that an algorithm terminates, preserves some invariant or has a given complexity.

In this chapter we will describe three of these minimalistic languages: term rewriting, the lambda-calculus, and Turing machines.

G. Dowek, *Proofs and Algorithms*, Undergraduate Topics in Computer Science, DOI 10.1007/978-0-85729-121-9_4, © Springer-Verlag London Limited 2011

4.1 Rewriting

Rewriting is the simplest language that allows us to express computations as sequences of small steps. Terms are simply expressions in a language without binders, and computation steps are defined by a set of rules, called *rewriting rules*, which specify the way in which terms are transformed. For instance, the rule

$$0 + y \longrightarrow y$$

states that any term of the form $0 + t$ can be transformed into t.

Definition 4.1 (Rewriting rule) Let $\mathcal{L}$ be a language without binders. A *rewriting rule* in the language $\mathcal{L}$ is a pair l, r of terms in $\mathcal{L}$, written $l \longrightarrow r$.

Definition 4.2 (Reduction step at the root) Let $\mathcal{R}$ be a set of rewriting rules. An $\mathcal{R}$-*reduction step at the root* is a pair of terms in the language $\mathcal{L}$, written $t \longrightarrow u$, such that there exists a rewriting rule $l \longrightarrow r$ in $\mathcal{R}$ and a substitution σ such that $\sigma l = t$ and $\sigma r = u$.

Definition 4.3 (Redex) Let $\mathcal{R}$ be a set of rewriting rules. A term t is a *redex* if it is reducible by the relation $\longrightarrow$, that is, if there is a rewriting rule $l \longrightarrow r$ and a substitution σ such that $\sigma l = t$.

The relation $\longrightarrow$ can be extended to perform reductions in subterms.

Definition 4.4 (Reduction step) Let $\mathcal{R}$ be a set of rewriting rules. An $\mathcal{R}$-*reduction step* is the relation defined inductively by

– if $t \to u$ then $t \rhd u$,
– if $t \rhd u$, then $f(t_1, \ldots, t_{i-1}, t, t_{i+1}, \ldots, t_n) \rhd f(t_1, \ldots, t_{i-1}, u, t_{i+1}, \ldots, t_n)$.

Definition 4.5 (Reduction) The reduction relation $\rhd^*$ is the reflexive-transitive closure of the relation $\rhd$.

Exercise 4.1 Consider the following set of rewriting rules.

$$0 + y \longrightarrow y$$

$$S(x) + y \longrightarrow S(x + y)$$

Show that $S(S(0)) + S(S(0)) \rhd^* S(S(S(S(0))))$.

Definition 4.6 (Irreducibility, termination) Let R be a binary relation. An element t is *irreducible* by the relation R if there is no element u such that $t \ R \ u$.

An element t *is terminating* if there exists an irreducible element t' such that $t \ R^* \ t'$.

Definition 4.7 (Irreducibility and termination for terms) Let $\mathcal{R}$ be a set of rewriting rules. A term t is *irreducible* if it is irreducible by the relation $\triangleright$, that is, if neither of its subterms is a redex.

A term t *is terminating* if it is terminating for the relation $\triangleright$, that is, if there exists some irreducible term t' such that $t \triangleright^* t'$.

For example, if we have two rules $f(x) \longrightarrow a$ and $\omega \longrightarrow \omega$, then the term ω is non-terminating, since the only term that can be obtained by reduction is ω again. However, the term $f(\omega)$ is terminating. Indeed, we can reduce the subterm ω and obtain again $f(\omega)$ but we can also reduce at the root and obtain the irreducible term a.

Definition 4.8 (Confluence) A binary relation R is *confluent* if for any u and v such that $t \ R^* \ u$ and $t \ R^* \ v$, there exists some w such that $u \ R^* \ w$ and $v \ R^* \ w$.

If the relation $\triangleright$ is confluent, then each term u can be reduced to at most one irreducible term: if $t \triangleright^* u$ and $t \triangleright^* v$, and u and v are irreducible, then $u = v$. In general, if t, u and v are three terms such that $t \triangleright^* u$ and $t \triangleright^* v$, and v is irreducible, then $u \triangleright^* v$. However, as we have seen with the term $f(\omega)$, some reduction sequences might end with an irreducible term, whereas others are infinite.

Definition 4.9 (Orthogonal set of rules) A set $\mathcal{R}$ of rewriting rules is *orthogonal* if

- for each rewriting rule $l \longrightarrow r$ in $\mathcal{R}$, the variables occurring in r occur also in l,
- for each rewriting rule $l \longrightarrow r$ in $\mathcal{R}$, each variable x occurs at most once in l,
  - if $l \longrightarrow r$ and $l' \longrightarrow r'$ are two different rewriting rules in $\mathcal{R}$, and l'' is a non-variable subterm of l', then for any pair of substitutions σ and τ, $\sigma l \neq \tau l''$,
  - if $l \longrightarrow r$ is a rewriting rule in $\mathcal{R}$, and l'' is a strict subterm of l which is not a variable, then for any pair of substitutions σ and τ, $\sigma l \neq \tau l''$.

Exercise 4.2 Is the set consisting of the rule

$$c \longrightarrow x$$

orthogonal?

Show that the term c can be reduced to two different irreducible terms.

Exercise 4.3 Is the set consisting of the rules

$$g(h(x)) \longrightarrow a$$
$$f(g(x)) \longrightarrow b$$

orthogonal?

Show that the term $f(g(h(c)))$ can be reduced to two different irreducible terms.

Exercise 4.4 Is the set consisting of the rules

$$x - x \longrightarrow 0$$

$$S(x) - x \longrightarrow 1$$

$$\infty \longrightarrow S(\infty)$$

orthogonal?

Show that the term $\infty - \infty$ can be reduced to two different irreducible terms.

This definition of orthogonality is motivated by the following result (the proof is omitted).

Proposition 4.1 (Confluence of orthogonal sets of rules) *If $\mathcal{R}$ is an orthogonal set of rewriting rules, then the relation $\triangleright$ is confluent.*

Definition 4.10 (Representing natural numbers) If the language $\mathcal{L}$ contains a constant 0 and a unary symbol S and if p is a natural number, we denote by $\underline{p}$ the term $S(S(\ldots(S(0))\ldots))$ where the symbol S occurs p times.

Definition 4.11 (Representing functions) Let $\mathcal{L}$ be a language containing the symbols 0 and S, and let $\mathcal{R}$ be a confluent set of rewriting rules such that all the terms of the form $\underline{p}$ are irreducible. Let F be a symbol in $\mathcal{L}$ and f a partial function. The pair $\mathcal{R}$, F *represents the function* f if for all $p_1, \ldots, p_n$

- if $f(p_1, \ldots, p_n) = q$ then $F(\underline{p_1}, \ldots, \underline{p_n}) \triangleright^* \underline{q}$,
- if f is not defined for $p_1, \ldots, p_n$ then $F(\underline{p_1}, \ldots, \underline{p_n})$ is non-terminating.

This definition does not fit properly in the framework that we gave in the introduction to this chapter, because a term which contains several redexes might reduce to several terms. However, we can use a specific reduction strategy: *call by name* avoids this non-determinism if the set of rules is orthogonal.

Definition 4.12 (A reduction step under call by name) *An $\mathcal{R}$-reduction step under call by name* is defined by induction

- if $t \longrightarrow t'$, then $t \succ t'$,
- if $f(t_1, \ldots, t_n)$ is not a redex, $t_1, \ldots, t_{i-1}$ are irreducible, and $t_i \succ t_i'$ then $f(t_1, \ldots, t_{i-1}, t_i, t_{i+1}, \ldots, t_n) \succ f(t_1, \ldots, t_{i-1}, t_i', t_{i+1}, \ldots, t_n)$.

In other words, given a term with several redexes, we give priority to the leftmost one.

An irreducible term with respect to the relation $\triangleright$ does not contain any redex; it is therefore also irreducible with respect to the relation $\succ$. However, if a term can be reduced by $\triangleright$, then it contains at least a redex, and it can be reduced by $\succ$. In this case, if the set of rules is orthogonal, the call by name reduction strategy produces a unique result.

Definition 4.13 (Call by name reduction) The reduction relation $\succ^*$ is the reflexive-transitive closure of the relation $\succ$, inductively defined by

$- t \succ^* t$,
$-$ if $t \succ t'$ and $t' \succ^* t''$, then $t \succ^* t''$.

This strategy suggests another way to represent functions.

Definition 4.14 (Representation of functions under call by name) Let $\mathcal{L}$ be a language that contains the symbols 0 and S. Let $\mathcal{R}$ be a set of rewriting rules such that all terms of the form $\underline{p}$ are irreducible. Let F be a symbol in $\mathcal{L}$ and f a partial function. The pair $\mathcal{R}$, F *represents the function* f *under call by name* if for all $p_1, \ldots, p_n$,

$-$ if $f(p_1, \ldots, p_n) = q$, then $F(\underline{p_1}, \ldots, \underline{p_n}) \succ^* \underline{q}$,
$-$ if f is not defined for $p_1, \ldots, p_n$, then $F(\underline{p_1}, \ldots, \underline{p_n})$ is non-terminating under call by name.

If we use call by name reduction, we are back in the framework defined in the introduction to this chapter. A program is simply a pair consisting of an orthogonal set of rewriting rules and a function symbol. From the program $(\mathcal{R}, F)$ and the natural numbers $p_1, \ldots, p_n$ we can build a pair consisting of a set $\mathcal{R}$ of rules and a term $F(\underline{p_1}, \ldots, \underline{p_n})$, and define a notion of computation where a computation step corresponds to a reduction step under call by name using the rules in $\mathcal{R}$.

Our aim now is to associate to each computable function f a set of rewriting rules representing this function, both in general and under call by name.

The following example illustrates the main difficulty we face. If g is a function undefined for the argument 4 and h is the constant function equal to 0 then the function $f = h \circ g$ is not defined for 4. However, if we simply write the rules $H(x) \longrightarrow 0$ and $F(x) \longrightarrow H(G(x))$, then the term $F(\underline{4})$ reduces to $H(G(\underline{4}))$ and then to 0, instead of producing a non-terminating computation. To solve this problem, we can replace the rule $H(x) \longrightarrow 0$ by $H(x) \longrightarrow 0 \& x$ and the rule $F(x) \longrightarrow H(G(x))$ by $F(x) \longrightarrow H(G(x)) \& x$, introducing a binary symbol $\&$ such that $t \& u$ reduces to t if u reduces to a natural number, and $t \& u$ is non-terminating if u is non-terminating. This property can be obtained with the rules $x \& 0 \longrightarrow x$ and $x \& S(y) \longrightarrow x \& y$, which erase the term u step by step, provided that it represents a natural number.

Definition 4.15 (Representing computable functions) Let f be a computable function with n arguments. We associate to f a symbol F and a set of rewriting rules as follows. All the sets contain the rules

$$x \& 0 \longrightarrow x$$

$$x \& S(y) \longrightarrow x \& y$$

$$Ifz(0, y, z) \longrightarrow y$$

$$Ifz(S(x), y, z) \longrightarrow z \& x$$

To these rules we add specific rules depending on the function f, defined by induction over its construction.

– If the function f is the ith projection, we add the rule

$$F(x_1, \ldots, x_n) \longrightarrow ((((x_i \& x_1) \& \ldots \& x_{i-1}) \& x_{i+1}) \& \ldots \& x_n)$$

– If the function f is a zero function, we add the rule

$$F(x_1, \ldots, x_n) \longrightarrow ((0 \& x_1) \& \ldots \& x_n)$$

– If the function f is the successor function, we add the rule

$$F(x) \longrightarrow S(x)$$

– If the function f is addition, we add the rules

$$F(0, y) \longrightarrow y$$

$$F(S(x), y) \longrightarrow S(F(x, y))$$

– If the function f is multiplication, we add the rules

$$F(0, y) \longrightarrow 0 \& y$$

$$F(S(x), y) \longrightarrow F'(F(x, y), y)$$

$$F'(0, y) \longrightarrow y$$

$$F'(S(x), y) \longrightarrow S(F'(x, y))$$

– If the function f is the characteristic function of the ordering relation, we add the rules

$$F(0, y) \longrightarrow S(0) \& y$$

$$F(S(x), 0) \longrightarrow 0 \& x$$

$$F(S(x), S(y)) \longrightarrow F(x, y)$$

– If the function f is obtained by composition from h and $g_1, \ldots, g_m$, then we take the sets of rules associated to these functions, and rename the symbols so that the sets share at most the symbols 0, S, $\&$ and Ifz; to the union of the sets of rules obtained we add the rule

$$F(x_1, \ldots, x_n) \longrightarrow (H(G_1(x_1, \ldots, x_n), \ldots, G_m(x_1, \ldots, x_n))) \& x_1 \& \ldots \& x_n$$

– If the function f is defined by minimisation of the function g, then we consider the set of rewriting rules associated to this function, and we add the rules

$$F(x_1, \ldots, x_n) \longrightarrow F'(x_1, \ldots, x_n, 0)$$

$$F'(x_1, \ldots, x_n, y) \longrightarrow Ifz(G(x_1, \ldots, x_n, y), y, F'(x_1, \ldots, x_n, S(y)))$$

Proposition 4.2 *The set of rules given in Definition 4.15 is confluent.*

Proof It is an orthogonal set, therefore by Proposition 4.1 it is confluent. $\square$

Proposition 4.3 *If $f(p_1, \ldots, p_n) = q$ and the terms $u_1, \ldots, u_n$ reduce to $\underline{p_1}$, $\ldots, \underline{p_n}$ under call by name, then the term $F(u_1, \ldots, u_n)$ reduces to $\underline{q}$ under call by name.*

Proof By induction over the definition of f. If f is a projection $F(u_1, \ldots, u_n)$ reduces to $((((u_i \& u_1) \& \ldots \& u_{i-1}) \& u_{i+1}) \& \ldots \& u_n)$ which under call by name reduces to $\underline{p_i}$. The cases corresponding to a zero function, the successor function, addition, multiplication and the characteristic function of the ordering relation are similar.

If the function f is defined by composition using h and $g_1, \ldots, g_m$, then $F(u_1, \ldots, u_n)$ reduces to $(H(G_1(u_1, \ldots, u_n), \ldots, G_m(u_1, \ldots, u_n))) \& u_1 \& \ldots \& u_n$ under call by name. By induction hypothesis, this term reduces under call by name to $q \& u_1 \& \ldots \& u_n$, then to $\underline{q}$.

If the function f is obtained by minimising the function g, then $g(p_1, \ldots, p_n, r)$ is defined and its value is different from zero for all natural number r strictly less than q, and $g(p_1, \ldots, p_n, q) = 0$. The term $F(u_1, \ldots, u_n)$ reduces under call by name to $F'(u_1, \ldots, u_n, 0)$, which reduces to $F'(u_1, \ldots, u_n, \underline{1}) \& v_0, \ldots, F'(u_1, \ldots, u_n, \underline{q}) \& v_{q-1} \& \ldots \& v_0$, where v_0 reduces to $g(p_1, \ldots, p_n, 0), \ldots, v_{q-1}$ reduces to $g(p_1, \ldots, p_n, q-1)$, and then to $Ifz(G(u_1, \ldots, u_n, \underline{q}), \underline{q}, F'(u_1, \ldots, u_n, \underline{q+1})) \& v_{q-1} \& \ldots \& v_0$, to $Ifz(0, \underline{q}, F'(u_1, \ldots, u_n, \underline{q+1})) \& v_{q-1} \& \ldots \& v_0$, to $\underline{q} \& v_{q-1} \& \ldots \& v_0$ and finally to $\underline{q}$. $\qquad\square$

We will now prove that if the function f is undefined for $p_1, \ldots, p_n$ then the term $F(\underline{p_1}, \ldots, \underline{p_n})$ is non-terminating. We start by proving the following proposition.

Proposition 4.4 *If any of the terms $u_1, \ldots, u_n$ is non-terminating, then $F(u_1, \ldots, u_n)$ is non-terminating. In other words, if $F(u_1, \ldots, u_n) \rhd^* t'$, then t' is not irreducible.*

Proof First, we remark that if a term $S(u)$ is non-terminating, so is the term u. Then, we define the set of *strict subterms* of a term t, denoted by $SST(t)$, by induction over the structure of t:

- if $t = x$, then $SST(t) = \{t\}$,
- if f is a function symbol different from Ifz (that is, one of the symbols 0, S, $\&$ or a symbol F representing a computable function) and $t = f(u_1, \ldots, u_n)$, then $SST(t) = \{t\} \cup \bigcup_i SST(u_i)$,
- if $t = Ifz(u_1, u_2, u_3)$, then $SST(t) \doteq \{t\} \cup SST(u_1)$.

First we show that for a set of rewriting rules as in Definition 4.15, if $t \longrightarrow t'$ and $SST(t)$ contains a non-terminating term, then so does $SST(t')$. Let u be a non-terminating member of $SST(t)$. If the term u is t itself, then t' is non-terminating and therefore $SST(t')$ contains a non-terminating element. If u is different from t, then by inspection of the rules, we verify that either u is in $SST(t')$ and therefore this set has a non-terminating element, or it is of the form $S(u')$ and $SST(t')$ contains u' that is non-terminating by the remark above.

Similarly we can show by induction over the structure of t that if $t \rhd t'$ and $SST(t)$ contains a non-terminating subterm, then so does $SST(t')$, and also if $t \rhd^* t'$ and $SST(t)$ contains a non-terminating subterm, then so does $SST(t')$.

As a consequence, we deduce that if one of the terms u_i is non-terminating, and $F(u_1, \ldots, u_n) \triangleright^* t'$, then $SST(t')$ contains a non-terminating term. This means that a subterm of t' is a redex, and therefore t' is not irreducible. $\square$

We can now prove that if the function f is undefined for $p_1, \ldots, p_n$ then the term $F(\underline{p_1}, \ldots, \underline{p_n})$ is non-terminating.

Proposition 4.5 *If the terms $u_1, \ldots, u_n$ reduce to $\underline{p_1}, \ldots, \underline{p_n}$, respectively, and f is undefined for $p_1, \ldots, p_n$, then $F(u_1, \ldots, u_n)$ is non-terminating, that is, if $F(u_1, \ldots, u_n) \triangleright^* t'$, then t' is not irreducible.*

Proof Let t' be a term such that $F(u_1, \ldots, u_n) \triangleright^* t'$. We prove that t' is not irreducible by induction over the definition of f.

The projections, the zero functions, the successor function, addition, multiplication and the characteristic function of the ordering relation are all total.

If the function f is defined by composition, using h and $g_1, \ldots, g_m$, and if in the sequence of reductions from $F(u_1, \ldots, u_n)$ to t' we never reduce a term at the root, then t' is itself a redex. If we do reduce a redex at the root, after some steps we obtain the term $H(G_1(u'_1, \ldots, u'_n), \ldots, G_m(u'_1, \ldots, u'_n))\&u'_1\&\ldots\&u'_n$ where the u'_i are reducts of u_i and t' is a reduct of this term. By confluence, u'_i reduces to $\underline{p_i}$. If one of the functions g_i is undefined for $p_1, \ldots, p_n$, then by induction one of the terms $G_i(u'_1, \ldots, u'_n)$ is non-terminating and therefore so is the term $H(G_1(u'_1, \ldots, u'_n), \ldots, G_m(u'_1, \ldots, u'_n))\&u'_1\&\ldots\&u'_n$ by Proposition 4.4.

Otherwise, $g_i(p_1, \ldots, p_n) = q_i$, and h is undefined for $q_1, \ldots, q_m$. In this case, $G_i(u'_1, \ldots, u'_n)$ reduces to $\underline{q_i}$ and $H(G_1(u'_1, \ldots, u'_n), \ldots, G_m(u'_1, \ldots, u'_n))$ is non-terminating by induction.

Thus, the term $H(G_1(u'_1, \ldots, u'_n), \ldots, G_m(u'_1, \ldots, u'_n))\&u'_1\&\ldots\&u'_n$ is non-terminating. Since the term $H(G_1(u'_1, \ldots, u'_n), \ldots, G_m(u'_1, \ldots, u'_n))\&u'_1\&\ldots\&u'_n$ is non-terminating, t' is not irreducible.

If f is defined by minimisation of the function g, then either the function g is defined everywhere and never returns 0, or it gives a non-zero result up to a certain value $q - 1$ and is undefined for q.

In the first case, by induction if the terms $u'_1, \ldots, u'_n$ reduce to $\underline{p_1}, \ldots, \underline{p_n}$ and u' reduces to a number, the term $G(u'_1, \ldots, u'_n, u')$ reduces to a number different from 0. We build inductively a set of terms containing

- the terms of the form $F(u'_1, \ldots, u'_n)$ where the terms $u'_1, \ldots, u'_n$ reduce to $\underline{p_1}, \ldots, \underline{p_n}$,
- the terms of the form $F'(u'_1, \ldots, u'_n, u')\&w_1\&\ldots\&w_s$ where the terms $u'_1, \ldots, u'_n$ reduce to $\underline{p_1}, \ldots, \underline{p_n}$ and $u', w_1, \ldots, w_s$ to arbitrary natural numbers,
- the terms of the form $Ifz(t, u, v)\&w_1\&\ldots\&w_s$, where the term t reduces to a number different from 0, u is arbitrary, v is in the set and $w_1, \ldots, w_s$ reduce to arbitrary natural numbers.

We can show that this set is closed under reduction, and therefore the term t' is in this set, thus it is not irreducible.

In the second case, by induction if the terms $u'_1, \ldots, u'_n$ reduce to $\underline{p_1}, \ldots, \underline{p_n}$ and u' reduces to $\underline{r}$ for some $r < q$, the term $G(u'_1, \ldots, u'_n, u')$ reduces to a number different from 0. We build inductively a set of terms containing

- the terms of the form $F(u'_1, \ldots, u'_n)$ where the terms $u'_1, \ldots, u'_n$ reduce to $\underline{p_1}, \ldots, \underline{p_n}$,
- the terms of the form $F'(u'_1, \ldots, u'_n, u')\&w_1\&\ldots\&w_s$ where the terms $u'_1, \ldots, u'_n$ reduce to $\underline{p_1}, \ldots, \underline{p_n}$, u' to $\underline{r}$ for some $r < q$ and $w_1, \ldots, w_s$ reduce to arbitrary natural numbers,
- the terms of the form $Ifz(t, u, v)\&w_1\&\ldots\&w_s$ where the term t reduces to a number different from 0, u is arbitrary, v is in the set and $w_1, \ldots, w_s$ reduce to arbitrary natural numbers,
- the terms of the form $Ifz(t, u, v)\&w_1\&\ldots\&w_s$ where the term t is non-terminating, u and v are arbitrary and $w_1, \ldots, w_s$ reduce to arbitrary natural numbers,
- the terms of the form $v\&t\&w_1\&\ldots\&w_s$ where the term t is non-terminating, v is arbitrary and $w_1, \ldots, w_s$ reduce to arbitrary natural numbers.

We can show that this set is closed under reduction, and therefore the term t' is in this set, thus it is not irreducible. □

We can finally conclude.

Theorem 4.1 *Every computable function can be represented by a set of rewriting rules in general and under call by name.*

The converse of this theorem states that all the functions that can be represented by a set of rewriting rules under call by name are computable. Indeed, the terms in the language $\mathcal{L}$ are trees, and therefore can be enumerated. It is sufficient then to show that the function that describes a basic step of computation, that is the function that associates to t the term u such that $t \succ u$, is computable.

Exercise 4.5 Give a direct proof of the fact that the set of functions that can be represented by a set of rewriting rules is closed under recursive definitions.

Exercise 4.6 A relation R defined over a set E is *strongly confluent* if each time we have $t\ R\ u$ and $t\ R\ v$, there exists an element w such that ($u\ R\ w$ or $u = w$) and ($v\ R\ w$ or $v = w$).
Show that a strongly confluent relation is confluent.

Exercise 4.7 This exercise relies on Exercise 4.6, which should be done prior to this one.
The goal of this exercise is to show a particular case of the theorem that states that a set of orthogonal rules defines a confluent relation $\triangleright$. Consider the language built out of the constants a and b, the unary function symbol f and the binary function symbol g. Assume we have the set of rules

$$a \longrightarrow b$$

$$f(x) \longrightarrow g(x, x)$$

1. The relation $\triangleright$ induced by this set of rules is inductively defined by the rules

$$\overline{a \triangleright b}$$

$$\overline{f(t) \triangleright g(t, t)}$$

$$\frac{t \triangleright t'}{f(t) \triangleright f(t')}$$

$$\frac{t_1 \triangleright t_1'}{g(t_1, t_2) \triangleright g(t_1', t_2)}$$

$$\frac{t_2 \triangleright t_2'}{g(t_1, t_2) \triangleright g(t_1, t_2')}$$

   Is it the case that $g(a, a) \triangleright g(b, b)$? Is the relation $\triangleright$ defined by this set of rules strongly confluent?
2. Consider a variant of this relation, *parallel reduction*, inductively defined by the rules

$$\overline{t \triangleright^{\|} t}$$

$$\overline{a \triangleright^{\|} b}$$

$$\overline{f(t) \triangleright^{\|} g(t, t)}$$

$$\frac{t \triangleright^{\|} t'}{f(t) \triangleright^{\|} f(t')}$$

$$\frac{t_1 \triangleright^{\|} t_1' \quad t_2 \triangleright^{\|} t_2'}{g(t_1, t_2) \triangleright^{\|} g(t_1', t_2')}$$

   Is it the case that $g(a, a) \triangleright^{\|} g(b, b)$? Show that the relation $\triangleright^{\|}$ is strongly confluent. Show that the relation $\triangleright^{\|}$ is confluent.
3. Show that if $t \triangleright u$ then $t \triangleright^{\|} u$. Show that if $t \triangleright^* u$ then $t \triangleright^{\|*} u$. Show that if $t \triangleright^{\|} u$ then $t \triangleright^* u$. Show that if $t \triangleright^{\|*} u$ then $t \triangleright^* u$. Show that the relation $\triangleright$ is confluent.

Exercise 4.8 (Noetherian Induction) Let R be a relation defined over a set E. A *reduction sequence* for this relation is a finite or infinite sequence $x_0, x_1, x_2, \ldots$ such that for all i, $x_i \ R \ x_{i+1}$. An element x in E is *strongly terminating* if every reduction sequence out of x is finite.

   The relation R is *strongly terminating* or *well founded*, also called *Noetherian*, if every element is strongly terminating.

1. Show that a strongly terminating element is terminating.

2. Give an example of a relation for which every element is terminating, but some elements are not strongly terminating.
3. Let R be a relation over a set E. An element u is a reduct of t, t R^+ u, if there exists a finite reduction sequence with more than one step from t to u. Let A be a subset of E such that

$$for\ every\ element\ x\ in\ E$$

$$if\ all\ the\ reducts\ of\ x\ are\ in\ A,\ then\ x\ is\ in\ A$$

Show that if x is not in A, it is not strongly terminating. Show that if x is strongly terminating, it is in A. Show that if R is well founded then all the elements in E are in A.

Exercise 4.9 (Newman's theorem) This exercise relies on Exercise 4.8, which should be done prior to this one.

A relation R over a set E is *locally confluent* if whenever we have t R u and t R v, there exists an element w such that u R^* w and v R^* w.

1. Consider a set with four elements a, b, c and d and the relation defined by a R b, b R a, a R c and b R d. Is this relation locally confluent? Is it confluent? Is every locally confluent relation also confluent?
2. Show that a well founded and locally confluent relation is confluent.

4.2 The Lambda-Calculus

The goal of the lambda-calculus is to bring programming languages closer to the language used in mathematics to express functions.

If e is a function associating to a natural number p the number 2^p, then the function that associates to p the number 2^{2^p} can be represented in the language defined in Sect. 3.4.2 by the term $\circ_1^1(e, e)$ or by the term $\circ_1^1(e, \circ_1^1(e, \pi_1^1))$. We can also represent it simply as $x \mapsto App(e, App(e, x))$, or $\lambda x App(e, App(e, x))$, or even *fun* $x \rightarrow App(e, App(e, x))$, using a binary symbol App that does not bind any variables in its arguments, and a unary symbol $\mapsto$, also written λ or *fun*, that binds a variable in its argument. If we write $(t\ u)$ for the term $App(t, u)$, the expression above can be simply written *fun* $x \rightarrow (e\ (e\ x))$.

There is no need to extend the notation *fun* to represent functions with more than one argument: we can build such functions using functions with one argument, thanks to the isomorphism $(A \times B) \rightarrow C = A \rightarrow (B \rightarrow C)$. For example, the function that associates to x and y the number $x \times x + y \times y$ is defined as the function that associates to x the function that associates to y the number $x \times x + y \times y$: *fun* $x \rightarrow$ *fun* $y \rightarrow (x \times x + y \times y)$. We can now apply this function f to the numbers 3 and 4; we first apply it to 3, that is, we build the term $(f\ 3)$ representing the function that associates to y the number $3 \times 3 + y \times y$, and then to 4, obtaining the term $((f\ 3)\ 4)$.

Definition 4.16 (The language of the lambda-calculus) The language of the lambda-calculus is built out of a binary symbol *App* that does not bind any variable, and a unary symbol *fun* that binds a variable in its argument.

If a function *fun* $x \rightarrow t$ is applied to a term u, we should be able to transform the obtained expression into $(u/x)t$ where the formal argument x is substituted by the actual argument u. This transformation is a basic computation step in the lambda-calculus.

Definition 4.17 (A beta-reduction step at the root) *A beta-reduction step at the root* is a relation $\longrightarrow$ over lambda-calculus terms defined by

$$((fun\ x \rightarrow t)\ u) \longrightarrow (u/x)t$$

Definition 4.18 (Redex) A *redex* is a term that can be reduced by $\longrightarrow$, that is, a term of the form $((fun\ x \rightarrow t)\ u)$.

The relation $\longrightarrow$ can be extended in order to reduce terms of the form $((fun\ x \rightarrow t)\ u)$ inside subterms.

Definition 4.19 (A beta-reduction step) *A beta-reduction step* is a relation $\triangleright$ over lambda-calculus terms, inductively defined by

- if $t \longrightarrow t'$, then $t \triangleright t'$,
- if $t \triangleright t'$, then $(t\ u) \triangleright (t'\ u)$,
- if $u \triangleright u'$, then $(t\ u) \triangleright (t\ u')$,
- if $t \triangleright t'$, then $(fun\ x \rightarrow t) \triangleright (fun\ x \rightarrow t')$.

Definition 4.20 (Beta-reduction) The reflexive-transitive closure of the relation $\triangleright$ is called beta-reduction, and denoted by $\triangleright^*$.

Definition 4.21 (Irreducibility, termination) A term t is *irreducible* if it cannot be reduced by the relation $\triangleright$, that is, if neither of its subterms is a redex.

A term t *is terminating* if it is terminating by the relation $\triangleright$, that is, if there exists an irreducible term t' such that $t \triangleright^* t'$.

For example, the term $((fun\ x \rightarrow (x\ x))\ y)$ is terminating since it can be reduced to the irreducible term $(y\ y)$. However, the term $\omega = ((fun\ x \rightarrow (x\ x))\ (fun\ x \rightarrow (x\ x)))$ is non-terminating, since the only term that can be obtained by reduction is ω itself. The term $((fun\ x \rightarrow y)\ \omega)$ is also terminating, since it reduces to the irreducible term y.

Since a term may contain several redexes, *a priori* it may seem that a term could be reduced to several different irreducible terms. However, it can be shown that this is not possible since the relation $\triangleright$ is confluent. This property can be proved by showing that the parallel beta-reduction relation is strongly confluent. The proof is similar to the one in Exercise 4.7 and will be omitted here.

Proposition 4.6 (Confluence of beta-reduction) *The relation $\rhd$ is confluent.*

Since the relation $\rhd$ is confluent, a term u can be reduced to at most one irreducible term: if $t \rhd^* u$ and $t \rhd^* v$ and u and v are irreducible, then $u = v$. In general, if t, u and v are three terms such that $t \rhd^* u$ and $t \rhd^* v$ and v is irreducible, then $u \rhd^* v$. Notice that there are some terms, such as the term $((fun\ x \to y)\ \omega)$ mentioned above, that can be reduced to an irreducible term if we reduce one of the redexes but produce an infinite reduction sequence if we choose to reduce the other redex.

The lambda-calculus cannot be seen as a particular case of the rewriting systems studied in the previous section, since the symbol *fun* binds a variable (the languages considered in the previous section did not include binders). Moreover, the right-hand side of the beta-reduction rule uses an auxiliary operation: substitution. Note also that the terms t and u mentioned in the left-hand side of the beta-reduction rule are not variables to be instantiated using a substitution σ: substitutions avoid capture of variables and this would mean that x cannot occur in the term t. For this, we would need to distinguish variables such as x from variables such as t so that the substitution for the variable t can capture x—the same mechanism is needed if we extend predicate logic to permit the use of binders in terms. There are extensions of the notion of rewriting to deal with languages with binders, but they are out of the scope of this book.

Assume we associate to each natural number p an irreducible lambda-term $\underline{p}$. We can now represent functions in the lambda-calculus.

Definition 4.22 (Representing functions in the lambda-calculus) A term F in the lambda-calculus *represents* a function f from natural numbers to natural numbers if for all natural numbers $p_1, \ldots, p_n$

- if $f(p_1, \ldots, p_n) = q$, then $(F\ \underline{p_1}\ \ldots\ \underline{p_n}) \rhd^* \underline{q}$,
- if f is undefined for $p_1, \ldots, p_n$, then the term $(F\ \underline{p_1}\ \ldots\ \underline{p_n})$ is non-terminating.

As in the case of rewriting, this definition does not fit properly in the framework that we gave in the introduction to this chapter, because a term which contains several redexes might reduce to several terms. However, we can use a specific reduction strategy: *call by name* avoids this non-determinism. Moreover, the standardisation theorem shows that no expressive power is lost by restricting reductions in this way.

Definition 4.23 (A beta-reduction step under call by name) *A beta-reduction step under call by name* is defined by the relation $\succ$ over lambda-terms, inductively defined as follows

- if $t \longrightarrow t'$, then $t \succ t'$,
- if $(t\ u)$ is not a redex (that is, if t is not of the form *fun*) and if $t \succ t'$, then $(t\ u) \succ (t'\ u)$,
- if $(t\ u)$ is not a redex and no subterm of t is a redex and $u \succ u'$, then $(t\ u) \succ (t\ u')$,
- if $t \succ t'$, then $(fun\ x \to t) \succ (fun\ x \to t')$.

In other words, if a term contains several redexes, we give priority to certain reductions. For a term of the form *fun x → t*, the priority redex is the one that has priority in *t*. For a term of the form (*t u*), we give priority to the redex at the root if there is one, otherwise we give priority to the reduction that has priority in *t*, if there is one, otherwise to the priority redex in *u*. Thus, the priority redex is the leftmost redex in the term.

Note that if a term is irreducible by $\triangleright$, it has no redexes and therefore it is also irreducible by $\succ$. However, if a term can be reduced by $\triangleright$, then it contains at least one redex and it can also be reduced by $\succ$. In the latter case, there exists a unique reduct under call by name.

Definition 4.24 (Call-by-name beta-reduction) The beta-reduction relation $\succ^*$ is the reflexive transitive closure of the relation $\succ$, inductively defined by

– $t \succ^* t$,
– if $t \succ t'$ and $t' \succ^* t''$, then $t \succ^* t''$.

We have seen that some terms, such as ((*fun x → y*) ω), can be reduced to an irreducible term if we choose to reduce one of the redexes but produce an infinite reduction sequence if we choose the other redex. The standardisation theorem states that for those terms the call-by-name reduction is always terminating. We will not give the proof of this theorem here.

Proposition 4.7 (Standardisation theorem) *If $t \triangleright^* t'$ and t' is irreducible, then $t \succ^* t'$.*

As a consequence of the standardisation theorem we deduce that if a term is non-terminating under call by name, then it is non-terminating in general. We can therefore consider only call-by-name reductions and give alternative definitions of irreducibility, termination and the representation of functions.

Proposition 4.8

– *A term is irreducible if and only if it cannot be reduced by the relation $\succ$.*
– *A term t is terminating if and only if there exists an irreducible term t' such that $t \succ^* t'$.*
– *A lambda-term F represents a function f from natural numbers to natural numbers if and only if for any tuple of natural numbers $p_1, \ldots, p_n$*
  – *if $f(p_1, \ldots, p_n) = q$, then $(F \, \underline{p_1} \, \ldots \, \underline{p_n}) \succ^* \underline{q}$,*
  – *if f is undefined for $p_1, \ldots, p_n$, then the term $(F \, \underline{p_1} \, \ldots \, \underline{p_n})$ is non-terminating under call by name.*

Using call by name reduction we are back in the framework defined in the introduction to this chapter. A program is a lambda-calculus term; the term consisting of a program F and the natural numbers $p_1, \ldots, p_n$ is simply $(F \, \underline{p_1} \, \ldots \, \underline{p_n})$ and a basic computation step corresponds to a reduction under call by name.

We will now prove that all the computable functions can be represented in the lambda-calculus. The representation of a natural number p by the term $\underline{p}$, originally motivated by the need to represent functions defined using recursion, provides a new answer to the question: what is a natural number? Instead of saying that the natural number 3 is the property that all the sets with three elements share, which leads to a definition of natural numbers as cardinals, we answer the question by saying that the natural number 3 is an algorithm that iterates three times a function. This leads us to the definition

$$\underline{3} = fun\ x \to fun\ f \to (f\ (f\ (f\ x)))$$

and more generally, to the following definition.

Definition 4.25 (Church numerals) The term $\underline{p}$ is defined as

$$\underline{p} = fun\ x \to fun\ f \to (\underbrace{f\ (f\ \dots\ (f\ x)\dots))}_{p\ times}$$

If the term t is the Church numeral $\underline{p}$ and u and v are arbitrary terms, then the term $(t\ u\ v)$ reduces in two steps under call by name to the term $w = (v\ (v\ \dots\ (v\ u)\dots))$, where the term v occurs p times. However, if t reduces to $\underline{p}$ under call by name but is not equal to $\underline{p}$, we cannot prove that $(t\ u\ v)$ reduces to the term $(v\ (v\ \dots\ (v\ u)\dots))$. This is because when we reduce $(t\ u\ v)$ under call by name, after reducing the term t to a term of the form fun, the priority redex is no longer in t but at the root. However, we can prove that if the term t reduces to $\underline{p}$ then the term $(t\ u\ v)$ is in the set $\mathcal{I}_p^{u,v}$; the family of sets $(\mathcal{I}_p^{u,v})_p$ is defined by induction on p as follows.

Definition 4.26 The set $\mathcal{I}_0^{u,v}$ is the set of terms that reduce to u under call by name, and the set $\mathcal{I}_{p+1}^{u,v}$ is the set of terms that reduce under call by name to a term of the form $(v\ w)$ where $w \in \mathcal{I}_p^{u,v}$.

Proposition 4.9 *If the term t reduces to $\underline{p}$ under call by name then the term $(t\ u\ v)$ is in $\mathcal{I}_p^{u,v}$.*

Proof We show a more general property: there exists a term w in $\mathcal{I}_p^{u,v}$ such that the term $(t\ u\ v)$ reduces to w under call by name in two steps. This is proved by a double induction on p and on the length of the reduction from t to $\underline{p}$.

If $t = \underline{p}$ then the term $(t\ u\ v)$ reduces in two steps, under call by name, to the term $w = (v\ (v\ \dots\ (v\ u)\dots))$ with p occurrences of the term v, which is in $\mathcal{I}_p^{u,v}$.

Otherwise, there exists a term t' such that $t \succ t'$ and t' reduces to $\underline{p}$ under call by name with a shorter reduction. The case where the term t is not of the form fun is easy because in this case the term $(t\ u\ v)$ reduces to $(t'\ u\ v)$ under call by name and the result follows directly by induction.

However, if t is of the form fun, more precisely, $fun\ y_1 \to \dots\ fun\ y_n \to t_1$ where t_1 is not a term of the form fun and $n \neq 0$, then since t reduces to a Church numeral we have $n = 1$ or $n = 2$. Let us write $t_1 = (r \; s_1 \; \ldots \; s_m)$ where r is not an application. The term r is either a variable or a term of the form *fun*.

If the term r is a variable, then the term t reduces to a Church numeral, but since it is not irreducible, then $n = 2$, $r = y_2$, $m = 1$. The term $(t \; u \; v)$ is therefore equal to $((\text{fun } y_1 \to \text{fun } y_2 \to (y_2 \; s_1)) \; u \; v)$ and reduces under call by name in two steps to the term $w = (v \; (u/y_1, v/y_2)s_1)$. Define $w' = (u/y_1, v/y_2)s_1$. The term $\text{fun } y_1 \to \text{fun } y_2 \to s_1$ reduces to $p - 1$ under call by name, and the term $((\text{fun } y_1 \to \text{fun } y_2 \to s_1) \; u \; v)$ reduces to w' under call by name in two steps. By induction hypothesis, the term w' is in $\mathcal{I}_{p-1}^{u,v}$ and therefore w is in $\mathcal{I}_p^{u,v}$.

If the term r is of the form $\text{fun } z \to r'$, then $t_1 = ((\text{fun } z \to r') \; s_1 \; \ldots \; s_m)$ and since this term is not of the form *fun*, $m \neq 0$. The term t is thus of the form $\text{fun } y_1 \to \text{fun } y_2 \to \ldots \text{fun } y_n \to ((\text{fun } z \to r') \; s_1 \; s_2 \; \ldots \; s_m)$ and the term t' obtained by one step of call by name reduction is $\text{fun } y_1 \to \text{fun } y_2 \to \ldots \text{fun } y_n \to ((s_1/z)r' \; s_2 \; \ldots \; s_m)$. If $n = 1$, the term $(t' \; u \; v)$ is equal to $((\text{fun } y_1 \to ((s_1/z)r' \; s_2 \; \ldots \; s_m)) \; u \; v)$ and reduces in one step under call by name to $w = (((u/y_1, (u/y_1)s_1/z)r' \; (u/y_1)s_2 \; \ldots \; (u/y_1)s_m) \; v)$. By induction hypothesis, this term is in $\mathcal{I}_p^{u,v}$. The term $(t \; u \; v)$ is equal to $((\text{fun } y_1 \to ((\text{fun } z \to r') \; s_1 \; \ldots \; s_m)) \; u \; v)$; it reduces in two steps under call by name to w, and we have already proved that w is in $\mathcal{I}_p^{u,v}$. If $n = 2$, the term $(t' \; u \; v)$ is equal to $((\text{fun } y_1 \to \text{fun } y_2 \to ((s_1/z)r' \; s_2 \; \ldots \; s_m)) \; u \; v)$; it reduces in two steps under call by name to $b = ((u/y_1, v/y_2, (u/y_1, v/y_2)s_1/z)r' \; (u/y_1, v/y_2)s_2 \ldots (u/y_1, v/y_2)s_m)$. By induction hypothesis, this term is in $\mathcal{I}_p^{u,v}$. The term $(t \; u \; v)$ is equal to $((\text{fun } y_1 \to \text{fun } y_2 \to ((\text{fun } z \to r') \; s_1 \; \ldots \; s_m)) \; u \; v)$; it reduces in three steps under call by name to b. The term $(t \; u \; v)$ reduces therefore in two steps to a term w that reduces to b. We have already proved that the term b is in $\mathcal{I}_p^{u,v}$, and so is the term w.   □

Proposition 4.10 *If t and u are terms that reduce under call by name to Church numerals $\underline{n}$ and $\underline{p}$, and x, y and f are variables that do not occur in t and u, then*

- *the term $\text{fun } x \to \text{fun } f \to (f \; (t \; x \; f))$ reduces to the term $\underline{n+1}$ under call by name,*
- *the term $\text{fun } x \to \text{fun } f \to (t \; (u \; x \; f) \; f)$ reduces to the term $\underline{n+p}$ under call by name,*
- *the term $\text{fun } x \to \text{fun } f \to (t \; x \; (\text{fun } y \to (u \; y \; f)))$ reduces to the term $\underline{n \times p}$ under call by name,*
- *the term $(t \; (K \; \underline{1}) \; T \; (u \; (K \; \underline{0}) \; T))$, where $K = \text{fun } x \to \text{fun } y \to x$ and $T = \text{fun } g \to \text{fun } h \to (h \; g)$, reduces to the term $\underline{\chi_{\leq}(n, p)}$ under call by name.*

Proof We first prove an auxiliary lemma, by induction on n: if a term is in $\mathcal{I}_n^{v,f}$ where f is a variable and v is an arbitrary term, then it reduces under call by name to $(f \; (f \; \ldots \; (f \; v) \ldots))$ with n occurrences of the symbol f. We then prove the four propositions.

- The term $(t \; x \; f)$ reduces under call by name to $(f \; (f \; \ldots \; (f \; x) \ldots))$ where the symbol f occurs n times, the term $(f \; (t \; x \; f))$ to $(f \; (f \; \ldots \; (f \; x) \ldots))$ where the symbol f occurs $n + 1$ times, and the term $fun\ x \to fun\ f \to (f\ (t\ x\ f))$ to $n + 1$.

- By Proposition 4.9, the term $v = (u\ x\ f)$ is in $\mathcal{I}_p^{x,f}$ and the term $(t\ (u\ x\ f)\ f)$ is in $\mathcal{I}_p^{v,f}$. Using the lemma above, the term $(t\ (u\ x\ f)\ f)$ reduces under call by name to $(f\ (f\ \dots\ (f\ v)\dots))$ where the symbol f occurs n times, then to $(f\ (f\ \dots\ (f\ x)\dots))$ where the symbol f occurs $n + p$ times. Thus, the term $fun\ x \to fun\ f \to (t\ (t\ x\ f)\ f)$ reduces under call by name to $n + p$.

- We show by induction on n that if a term v is in $\mathcal{I}_n^{x,fun\ y \to (u\ y\ f)}$, then it reduces under call by name to $(f\ (f\ \dots\ (f\ x)\dots))$, where the symbol f occurs $n \times p$ times. If $n = 0$, the term v reduces under call by name to x. Otherwise, it reduces under call by name to $((fun\ y \to (u\ y\ f))\ v')$ and then to $(u\ v'\ f)$ where v' is in $\mathcal{I}_{n-1}^{x,fun\ y \to (u\ y\ f)}$. By Proposition 4.9 this term is in $\mathcal{I}_p^{v',f}$ and, using the lemma above, it reduces under call by name to $(f\ (f\ \dots\ (f\ v')\dots))$ where the symbol f occurs p times. Therefore, by induction hypothesis, it reduces to $(f\ (f\ \dots\ (f\ x)\dots))$ where the symbol f occurs $p + (n - 1) \times p = n \times p$ times. By Proposition 4.9, the term $(t\ x\ (fun\ y \to (u\ y\ f)))$ is in $\mathcal{I}_n^{x,fun\ y \to (u\ y\ f)}$, and thus it reduces under call by name to $(f\ (f\ \dots\ (f\ x)\dots))$ where the symbol f occurs $n \times p$ times. Hence, the term $fun\ x \to fun\ f \to (t\ x\ (fun\ y \to (u\ y\ f)))$ reduces under call by name to $n \times p$.

- We show by induction on $n + p$ that if a is a term in $\mathcal{I}_n^{(K\ \underline{\alpha}),T}$ and b a term in $\mathcal{I}_p^{(K\ \underline{\beta}),T}$, then $(a\ b)$ reduces under call by name to $\underline{\alpha}$, if $n \leq p$, and to $\underline{\beta}$, if $p + 1 \leq n$. If $n = 0$, then the term a reduces under call by name to $(K\ \underline{\alpha})$ and since this term is not of the form fun, the term $(a\ b)$ reduces under call by name to $(K\ \underline{\alpha}\ b)$, which in turn reduces under call by name to $\underline{\alpha}$. Otherwise, the term a reduces under call by name to $(T\ a')$, where a' is an element of $\mathcal{I}_{n-1}^{(K\ \underline{\alpha}),T}$, and since this term is not of the form fun, the term $(a\ b)$ reduces under call by name to $(T\ a'\ b)$, which in turn reduces under call by name to $(b\ a')$. By induction, this term reduces under call by name to $\underline{\beta}$, if $p \leq n - 1$, that is, if $p + 1 \leq n$, and to $\underline{\alpha}$, if $n \leq p$. By Proposition 4.9, the term $(t\ (K\ \underline{1})\ T)$ is in $\mathcal{I}_n^{(K\ \underline{1}),T}$ and the term $(u\ (K\ \underline{0})\ T)$ is in $\mathcal{I}_p^{(K\ \underline{0}),T}$. The term $(t\ (K\ \underline{1})\ T\ (u\ (K\ \underline{0})\ T))$ reduces therefore to $\underline{1}$, if $n \leq p$ and to $\underline{0}$ otherwise, that is, to $\chi_{\leq}(n, p)$. $\qquad\square$

Definition 4.27 (Test) We define

$$Ifz(t, u, v) = (t\ u\ fun\ x \to v)$$

where x is a variable that does not occur in v.

Proposition 4.11 *Let t, u and v be three lambda-terms such that t reduces under call by name to a Church numeral $\underline{p}$. If $p = 0$, then $Ifz(t, u, v) \succ^* u$, and if $p \neq 0$, $Ifz(t, u, v) \succ^* v$.*

Proof By Proposition 4.9. $\qquad\square$

As in the case of rewriting, if G is a term representing a function g that is undefined for the argument 4 and H is a term representing the function h, that returns 0 for all its arguments, then the term representing the function $h \circ g$ should be non-terminating if applied to 4. To achieve this, the function h cannot be represented by the term $fun\ x \to \underline{0}$; as in the case of rewriting, it will be represented by a slightly more complicated term, which checks that its argument reduces to a Church numeral: $fun\ x \to \underline{0}\&x$. In a similar way, the function $f \circ g$ will be represented by the term $fun\ x \to (H(G\ x))\&x$.

Definition 4.28 For all terms t and u,

$$t\&u = Ifz(u, t, t) = (u\ t\ (fun\ x \to t))$$

where x is a variable that does not occur in t.

Proposition 4.12 *Let t and u be lambda-terms such that u reduces under call by name to a Church numeral. Then $t\&u \succ^* t$.*

Proof By Proposition 4.11. $\square$

Finally, to represent in the lambda-calculus functions defined by minimisation, we need a mechanism allowing us to iterate a function and compute the values of $g(0)$, $g(1)$, $g(2)$, ... until the value 0 is obtained. In order to achieve this, we will rely on the fact that in the lambda-calculus a function can be applied to itself.

Definition 4.29 (Fixed point) For any term t,

$$Y_t = ((fun\ x \to (t\ (x\ x)))\ (fun\ x \to (t\ (x\ x))))$$

Proposition 4.13 $Y_t \succ (t\ Y_t)$.

Now we are ready to define a representation in the lambda-calculus for each computable function.

Definition 4.30 (Representing computable functions) Let f be a computable function with n arguments. The lambda-term associated to f is defined by induction over the definition of f.

If f is the ith projection, the term associated to it is

$$fun\ x_1 \to\ \ldots\ fun\ x_n \to ((((x_i\&x_1)\&\ldots\&x_{i-1})\&x_{i+1})\&\ldots\&x_n)$$

If f is a zero function, the term associated to it is

$$fun\ x_1 \to\ \ldots\ fun\ x_n \to ((\underline{0}\&x_1)\&\ldots\&x_n)$$

If f is the successor function, the term associated to it is

$$S = fun\ n \to ((fun\ x \to fun\ f \to (f\ (n\ x\ f)))\&n)$$

If f is addition, the term associated to it is

$$fun\ p \to fun\ q \to ((fun\ x \to fun\ f \to (p\ (q\ x\ f)\ f))\&p\&q)$$

If f is multiplication, the term associated to it is

$$fun\ p \to fun\ q \to ((fun\ x \to fun\ f \to (p\ x\ (fun\ y \to (q\ y\ f))))\&p\&q)$$

If f is the characteristic function of the ordering relation, the term associated to it is

$$fun\ p \to fun\ q \to ((p\ (K\ \underline{1})\ T\ (q\ (K\ \underline{0})\ T))\&p\&q)$$

where $K = fun\ x \to fun\ y \to x$ and $T = fun\ g \to fun\ h \to (h\ g)$.

If f is defined as the composition of the functions h and $g_1, \ldots, g_m$, then let $G_1, \ldots, G_m$ and H be the terms associated to these functions, the term associated to f is

$$fun\ x_1 \to\ \ldots\ fun\ x_n \to ((H\ (G_1\ x_1\ \ldots\ x_n)\ \ldots\ (G_m\ x_1\ \ldots\ x_n))\&x_1\&\ldots\&x_n)$$

If f is defined by minimisation of the function g, then let G be the term associated to these function and G' the term $fun\ f \to fun\ x_1 \to\ \ldots\ fun\ x_n \to fun\ x_{n+1} \to (Ifz((G\ x_1\ \ldots\ x_n\ x_{n+1}), x_{n+1}, (f\ x_1\ \ldots\ x_n\ (S\ x_{n+1}))))$, the term associated to f is

$$fun\ x_1 \to\ \ldots\ fun\ x_n \to ((Y_{G'}\ x_1\ \ldots\ x_n\ \underline{0})\&x_1\&\ldots\&x_n)$$

We will now show that these terms represent indeed the computable functions associated to them.

Proposition 4.14 *Let F be the lambda-term associated to the computable function f and let $p_1, \ldots, p_n$ be natural numbers such that $f(p_1, \ldots, p_n) = q$, then*

$$(F\ \underline{p_1}\ \cdots\ \underline{p_n}) \succ^* \underline{q}$$

Proof We show a more general property, by induction over the definition of the function f: if $u_1, \ldots, u_n$ are terms that reduce under call by name to $\underline{p_1}, \ldots, \underline{p_n}$, then $(F\ u_1\ \ldots\ u_n) \succ^* \underline{q}$.

If f is a projection, a zero function, the successor function, addition, multiplication or the characteristic function of the ordering relation, the property follows directly from Propositions 4.10 and 4.12.

If f is a function defined by composition using functions h and $g_1, \ldots, g_m$, then there are natural numbers $r_1, \ldots, r_m$ such that $g_1(p_1, \ldots, p_n) = r_1, \ldots, g_m(p_1, \ldots, p_n) = r_m$ and $h(r_1, \ldots, r_m) = q$. By Proposition 4.12, the term $(F\ u_1\ \ldots\ u_n)$ reduces to $(H\ (G_1\ u_1\ \ldots\ u_n)\ \ldots\ (G_m\ u_1\ \ldots\ u_n))$ under call by name. By induction hypothesis, $(G_1\ u_1\ \ldots\ u_n)$ reduces under call by name to $\underline{r_1}, \ldots, (G_m\ u_1\ \ldots\ u_n)$ reduces under call by name to $\underline{r_m}$ and $(H\ (G_1\ u_1\ \ldots\ u_n)\ \ldots\ (G_m\ u_1\ \ldots\ u_n))$ reduces under call by name to $\underline{q}$.

If f is a function defined by minimisation of the function g, then for all r strictly less than q, $g(p_1, \ldots, p_n, r)$ is different from 0, and $g(p_1, \ldots, p_n, q) = 0$. If u reduces under call by name to a Church numeral $\underline{r}$ for some r strictly less than q, then the term $(Y_{G'}\ u_1\ \ldots\ u_n\ u)$ reduces under call by name to

$$Ifz((G\ u_1\ \ldots\ u_n\ u), u, (Y_{G'}\ u_1\ \ldots\ u_n\ (S\ u)))$$

By induction hypothesis, $(G\ u_1\ \ldots\ u_n\ u)$ reduces under call by name to a non-zero Church numeral, and therefore by Proposition 4.11 the term $(Y_{G'}\ u_1\ \ldots\ u_n\ u)$ reduces under call by name to $(Y_{G'}\ u_1\ \ldots\ u_n\ (S\ u))$. Thus, using Proposition 4.12, the term $(F\ u_1\ \ldots\ u_n)$ reduces under call by name to $(Y_{G'}\ u_1\ \ldots\ u_n\ \underline{0})$, then to $(Y_{G'}\ u_1\ \ldots\ u_n\ (S\ \underline{0}))$, $(Y_{G'}\ u_1\ \ldots\ u_n\ (S\ (S\ \underline{0})))$, $\ldots (Y_{G'}\ u_1\ \ldots\ u_n\ (S^q\ \underline{0}))$. Finally, this term reduces under call by name to

$$Ifz((G\ u_1\ \ldots\ u_n\ (S^q\ \underline{0})), (S^q\ \underline{0}), (Y_{G'}\ u_1\ \ldots\ u_n\ (S\ (S^q\ \underline{0}))))$$

By induction hypothesis, the term $(G\ u_1\ \ldots\ u_n\ (S^q\ \underline{0}))$ reduces under call by name to $\underline{0}$ and therefore by Proposition 4.11, it reduces under call by name to $(S^q\ \underline{0})$ and finally to $\underline{q}$.   □

We now need to prove that if F is the lambda-term associated to a computable function f and $u_1, \ldots, u_n$ are terms that reduce under call by name to Church numerals $\underline{p_1}, \ldots, \underline{p_n}$ such that f is undefined for $p_1, \ldots, p_n$, then the term $(F\ u_1\ \ldots\ u_n)$ is non-terminating. Unfortunately, non-termination is a property not preserved by composition. For example, the term $fun\ f \to (f\ \omega)$ is non-terminating, but if we apply it to $fun\ x \to y$ we obtain a terminating term. We will therefore show a stronger property, namely that the term $(F\ u_1\ \ldots\ u_n)$ is *isolated*.

Definition 4.31 (Isolated term) A term t is *isolated*, if for any term t' such that $t \succ^* t'$, the term t' is neither irreducible nor of the form *fun*.

Proposition 4.15 *If* $t \succ^* u$ *and* u *is isolated, then so is* t.

Proof Let t' be a term such that $t \succ^* t'$. Since t reduces under call by name both to u and t', either $u \succ^* t'$ or $t' \succ^* u$. In the first case, t' is neither irreducible nor of the form *fun*. In the second case, t' is not irreducible and if it were of the form *fun*, then the term u would also be of the form *fun*, a contradiction since it is isolated.   □

Proposition 4.16 *If* t *is isolated then so are the terms* $(t\ u)$, $Ifz(t, u, v)$ *and* $u\&t$.

Proof If t is isolated then the sequence of call-by-name reductions $t = t_0, t_1, \ldots$ contains only terms that have a redex and are not of the form *fun*. It follows that the sequence of reductions starting from $(t\ u)$ is $(t_0\ u), (t_1\ u), \ldots$ Indeed, for all i, t_i has a redex and is not of the form *fun*, therefore the priority redex in $(t_i\ u)$ is the one in t_i. Hence, $(t\ u)$ is isolated.

The terms $Ifz(t, u, v)$ and $u\&t$ are therefore isolated.   □

Proposition 4.17 *Let* F *be a lambda-term associated to a computable function* f. *Let* $u_1, \ldots, u_n$ *be terms such that each* u_i *reduces to a Church numeral or is isolated. If at least one of the* u_i *is isolated, then* $(F\ u_1\ \ldots\ u_n)$ *is isolated.*

Proof By case analysis: we consider the different cases for the function f, and use Propositions 4.15 and 4.16 in each case.   □

Proposition 4.18 *Let F be the lambda-term associated to a computable function f and $p_1, \ldots, p_n$ natural numbers such that f is undefined for $p_1, \ldots, p_n$. Then the term $(F \ \underline{p_1} \ \ldots \ \underline{p_n})$ is non-terminating.*

Proof We will prove by induction over the definition of the function f a more general property: if $u_1, \ldots, u_n$ are terms that reduce under call by name to the Church numerals $\underline{p_1}, \ldots, \underline{p_n}$, then the term $(F \ u_1 \ \ldots \ u_n)$ is isolated.

The projections, zero functions, successor function, addition, multiplication and the characteristic function of the ordering relation are total.

If the function f is defined by composition using the functions h and $g_1, \ldots, g_m$, then, by Proposition 4.12, the term $(F \ u_1 \ \ldots \ u_n)$ reduces under call by name to

$$(H \ (G_1 \ u_1 \ \ldots \ u_n) \ \ldots \ (G_m \ u_1 \ \ldots \ u_n))$$

and if any of the functions g_i is undefined for $p_1, \ldots, p_n$, then by induction hypothesis the corresponding term $(G_i \ u_1 \ \ldots \ u_n)$ are isolated and therefore by Proposition 4.17 so is the term $(H \ (G_1 \ u_1 \ \ldots \ u_n) \ \ldots \ (G_m \ u_1 \ \ldots \ u_n))$. By Proposition 4.15, the term $(F \ u_1 \ \ldots \ u_n)$ is also isolated. However, if there are natural numbers $r_1, \ldots, r_m$ such that $r_1 = g_1(p_1, \ldots, p_n), \ldots, r_m = g_m(p_1, \ldots, p_n)$, then h is undefined for $r_1, \ldots, r_m$. The terms $(G_i \ u_1 \ \ldots \ u_n)$ reduce to $\underline{r_i}$ and by induction hypothesis the term $(H \ (G_1 \ u_1 \ \ldots \ u_n) \ \ldots \ (G_m \ u_1 \ \ldots \ u_n))$ is isolated. Thus, by Proposition 4.15, so is the term $(F \ u_1 \ \ldots \ u_n)$.

If the function f is defined by minimisation of the function g, then if g returns a non-zero value for $(p_1, \ldots, p_n, 0), (p_1, \ldots, p_n, 1), \ldots$, the term $(F \ u_1 \ \ldots \ u_n)$ reduces under call by name to $(Y_{G'} \ u_1 \ \ldots \ u_n \ \underline{0}), (Y_{G'} \ u_1 \ \ldots \ u_n \ (S \ \underline{0})), \ldots$ and is therefore isolated.

If the function g returns a non-zero value for $(p_1, \ldots, p_n, 0), (p_1, \ldots, p_n, 1), \ldots, (p_1, \ldots, p_n, q-1)$ and is undefined for $(p_1, \ldots, p_n, q)$, the term $(F \ u_1 \ \ldots \ u_n)$ reduces under call by name to $Ifz((G \ u_1 \ \ldots \ u_n \ (S^q \ \underline{0})), (S^q \ \underline{0}), (Y_{G'} \ u_1 \ \ldots \ u_n \ (S^q \ \underline{0})))$ where the term $(G \ u_1 \ \ldots \ u_n \ (S^q \ \underline{0}))$ is isolated. By Proposition 4.16, the term $Ifz((G \ u_1 \ \ldots \ u_n \ (S^q \ \underline{0})), (S^q \ \underline{0}), (Y_{G'} \ u_1 \ \ldots \ u_n \ (S^q \ \underline{0})))$ is isolated. Therefore, by Proposition 4.15, so is the term $(F \ u_1 \ \ldots \ u_n)$. □

We can finally conclude.

Theorem 4.2 *Every computable function can be represented in the lambda-calculus.*

The converse of this theorem states that all the functions that can be represented in the lambda-calculus are computable. Indeed, lambda-terms are trees, and therefore they can be enumerated. It is sufficient then to show that the function that describes a basic step of computation, that is the function that associates to t the term u such that $t \succ u$, is computable.

4.3 Turing Machines

As the lambda-calculus brought the notation of programs closer to that of mathematical functions, it could be said that Turing machines highlight the fact that computations take place not only over time but also in a given space.

A *Turing machine* consists of a certain number k of tapes. Each tape contains an infinite number of cells, more precisely, each tape has a first cell, followed by an unlimited number of cells to the right of the first one.

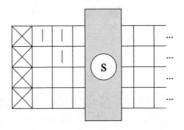

Each cell contains a symbol from a finite set Σ. This set contains, amongst others, two distinguished symbols: b (blank) and $\times$ (cross). When the machine starts, only a finite number of cells in each tape contain a symbol different from b, and this property is an invariant of the machine. The crosses mark the first cell of each tape.

Another ingredient in the definition of a Turing machine is the *reading and writing head*. At each moment in time, the head is in a certain position over the tapes and in a certain state s (there is a finite set of states).

The final ingredient is the *transition table* describing the evolution of the machine. At each computation step, the head reads the contents of the k tapes (in the current position), and depending on the head's state and the symbols read, the transition table specifies a k-tuple of symbols to be written on the tapes, a new state, and a new position for the head (-1: move to the left, 0: stay in the same position, $+1$: move to the right). The head then writes the k symbols, changes state and position, and performs the next step. The transition table is in fact a function from $\Sigma^k \times S$ to $\Sigma^k \times S \times \{-1, 0, +1\}$. We will assume that the transition table never specifies that the machine should write or erase a cross, and never specifies a movement towards the left if the machine has read k crosses.

When the machine starts, the head is always at the leftmost position, that is, over the first cell of each tape, and in a distinguished state, called *initial state*. There is another distinguished state called *final state*; if the machine reaches the final state, it stops the computation.

Summarising, a machine is defined by a finite set Σ of symbols, a natural number (the number of tapes it has), a finite set of states that contains two distinguished states—the initial and final states, and a transition table.

How can we compute with such a machine? We will assume that the set of symbols Σ contains, in addition to the symbols b and $\times$, a symbol | (bar). A function f from $\mathbb{N}^n$ to $\mathbb{N}$ will be computed using a machine with at least $n + 1$ tapes. To compute the value of this function for the arguments $p_1, \ldots, p_n$, we start the machine in an initial configuration where the first tape contains a cross followed by p_1 bars, the second tape contains a cross followed by p_2 bars, ..., the nth tape contains a cross followed by p_n bars. All the other tapes contain simply a cross in the first cell. The machine's head starts in the leftmost position, and in the initial state.

The machine's execution is defined as a series of small steps. When it stops, the $(n + 1)$th tape should contain a cross followed by q bars and all the other tapes should be as they were when the machine started. The integer q is the result of the computation: $f(p_1, \ldots, p_n)$.

The language of Turing machines fits well within the framework defined in the introduction to this chapter. A function is represented by a natural number k—the number of tapes—, a set of states, and a transition table. Given a tuple (k, S, M) and natural numbers $p_1, \ldots, p_n$, a term can be built to represent the machine with k tapes containing the numbers $p_1, \ldots, p_n$ and the other tapes containing simply a crosses, with a set S of states and transition table M. The basic step of computation is a transition, consisting of a reading operation, a writing operation, a change of state and a movement of the head.

A function is *representable* by a Turing machine if there exists a machine that computes it.

Let us define, for example, a machine to compute the successor of a natural number. The machine will have two tapes and three states: s_0 (initial state), s_1 and s_2 (final state). The machine starts by moving the head towards the right-hand side, and writing a bar in the second tape for each bar read in the first tape. When no more bars are left, the machine writes a bar in the second tape, changes state, moves the head towards the left, and moves to the final state. The transition table is therefore as follows.

$$M((\times, \times), s_0) = ((\times, \times), s_0, 1)$$
$$M((|, b), s_0) = ((|, |), s_0, 1)$$
$$M((b, b), s_0) = ((b, |), s_1, -1)$$
$$M((|, |), s_1) = ((|, |), s_1, -1)$$
$$M((\times, \times), s_1) = ((\times, \times), s_2, 0)$$

Of course, in order to have a complete definition of the machine we need to complete the table so that it specifies what the machine should do in all the other configurations. However, since they are not reachable, it does not matter how we complete the table.

To show that every computable function can be computed using a Turing machine, we need to show that the set of functions that can be computed using Turing machines contains the projections, zero functions, successor, addition multiplication, the characteristic function of the ordering relation, and that it is closed under composition and minimisation.

We start by showing how to compute the composition of functions, which requires a combination of Turing machines.

First, notice that a machine that computes a function f from $\mathbb{N}^n$ to $\mathbb{N}$ can be easily transformed by adding tapes whose contents do not change the evolution of the machine and where the head does not write anything. We can transform it so that the arguments are read from tapes $b_1, \ldots, b_n$ that are not necessarily the first n tapes and the result is left on the tape b_{n+1}, which is not necessarily the $(n + 1)$th tape.

After this remark, we can show that the set of functions that can be computed using Turing machines is closed under composition. Let h, $g_1, \ldots, g_m$ be functions computed by machines N and $M_1, \ldots, M_m$, respectively. These machines may use, in addition to the tapes that contain the arguments and the tape where the result is left, a certain number of auxiliary tapes for intermediate computations. We start by modifying them so that all the machines work on $n + m + 1 + r$ tapes, where r is the greatest number of auxiliary tapes used by the machines $M_1, \ldots, M_n, N$, each machine M_i reads its arguments from the tapes $1, \ldots, n$ and writes the result on the tape $n + 1 + i$, N reads its arguments from the tapes $n + 2, \ldots, n + m + 1$ and writes its result on the tape $n + 1$, and the remaining tapes (after the $n + m + 1$ first tapes) are the auxiliary tapes used by the machines.

We then build a machine whose set of states is the disjoint union of the sets of states of these $m + 1$ machines and an additional set of states specific to this machine, containing an initial state and a final state. The transition table is the union of the tables of all these machines; this is still a function since the tables are functions with disjoint domains. We add transitions so that when the machine is in the initial state, it performs a transition to M_1's initial state and when it reaches M_1's final state it performs a transition to M_2's initial state, $\ldots$, when it reaches M_m's final state it performs a transition to N's initial state, and when it reaches N's final state it performs a transition to its own final state. In this way, we obtain a machine that, starting in a configuration with the numbers $p_1, \ldots, p_n$ in the first n tapes, computes $q_1 = g_1(p_1, \ldots, p_n)$, $q_2 = g_2(p_1, \ldots, p_n)$, $\ldots$, $q_m = g_m(p_1, \ldots, p_n)$ and writes the results on the tapes $n + 2, \ldots, m + n + 1$, and finally computes $h(q_1, \ldots, q_m)$ and leaves the result on the $n + 1$'th tape. It is now easy to modify this machine to erase the numbers written in the tapes $n + 2, \ldots, n + m + 1$ and move the head to the leftmost position; we obtain in this way a machine that computes the composition of h and $g_1, \ldots, g_m$.

The machine to compute a function defined by minimisation is built similarly: first it computes $g(p_1, \ldots, p_n, 0)$, simulating the machine that computes the function g using the tapes $1, \ldots, n, n + 1$ to store the arguments and the tape $n + 2$ for the result. If the second cell in the $n + 2$'th tape is b then the machine moves its head to the left and reaches a final state, otherwise it writes an additional bar on the $n + 1$'th tape and re-starts the computation of g reading the arguments from the tapes $1, \ldots, n, n + 1, \ldots$.

We have already built a machine to compute the successor function. The machines that compute projections can be built similarly. The machine that computes π_i^n consists of $n + 1$ bands; it starts by moving its head to the right and writing a bar on the $n + 1$'th tape for each bar found in the i'th tape. When there are no more bars, it moves the head towards the left and reaches a final state.

It is even easier to define a machine that computes a zero function: it suffices to move directly from the initial state to the final state.

We now show the construction of a machine to compute addition. This machine starts by copying the contents of the first tape onto the fourth, and the contents of the second tape onto the third. Then, it erases one by one the bars in the fourth tape, adding a bar on the third tape for each erased bar.

To build a machine to compute multiplication we proceed as follows. The machine starts by copying the contents of the first tape onto the fourth, then it erases one by one the bars on the fourth tape, writing on the third tape as many bars as there are in the second tape. To do this, it is sufficient to copy the contents of the second tape onto the fifth, and then erase one by one the bars from the fifth tape, adding each time a bar on the third tape.

The machine that computes the characteristic function of the ordering relation can be built as follows. While the first two tapes contain bars, the machine moves its head towards the right, if it finds a configuration $(b, |)$ or (b, b) it changes state to s, if it finds the configuration $(|, b)$ it changes state to s'. In both cases, the machine moves its head to the left. If it is in state s' it moves to the final state, and if it is in state s it moves the head towards the right and writes a bar on the third tape, then it moves to the left and reaches a final state.

We can now conclude.

Theorem 4.3 *Every computable function can be represented by a Turing machine.*

The converse of this proposition states that all the functions that can be represented by a Turing machine are computable. Indeed, there are many ways to represent, using trees, the state of a Turing machine, more precisely, the contents of its tapes, the position of the head and its state. For instance, we can represent each state by a constant, and the elements of Σ can also be represented by constants. The part of the tapes to the left-hand side of the head can be represented as a list of k-tuples— the first element of the list denotes the k-tuple of symbols that are just to the left of the head—and, similarly, the right-hand side of the tapes can be represented as a list of k-tuples—the first element of the list denotes the k-tuple of symbols that are just to the right of the head. Thus, a term is a tuple consisting of three elements: a state, a k-tuple representing the cells at the current position of the head in the tapes, and a pair of lists of k-tuples representing the left- and right-hand sides of the tapes. These states can be indexed; it remains then to show that the function that describes a basic computation step is computable.

Exercise 4.10 Give a direct proof of the fact that the set of functions that can be computed using Turing machines is closed under recursive definitions.

Exercise 4.11 So far we have used the idea that trees can be indexed in order to prove the existence of algorithms to solve certain problems. However, if instead of focusing on the existence of an algorithm we want to study its complexity, the use of tree encodings is not ideal: encodings can change the complexity of the algorithm. In this exercise we consider Turing machines that compute directly on trees. For this, we consider a set Σ of symbols containing, in addition to b and $\times$, an arbitrary number of symbols. We can then represent a tree, from an articulated set, on a tape using prefix or postfix notation.

If the first tape of a machine contains a sequence $u_0, u_1, \ldots$ of symbols and the second contains the number k represented by k bars, the pair of tapes describes a *marked sequence of symbols*, that is, the sequence $u_0, u_1, \ldots$ where the element u_k is marked.

marked element

	0	1	P	1	1	0	1	P		
	I	I	I							

1. Show that there exists a Turing machine that reads a natural number n, represented by n bars on the first tape, and writes $2n$ bars in the second tape.
2. Show that there exists a Turing machine that reads a natural number n in binary notation (least significant digit first) from the first tape, starting at the position k indicated by the number of bars in the second tape, writes n bars on the third tape and writes additional bars in the second tape until the corresponding position in the first tape is not a binary digit.
3. Show that there exists a Turing machine that reads a sequence of 0 and 1 on the first tape, erases the last two symbols and writes 1 at the end of the sequence obtained if the two symbols are 1, and 0 otherwise.

	0	1	1	1	0					

	0	1	1	0						

Propositional logic is the fragment of predicate logic consisting of all the propositions built out of predicate symbols without arguments, called *proposition symbols*, and symbols $\top$, $\bot$, $\neg$, $\wedge$, $\vee$ and $\Rightarrow$. For example,

$$P_1 \Rightarrow (P_0 \wedge P_2)$$

is a proposition.

We will use the proposition symbols P_0, P_1, ..., P_n, and assume that the indices of the symbols that occur in a proposition are an initial segment of the set of natural numbers. Propositions will be written on a tape in postfix notation using binary notation for the indices, with the least significant digit first. Thus, the proposition shown above is written

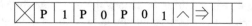

A model for a proposition is a function that associates a truth value 0 or 1 to each propositional symbol. A model for a proposition can be written on the tape of a Turing machine, for example, by writing the sequence of truth values associated to $P_0, P_1, P_2, \ldots$.

✕	0	1	1	1	0					

4. Show that there exists a Turing machine that reads a proposition symbol P_n written on the first tape starting from the position k indicated by the number of bars in the second tape, and a model on the third tape, and writes the truth value of this proposition symbol in the fourth tape.

✕				P	0	1					
✕	I	I	I								
✕	0	1	1	0							
✕											

✕				P	0	1					
✕	I	I	I								
✕	0	1	1	0							
✕	1										

5. Show that there exists a Turing machine that reads a proposition from the first tape and a model from the second and writes the truth value of the proposition on the third tape.

✕	P	1	P	0	P	0	1	∧	⇒		
✕	0	1	1	0							
✕											

✕	P	1	P	0	P	0	1	∧	⇒		
✕	0	1	1	0							
✕	0										

6. Let n be the number of symbols in a proposition. Show that all the indices of proposition symbols are bounded by n. Show that the length of the representation of the proposition on a machine tape is a number between n and $n(2 + \log_2(n))$.

Let E be a set of trees labelled by elements of a finite set. The set E is *in the class P* if there exists a Turing machine that always terminates and such that

- for any tree a, a is in E if and only if the execution of the machine on the tree a gives the result 1, and
- there exists a polynomial f such that the number of computation steps of the machine for a tree of size p is bounded by $f(p)$.

7. Show that the set of pairs consisting of a proposition A and a model $\mathcal{M}$ such that A is valid in $\mathcal{M}$ is in the class P.

Exercise 4.12 This exercise relies on Exercise 4.11, which should be done prior to this one.

We extend Turing machines to introduce *non determinism*. The transition table of a standard Turing machine specifies, for each pair consisting of a sequence of symbols and a state, a unique transition involving a writing operation, a change of state and a movement of the head. In contrast, the transition table of a non-deterministic Turing machine specifies, for each pair, a finite set of transitions.

The table of a non-deterministic Turing machine is not a function from $\Sigma^k \times S$ to $\Sigma^k \times S \times \{-1, 0, +1\}$ but a function that associates to each element in $\Sigma^k \times S$ a finite and non-empty subset of $\Sigma^k \times S \times \{-1, 0, +1\}$.

The initial configuration of a standard machine determines a unique sequence of transitions. In contrast, the initial configuration of a non-deterministic machine determines a set of sequences of transitions, where at each step the machine performs one of the transitions specified in the table. These different sequences of transitions may lead to different results. A non-deterministic Turing machine defines a function that associates to the trees $p_1, \ldots, p_n$ a set of trees instead of just a tree.

Let E be a set of trees labelled by elements of a finite set. The set E is *in the class NP* if there exists a non-deterministic Turing machine that always terminates and such that

- for any tree a, a is in E if and only if *one of the* sequences of transitions of the machine starting on the tree a gives the result 1, and
- there exists a polynomial f such that the length of all the sequences of transitions of these machine on trees of size p are bound by $f(p)$.

Show that the set SAT of all the consistent—also called *satisfiable*—propositions, that is, propositions that have a model, is in the class *NP*.

The notion of computability is robust, in the sense that the functions that can be defined in languages as diverse as Turing machines, the lambda-calculus, or term rewriting, coincide: they are the computable functions.

However, this apparent diversity hides a deep unity: in all these languages the execution of a computation is defined as a sequence of small steps.

Part III
Proofs and Algorithms

Chapter 5
Church's Theorem

The design of algorithms to solve mathematical problems, such as the algorithm that computes the greatest common divisor of two integers, the algorithm that computes the solution of a linear system of equations, or the algorithm that permits to compute the primitive of a polynomial function, is an important mathematical activity without requiring the construction of a proof. Up to which point can the search for a proof be replaced by the execution of an algorithm? There is a set of results, some positive and some negative, which provide answers to this question.

In this chapter we describe two results, one negative and one positive, which show that the set of provable propositions in predicate logic is not decidable, but it is semi-decidable.

Since propositions are trees, they can be indexed. More precisely, these results show that the set of all the indices of provable propositions in predicate logic is not decidable but it is semi-decidable.

5.1 The Notion of Reduction

We start by showing that the set of propositions that are provable in predicate logic is not decidable. The proof is based on the following idea: it is possible to express the termination property of a program f by the proposition "The program f is terminating" and therefore, since the termination property is undecidable in general, so is the provability of propositions of this kind, and thus the provability of propositions in predicate logic is undecidable in general. But what is the proposition "The program f is terminating"?

To answer this question we need to associate to each program f a proposition that is provable if and only if the program f terminates. As we shall see, the function T that associates to the program f the proposition "The program f is terminating" is computable. Therefore, if there exists a computable function F that decides whether a proposition is provable or not, the function $F \circ T$ is computable, contradicting the theorem of undecidability of the halting problem.

G. Dowek, *Proofs and Algorithms*, Undergraduate Topics in Computer Science, DOI 10.1007/978-0-85729-121-9_5, © Springer-Verlag London Limited 2011

This idea gives rise to a general method to show that a problem is undecidable: it is sufficient to build an algorithm that reduces the problem in question to a problem that has already been shown to be undecidable (in this example, the halting problem). This method can be formulated in an abstract way: since the set of computable functions is closed under composition, if T is computable and $F \circ T$ is not, then F is not computable either.

5.2 Representing Programs

Each program f of arity n will be associated to an arithmetic proposition A, with free variables among $x_1, \ldots, x_n, y$, *representing* the program f. This means that the proposition $(\underline{p_1}/x_1, \ldots, \underline{p_n}/x_n, \underline{q}/y)A$, where $\underline{p}$ is the term $S^p(0)$, is provable if and only if f returns the value q for $p_1, \ldots, p_n$. To simplify the notation, the proposition $(t_1/x_1, \ldots, t_n/x_n, u/y)A$ will be written $A[t_1, \ldots, t_n, u]$.

If $f = \pi_i^n$, we define $A = (y = x_i)$. If $f = Z^n$, $A = (y = 0)$. If $f = Succ$, $A = (y = S(x_1))$. If $f = +$, $A = (y = x_1 + x_2)$. If $f = \times$, $A = (y = x_1 \times x_2)$. If $f = \chi_\leq$, $A = (x_1 \leq x_2 \wedge y = 1) \vee (x_2 < x_1 \wedge y = 0)$ where the proposition $x \leq y$ abbreviates $\exists z \ (z + x = y)$ and $x < y$ abbreviates $S(x) \leq y$.

If $f = \circ_m^n(h, g_1, \ldots, g_m)$, we first build the propositions $B_1, \ldots, B_m$ and C, representing the programs $g_1, \ldots, g_m$ and h, and then define

$$A = \exists w_1 \ldots \exists w_m \ (B_1[x_1, \ldots, x_n, w_1] \wedge \cdots \wedge B_m[x_1, \ldots, x_n, w_m]$$
$$\wedge \ C[w_1, \ldots, w_m, y])$$

Finally, if $f = \mu^n(g)$, we first build the proposition B representing the program g and then define

$$A = (\forall z \ (z < y \Rightarrow \exists w \ (B[x_1, \ldots, x_n, z, S(w)]))) \wedge B[x_1, \ldots, x_n, y, 0]$$

We can prove that f maps $p_1, \ldots, p_n$ to the value q if and only if the arithmetic proposition $A[\underline{p_1}, \ldots, \underline{p_n}, \underline{q}]$ is provable, and conclude that provability in arithmetic is undecidable.

However, before we prove this property we will extend the definition given above. Indeed, this definition assumes that the language contains the symbols 0, $S, +, \times$ and $=$, and it also assumes that the domain of discourse is limited to the set of integers. These two assumptions are correct in the case of arithmetic, but will be problematic when we try to generalise this result to other theories. For example, we have seen that in the language of set theory there is no symbol S representing the successor function, but there is a proposition with two free variables x and y stating that y is the successor of x

$$\forall z \ (z \in y \Leftrightarrow (z \in x \vee z = x))$$

We will assume then that we have an arbitrary language allowing us to build propositions N, $Null$, $Succ$, $Plus$, $Mult$ and Eq. We will write $N[t]$ for the proposition $(t/x)N$, $Succ[t, u]$ for the proposition $(t/x, u/y)Succ, \ldots$. For example, in arithmetic, N is the proposition $\top$, *Null* the proposition $x = 0$, *Succ* the proposition $y = S(x)$, *Plus* the proposition $z = x + y$, *Mult* the proposition $z = x \times y$ and *Eq* the proposition $x = y$. In set theory, the proposition N is the one built in Exercise 1.17, the proposition *Succ* is the proposition $\forall z \ (z \in y \Leftrightarrow (z \in x \lor z = x)), \ldots$.

The proposition *Inf*, for the *ordering relation*, is defined as $\exists z \ (N[z] \land Plus[z, x, y])$ and *InfS*, for the *strict ordering relation*, as $\exists x' \ (N[x'] \land Succ[x, x'] \land Inf[x', y])$.

In this language, we can associate a proposition to each program.

Definition 5.1 (Proposition representing a program) Let f be a program of arity n. The proposition A *representing* f is defined by induction over the construction of f.

- If $f = \pi_i^n$, then $A = Eq[x_i, y]$.
- If $f = Z^n$, then $A = Null[y]$.
- If $f = Succ$, then $A = Succ[x_1, y]$.
- If $f = +$, then $A = Plus[x_1, x_2, y]$.
- If $f = \times$, then $A = Mult[x_1, x_2, y]$.
- If $f = \chi_\leq$, then $A = (Inf[x_1, x_2] \land \exists z \ (Null[z] \land Succ[z, y])) \lor (InfS[x_2, x_1] \land Null[y])$.
- If $f = \circ_m^n(h, g_1, \ldots, g_m)$, and $B_1, \ldots, B_m$ and C are the propositions representing the programs $g_1, \ldots, g_m$ and h, then

$$A = \exists w_1 \ldots \exists w_m \ (N[w_1] \land \cdots \land N[w_m]$$
$$\land B_1[x_1, \ldots, x_n, w_1] \land \cdots \land B_m[x_1, \ldots, x_n, w_m]$$
$$\land C[w_1, \ldots, w_m, y])$$

- If $f = \mu^n(g)$, and B is the proposition representing the program g, then

$$A = (\forall z \ (N[z] \land InfS[z, y] \Rightarrow \exists w \exists w' \ (N[w'] \land Succ[w', w]$$
$$\land B[x_1, \ldots, x_n, z, w]))) \land (\forall w \ (Null[w] \Rightarrow B[x_1, \ldots, x_n, y, w]))$$

We will now prove that f maps $p_1, \ldots, p_n$ to q if and only if the proposition A relates the numbers $p_1, \ldots, p_n, q$. However, it is not possible to express this property simply by substituting variables by terms of the form $S^p(0)$ in A—the symbols 0 and S might not be in the language. Instead, we will define for each natural number n a proposition N_n characterising n, more precisely: $N_0 = Null[x]$ and $N_{n+1} = \exists y \ (N_n[y] \land Succ[y, x])$. If a proposition A contains a free variable x, we can state that the property represented by A holds for the number n using the proposition $\forall x \ (N_n[x] \Rightarrow A)$.

We can now prove that f associates the value q to $p_1, \ldots, p_n$ if and only if the proposition

$$\forall x_1 \ldots \forall x_n \forall y \ ((N_{p_1}[x_1] \land \cdots \land N_{p_n}[x_n] \land N_q[y]) \Rightarrow A[x_1, \ldots, x_n, y])$$

is provable. Of course, to prove this proposition we will need to rely on some properties of the propositions N, *Null*, *Succ*, *Plus*, *Mult* and *Eq*. Surprisingly, very few properties are needed; they are given in the theory T_0 below.

Definition 5.2 (Theory $\mathcal{T}_0$) The theory $\mathcal{T}_0$ is composed of the following axioms.
Predicate N:

$$\forall x\ (Null[x] \Rightarrow N[x])$$

$$\forall x \forall y\ ((N[x] \wedge Succ[x,y]) \Rightarrow N[y])$$

Existence of natural numbers:

$$\exists x\ Null[x]$$

$$\forall x\ (N[x] \Rightarrow \exists y\ Succ[x,y])$$

Equality:

$$\forall x\ Eq[x,x]$$

$$\forall x \forall y\ (Null[x] \Rightarrow (Null[y] \Leftrightarrow Eq[x,y]))$$

$$\forall x \forall y \forall x' \forall y'\ ((N[x] \wedge Succ[x,x'] \wedge Eq[x,y]) \Rightarrow (Succ[y,y'] \Leftrightarrow Eq[x',y']))$$

Injectivity of successor:

$$\forall x \forall y \forall x' \forall y'\ (Succ[x,x'] \wedge Succ[y,y'] \wedge Eq[x',y']) \Rightarrow Eq[x,y])$$

Zero is not a successor:

$$\forall x \forall x'\ (Succ[x,x'] \Rightarrow \neg Null[x'])$$

Every natural number is either zero or a successor:

$$\forall x\ (N[x] \Rightarrow (Null[x] \vee \exists y\ (N[y] \wedge Succ[y,x])))$$

Addition:

$$\forall x \forall y \forall z\ ((Null[x] \wedge N[y]) \Rightarrow (Eq[y,z] \Leftrightarrow Plus[x,y,z]))$$
$$\forall x \forall y \forall z \forall x' \forall z'\ ((N[x] \wedge N[y] \wedge Plus[x,y,z] \wedge Succ[x,x'])$$
$$\Rightarrow (Succ[z,z'] \Leftrightarrow Plus[x',y,z']))$$
$$\forall x \forall y \forall x' \forall y'\ ((N[x] \wedge N[y] \wedge Succ[x,x'] \wedge Succ[z,z'] \wedge Plus[x',y,z'])$$
$$\Rightarrow Plus[x,y,z])$$
$$\forall x \forall y \forall y' \forall z'\ ((N[x] \wedge N[y] \wedge N[y'] \wedge Succ[y,y'] \wedge Plus[x,y',z'])$$
$$\Rightarrow \exists z\ (Plus[x,y,z] \wedge Succ[z,z']))$$

Multiplication:

$$\forall x \forall y \forall z\ ((Null[x] \wedge N[y]) \Rightarrow (Null[z] \Leftrightarrow Mult[x,y,z]))$$
$$\forall x \forall y \forall z \forall x' \forall z'\ ((N[x] \wedge N[y] \wedge Mult[x,y,z] \wedge Succ[x,x'])$$
$$\Rightarrow (Plus[y,z,z'] \Leftrightarrow Mult[x',y,z']))$$

Proposition 5.1 *The following propositions are provable in the theory* T_0.

1. $\forall x \ (N_p[x] \Rightarrow N[x])$
2. $\exists x \ N_p[x]$
3. $\forall x \forall y \ (N_p[x] \Rightarrow (N_p[y] \Leftrightarrow Eq[x, y]))$
4. $\forall x \forall y \forall z \ ((N_p[x] \wedge N_q[y]) \Rightarrow (N_{p+q}[z] \Leftrightarrow Plus[x, y, z]))$
5. $\forall x \forall y \forall z \ ((N_p[x] \wedge N_q[y]) \Rightarrow (N_{p \times q}[z] \Leftrightarrow Mult[x, y, z]))$
6. $\forall x_1 \forall x_2 \ ((N_{p_1}[x_1] \wedge N_{p_2}[x_2]) \Rightarrow Inf[x_1, x_2])$, *où* $p_1 \leq p_2$
7. $\forall x_1 \forall x_2 \ ((N_{p_1}[x_1] \wedge N_{p_2}[x_2]) \Rightarrow InfS[x_1, x_2])$, *où* $p_1 < p_2$
8. $\forall x \forall y \forall y' \ ((N[x] \wedge Inf[x, y'] \wedge Succ[y, y']) \Rightarrow (Eq[x, y'] \vee Inf[x, y]))$
9. $\forall x \forall y \forall y' \ ((N[x] \wedge InfS[x, y'] \wedge Succ[y, y']) \Rightarrow (Eq[x, y] \vee InfS[x, y]))$
10. $\forall x \forall y \ ((N[x] \wedge InfS[x, y]) \Rightarrow \neg Null[y])$

Proof

1. By induction on p, using the axioms for the predicate N.
2. By induction on p, using the axioms stating the existence of natural numbers and (1.).
3. By induction on p, using the equality axioms and (1.).
4. By induction on p, using the first two axioms of addition, (1.), (2.) and (3.).
5. By induction on p, using the axioms of multiplication, (1.), (2.) and (4.).
6. Since $p_1 \leq p_2$, there exists a natural number q such that $q + p_1 = p_2$. From the assumptions $N_q[z]$, $N_{p_1}[x_1]$ and $N_{p_2}[x_2]$ we can deduce the propositions $N[z]$ and $Plus[z, x_1, x_2]$ using (1.) and (4.). Therefore $Inf[x_1, x_2]$. We can now eliminate the assumption $N_q[z]$ using (2.).
7. Since $p_1 < p_2$, we have $p_1 + 1 \leq p_2$. From the assumptions $N_{p_1}[x_1]$, $Succ[x_1, w]$ and $N_{p_2}[x_2]$ we can deduce $N_{p_1+1}[w]$ and then, using (1.) and (6.), the propositions $N[w]$ and $Inf[w, x_2]$ and hence $InfS[x_1, x_2]$. We can now eliminate the assumption $Succ[x_1, w]$ using $\exists w \ Succ[x_1, w]$, which can be proved using the second axiom of existence of natural numbers.
8. The proposition $Inf[x, y']$ is $\exists z' \ (N[z'] \wedge Plus[z', x, y'])$. We use the axiom *Every natural number is either zero or a successor* to distinguish two cases: z' equal to zero and z' equal to the successor of a number z. In the first case, the first axiom of addition implies $Eq[x, y']$. In the second case, the third axiom of addition implies $Plus[z, x, y]$ and therefore $Inf[x, y]$.
9. Consequence of (8.) and the axiom *Injectivity of successor*.
10. Consequence of the fourth axiom of addition and the axiom *Zero is not a successor*.

$\square$

Proposition 5.2 *Let A be a proposition. We denote by* $A[t]$ *the proposition* $(t/x)A$. *If the propositions* $\forall x \ (N_0[x] \Rightarrow A[x])$, $\forall x \ (N_1[x] \Rightarrow A[x]), \ldots, \forall x \ (N_{p-1}[x] \Rightarrow A[x])$ *are provable in the theory* T_0, *then so is the proposition* $\forall x \forall y \ ((N[x] \wedge N_p[y] \wedge InfS[x, y]) \Rightarrow A[x])$.

Proof By induction on p using Proposition 5.1(9.). $\square$

Definition 5.3 (N-model) Let $\mathcal{L}$ be a language and let N, *Null*, *Succ*, *Plus*, *Mult* be propositions in $\mathcal{L}$. A model $\mathcal{M}$ of this language is a N-*model* if

$$\{a \in \mathcal{M} \mid [\![N]\!]_{x=a} = 1\} = \mathbb{N}$$

$$\{a \in \mathbb{N} \mid [\![Null]\!]_{x=a} = 1\} = \{0\}$$

$$\{(a,b) \in \mathbb{N}^2 \mid [\![Succ]\!]_{x=a,y=b} = 1\} = \{(a,b) \in \mathbb{N}^2 \mid b = a+1\}$$

$$\{(a,b,c) \in \mathbb{N}^3 \mid [\![Plus]\!]_{x=a,y=b,z=c} = 1\} = \{(a,b,c) \in \mathbb{N}^3 \mid c = a+b\}$$

$$\{(a,b,c) \in \mathbb{N}^3 \mid [\![Mult]\!]_{x=a,y=b,z=c} = 1\} = \{(a,b,c) \in \mathbb{N}^3 \mid c = a \times b\}$$

$$\{(a,b) \in \mathbb{N}^2 \mid [\![Eq]\!]_{x=a,y=b} = 1\} = \{(a,b) \in \mathbb{N}^2 \mid a = b\}$$

If $\mathcal{T}$ is a theory in the language $\mathcal{L}$, an N-model of $\mathcal{T}$ is a N-model of $\mathcal{L}$ that is also a model of $\mathcal{T}$.

The axioms of the theory $\mathcal{T}_0$ are valid in all the N-models.
We can now prove the following proposition.

Proposition 5.3 *Let $\mathcal{L}$ be a language, and N, Null, Succ, Plus, Mult and Eq propositions in the language $\mathcal{L}$. Let $\mathcal{T}$ be a theory in $\mathcal{L}$ such that all the axioms of the theory $\mathcal{T}_0$ are provable in $\mathcal{T}$, and $\mathcal{T}$ has an N-model $\mathcal{M}$. If f is a program and A a proposition representing f, the following three propositions are equivalent*

- *f gives the value q for $p_1, \dots, p_n$,*
- *the proposition*

$$\forall x_1 \dots \forall x_n \forall y \, ((N_{p_1}[x_1] \wedge \cdots \wedge N_{p_n}[x_n] \wedge N_q[y]) \Rightarrow A[x_1, \dots, x_n, y])$$

is provable in the theory $\mathcal{T}$,
- *this proposition is valid in the model $\mathcal{M}$.*

Proof Assuming that f gives the value q for $p_1, \dots, p_n$, we show by induction over the structure of f that the proposition

$$\forall x_1 \dots \forall x_n \forall y \, ((N_{p_1}[x_1] \wedge \cdots \wedge N_{p_n}[x_n] \wedge N_q[y]) \Rightarrow A[x_1, \dots, x_n, y])$$

is provable in $\mathcal{T}$.

- If $f = \pi_i^n$ then $A = Eq[y, x_i]$ and the proposition

$$\forall x_1 \dots \forall x_n \forall y \, ((N_{p_1}[x_1] \wedge \cdots \wedge N_{p_n}[x_n] \wedge N_{p_i}[y]) \Rightarrow Eq[x_i, y])$$

is a consequence of Proposition 5.1(3.). We proceed in the same way for the programs zero, successor, addition and multiplication, using Proposition 5.1(4.) and (5.).

- If $f = \chi_{\leq}$, and $p_1 \leq p_2$, then by Proposition 5.1(6.), the proposition $Inf[x_1, x_2]$ is provable under the assumptions $N_{p_1}[x_1]$ and $N_{p_2}[x_2]$. The proposition $\exists z' \, (Null[z'] \wedge Succ[z', y])$ is provable under the assumption $N_1[y]$ and therefore the proposition A is provable assuming $N_{p_1}[x_1]$, $N_{p_2}[x_2]$ and $N_1[y]$. We proceed in the same way if $p_2 < p_1$, using Proposition 5.1(7.).

- If $f = o_m^n(h, g_1, \ldots, g_m)$, then, since f is terminating for $(p_1, \ldots, p_n)$, $g_1, \ldots,$ g_m are terminating for $(p_1, \ldots, p_n)$, and if we call r_i the number $g_i(p_1, \ldots, p_n)$, h is terminating for $r_1, \ldots, r_m$ and $q = h(r_1, \ldots, r_m)$. Let $B_1, \ldots, B_m$ and C be the propositions representing the programs $g_1, \ldots, g_m$ and h. By induction hypothesis, under the assumptions $N_{p_1}[x_1], \ldots, N_{p_n}[x_n], N_{r_1}[w_1], \ldots, N_{r_m}[w_m]$ and $N_q[y]$, the propositions $B_1[x_1, \ldots, x_n, w_1], \ldots, B_m[x_1, \ldots, x_n, w_m]$ and $C[w_1, \ldots, w_m, y]$ are provable, and by Proposition 5.1(1.), under the same assumptions the propositions $N[w_1], \ldots, N[w_n]$ are provable. As a consequence, the proposition A is provable. We can eliminate the assumptions $N_{r_1}[w_1], \ldots, N_{r_m}[w_m]$ using Proposition 5.1(2.).

- If $f = \mu^n(g)$ then, since f is terminating for $(p_1, \ldots, p_n)$ and gives the value q, g is terminating for $(p_1, \ldots, p_n, 0), \ldots, (p_1, \ldots, p_n, q - 1)$ and gives a value which is not zero, and g is defined for $(p_1, \ldots, p_n, q)$ and gives the value 0. Therefore, there are numbers $r_0, \ldots, r_{q-1}$ such that $g(p_1, \ldots, p_n, 0) = r_0 + 1, \ldots, g(p_1, \ldots, p_n, q - 1) = r_{q-1} + 1$.

  Let B be the proposition representing the program g. By induction hypothesis, under the assumptions $N_{p_1}[x_1], \ldots, N_{p_n}[x_n]$ and $N_q[y]$, the propositions

$$\forall v \forall w \, ((N_i[v] \wedge N_{r_i+1}[w]) \Rightarrow B[x_1, \ldots, x_n, v, w])$$

are provable for any i between 0 and $q - 1$. Using Proposition 5.1(1.) and (2.), we can deduce that the proposition

$$\forall v \, (N_i[v] \Rightarrow \exists w \exists w' \, (N[w'] \wedge Succ[w', w] \wedge B[x_1, \ldots, x_n, v, w]))$$

is provable. Using Proposition 5.2, we can deduce that the proposition

$$\forall v \, (InfS[v, y] \Rightarrow \exists w \exists w' \, (N[w'] \wedge Succ[w', w] \wedge B[x_1, \ldots, x_n, v, w]))$$

is provable, and, similarly, the proposition

$$\forall w \, (Null[w] \Rightarrow B[x_1, \ldots, x_n, y, w])$$

is provable. We conclude that the proposition A is provable.

Since the model $\mathcal{M}$ is a model of the theory $\mathcal{T}$, if the proposition

$$\forall x_1 \ldots \forall x_n \forall y \, ((N_{p_1}[x_1] \wedge \cdots \wedge N_{p_n}[x_n] \wedge N_q[y]) \Rightarrow A[x_1, \ldots, x_n, y])$$

is provable in $\mathcal{T}$ then it is valid in the model $\mathcal{M}$.

Finally, if the proposition

$$\forall x_1 \ldots \forall x_n \forall y \, ((N_{p_1}[x_1] \wedge \cdots \wedge N_{p_n}[x_n] \wedge N_q[y]) \Rightarrow A[x_1, \ldots, x_n, y])$$

is valid in $\mathcal{M}$, there are numbers $p_1, \ldots, p_n, q$ such that

$$[\![A[x_1, \ldots, x_n, y]\!]\!]_{x_1=p_1, \ldots, x_n=p_n, y=q} = 1$$

and, using the fact that $\mathcal{M}$ is an $\mathbb{N}$-model, we can show by induction over the structure of f that f gives the value q for $p_1, \ldots, p_n$.   □

5.3 Church's Theorem

Definition 5.4 Let f be a program and A the proposition representing it. The proposition "The program f is terminating for $p_1, \ldots, p_n$" corresponds to the closed proposition

$$\forall x_1 \ldots \forall x_n \, ((N_{p_1}[x_1] \wedge \cdots \wedge N_{p_n}[x_n]) \Rightarrow \exists y \, (N[y] \wedge A[x_1, \ldots, x_n, y]))$$

Proposition 5.4 *Let $\mathcal{L}$ be a language, N, Null, Succ, Plus, Mult and Eq propositions in $\mathcal{L}$, and T a theory in $\mathcal{L}$ such that the axioms of the theory T_0 are provable in T and T has an $\mathbb{N}$-model $\mathcal{M}$. If f is a program, the following three propositions are equivalent.*

- *the program f is terminating for $p_1, \ldots, p_n$,*
- *the proposition "The program f is terminating for $p_1, \ldots, p_n$" is provable in T,*
- *this proposition is valid in $\mathcal{M}$.*

Proof If the program f terminates for $p_1, \ldots, p_n$ then there exists a number q such that f gives the value q for $p_1, \ldots, p_n$. By Proposition 5.3, the proposition

$$\forall x_1 \ldots \forall x_n \forall y \, ((N_{p_1}[x_1] \wedge \cdots \wedge N_{p_n}[x_n] \wedge N_q[y]) \Rightarrow A[x_1, \ldots, x_n, y])$$

is provable in T. Therefore, by Proposition 5.1(1.) and (2.), the proposition $\forall x_1 \ldots \forall x_n \, ((N_{p_1}[x_1] \wedge \cdots \wedge N_{p_n}[x_n]) \Rightarrow \exists y \, (N[y] \wedge A[x_1, \ldots, x_n, y]))$ is provable in T.

Since the model $\mathcal{M}$ is a model of the theory T, if this proposition is provable in T then it is valid in the model $\mathcal{M}$.

Finally, if this proposition is valid in $\mathcal{M}$, there exists a natural number q such that

$$[\![A[x_1, \ldots, x_n, y]\!]\!]_{x_1=p_1, \ldots, x_n=p_n, y=q} = 1$$

The proposition

$$\forall x_1 \ldots \forall x_n \forall y \, ((N_{p_1}[x_1] \wedge \cdots \wedge N_{p_n}[x_n] \wedge N_q[y]) \Rightarrow A[x_1, \ldots, x_n, y])$$

is therefore valid in $\mathcal{M}$. By Proposition 5.3, f gives the value q for $p_1, \ldots, p_n$ and is therefore terminating for $p_1, \ldots, p_n$.   □

Proposition 5.5 *The function T that maps*

- *the index of a program f and $p_1, \ldots, p_n$ to the index of the proposition "The program f is terminating for $p_1, \ldots, p_n$", and*
- *all the numbers that are not indices of a program to the value 0*

is computable.

Proof The function T is defined by well-founded induction. $\square$

We have thus a first undecidability result for provability.

Proposition 5.6 *Let $\mathcal{L}$ be a language, N, Null, Succ, Plus, Mult and Eq propositions in the language $\mathcal{L}$ and T a theory in the language $\mathcal{L}$ such that the axioms of the theory T_0 are provable and it has an $\mathbb{N}$-model. Then the set of closed propositions in $\mathcal{L}$ that are provable in T is undecidable.*

Proof If there exists a computable function F that maps the index of a proposition to 1 or 0 depending on whether the proposition is provable in T or not, then the function $F \circ T$ is computable. This contradicts the theorem of undecidability of the halting problem. $\square$

We now generalise the result by dropping the assumption that the axioms of the theory T_0 can be proved in the theory T.

Proposition 5.7 *Let $\mathcal{L}$ be a language, N, Null, Succ, Plus, Mult and Eq propositions in $\mathcal{L}$ and T a theory in $\mathcal{L}$ that has an $\mathbb{N}$-model. Then, the set of closed propositions in $\mathcal{L}$ that are provable in T is undecidable.*

Proof The theory $T \cup T_0$ can prove the axioms of T_0 and has an $\mathbb{N}$-model. By Proposition 5.6, provability in this theory is undecidable.

We use again a reduction: let H be the conjunction of all the axioms of the theory T_0. The proposition $H \Rightarrow A$ is provable in the theory T if and only if the proposition A is provable in the theory $T \cup T_0$. Let T be the function that associates the index of the proposition $H \Rightarrow A$ to the index of the proposition A. The function T is computable and the proposition with index $T(\ulcorner A \urcorner)$ is provable in the theory T if and only if the proposition A is provable in $T \cup T_0$. If there exists a decision algorithm F for the theory T, then $F \circ T$ is a decision algorithm for $T \cup T_0$, contradicting the fact that $T \cup T_0$ is undecidable. $\square$

Proposition 5.8 *Let $\mathcal{L}$ be a language and N, Null, Succ, Plus, Mult and Eq propositions in $\mathcal{L}$. If $\mathcal{L}$ has an $\mathbb{N}$-model then the set of closed propositions in $\mathcal{L}$ that are provable in the empty theory is undecidable.*

Proof Consequence of Proposition 5.7, taking $T = \emptyset$. $\square$

Theorem 5.1 (Undecidability of arithmetic) *The set of closed propositions that are provable in arithmetic, or in any extension of arithmetic that has the model $(\mathbb{N}, 0, x \mapsto x + 1, +, \times, =)$, is undecidable.*

Proof Define $N = \top$, $Null = (x = 0)$, $Succ = (y = S(x))$, $Plus = (z = x + y)$, $Mult = (z = x \times y)$ and $Eq = (x = y)$. The model $\mathbb{N}$ is an $\mathbb{N}$-model. We can therefore apply Proposition 5.7. $\qquad\qquad\square$

This theorem can be generalised for any consistent extension of arithmetic, that is, any extension of arithmetic that has a model (whether this model is $\mathbb{N}$ or not). In this way, it is possible to prove the undecidability of exotic extensions of arithmetic such as the ones that we built in the proof of Löwenheim-Skolem's theorem, which are consistent although $\mathbb{N}$ is not a model for them. We will not present this proof here, but it is important to note that this result does not extend to extensions of arithmetic that are contradictory. If we add for instance the axiom $\bot$ then all propositions become provable and the theory is trivially decidable.

Theorem 5.2 (Church) *Consider a language containing at least one binary predicate symbol. The set of closed propositions in this language that are provable in the empty theory is undecidable.*

Proof We show that we can define the propositions N, $Null$, $Succ$, $Plus$, $Mult$ and Eq and an $\mathbb{N}$-model $\mathcal{M}$ for the language, and the result follows from Proposition 5.8. Let $\mathcal{M} = \mathbb{N} \uplus (\mathbb{N} \times \mathbb{N})$ and $\hat{R} = \{(a, (a, b)) \mid a \in \mathbb{N}, b \in \mathbb{N}\} \cup \{((a, b), b) \mid a \in \mathbb{N}, b \in \mathbb{N}\} \cup \{((a, b), (a + b, a \times b)) \mid a \in \mathbb{N}, b \in \mathbb{N}\}$. We define the propositions

$$Eq = \forall z \, (x \, R \, z \Leftrightarrow y \, R \, z)$$

$$N = \exists y_1 \exists y_2 \exists y_3 \, (\neg Eq[y_1, y_2] \wedge \neg Eq[y_1, y_3] \wedge \neg Eq[y_2, y_2]$$
$$\wedge \, x \, R \, y_1 \wedge x \, R \, y_2 \wedge x \, R \, y_3)$$

$$Plus = N[x] \wedge N[y] \wedge N[z] \wedge \exists w \exists w' \, (x \, R \, w \wedge w \, R \, y \wedge w \, R \, w' \wedge z \, R \, w')$$

$$Mult = N[x] \wedge N[y] \wedge N[z] \wedge \exists w \exists w' \, (x \, R \, w \wedge w \, R \, y \wedge w \, R \, w' \wedge w' \, R \, z)$$

$$Null = N[x] \wedge \forall y \, (N[y] \Rightarrow Plus[x, y, y])$$

$$One = N[x] \wedge \forall y \, (N[y] \Rightarrow Mult[x, y, y])$$

$$Succ = \exists u \, (One[u] \wedge Plus[x, u, y])$$

It is easy to show that $[\![Eq[x, y]]\!]_{x=u, y=v} = 1$ if and only if $u = v$ by considering first the case where u is a number and then the case where it is a pair, and also that $[\![N[x]]\!]_{x=u} = 1$ if and only if u is a number, $[\![Plus[x, y, z]]\!]_{x=p, y=q, z=r} = 1$ if and only if p, q and r are numbers and $p + q = r$, $[\![Mult[x, y, z]]\!]_{x=p, y=q, z=r} = 1$ if and only if p, q and r are numbers and $p \times q = r$, $[\![Null[x]]\!]_{x=p} = 1$ if and only if $p = 0$, and $[\![Succ[x, y]]\!]_{x=p, y=q} = 1$ if and only if p and q are numbers and $p + 1 = q$. $\quad\square$

If the language $\mathcal{L}$ contains a predicate of arity n, with $n \geq 2$, the construction of an $\mathbb{N}$-model is easy to generalise. A language that contains at least one unary predicate symbol P and a function symbol f of arity $n \geq 2$ is also undecidable, since using a unary predicate symbol P and an n-ary function symbol f we can build the proposition $P(f(x_1, \ldots, x_n))$ that simulates an n-ary predicate symbol.

The only remaining cases are the case where all predicate symbols have arity zero—then it does not matter which function symbols we have, since they cannot be used in the propositions—and the case where all function and predicate symbols are at most unary. In both cases provability is decidable.

Church's theorem highlights the huge leap in power introduced by G. Frege with the use of binary predicates. All the previous logics—the logic of syllogisms defined by Aristotle, ...—where all symbols were at most unary—Man, Mortal, ...—are decidable.

Note that although provability in predicate logic is undecidable if the language contains at least one binary predicate symbol, it might become decidable if we add axioms. For instance, it becomes trivially decidable if we add the axiom $\perp$ to make the theory contradictory. It is also decidable if we add the axiom $\forall x \forall y \ (x \ R \ y)$ which is consistent. Church's theorem does not preclude research on algorithms for specific theories *a priori*, even if the theories use binary predicate symbols, provided that they do not have an $\mathbb{N}$-model. For example, A. Tarski proved that elementary geometry is decidable, although it uses several binary predicates. We will see another example of a decidable theory in Chap. 7.

We finish this section with a generalisation of the undecidability theorem for arithmetic. We have already seen that when we have a program f and natural numbers $p_1, \ldots, p_n$, we can build a closed proposition in arithmetic that is provable if and only if the program f terminates for $p_1, \ldots, p_n$. In 1970, Y. Matiyasevich built a proposition of the form $\exists z_1 \ldots \exists z_m \ (t = u)$ for this purpose. As a consequence, we can deduce that the set of propositions of the form $\exists z_1 \ldots \exists z_m \ (t = u)$ that are provable in arithmetic is undecidable. Such a proposition states the existence of an integer solution for the polynomial equation $t = u$ where all the coefficients are also integers. This means that no algorithm can decide whether a polynomial equation with integer coefficients has an integer solution. This result solved negatively one of the problems posed by D. Hilbert in 1900, known as *Hilbert's tenth problem*: find an algorithm to decide whether a polynomial equation with integer coefficients has an integer solution or not. Building a proposition of the form $\exists z_1 \ldots \exists z_m \ (t = u)$ is not easy: although a link between Church's theorem and a negative solution to Hilbert's tenth problem had been suggested by M. Davis in 1953 (he had proposed a first simplification for propositions representing programs), it was only in 1970 that this result was proved, by Matiyasevich.

5.4 Semi-decidability

The set of provable propositions is undecidable for predicate logic, but the deduction rules are effective. By Proposition 3.14, this means that the set of provable propositions is semi-decidable. This result holds for all the theories that have a finite number of axioms, and can be generalised to all the theories that have a decidable set of axioms.

We give here the proof of this proposition starting from Proposition 3.13, which paves the way for Proposition 5.10.

Proposition 5.9 *Let T be a theory with a decidable set of axioms. The set of all the propositions that are provable in T is semi-decidable.*

Proof Since the deduction rules are effective, by Proposition 3.13 the set of proofs is decidable. Since the set of axioms of the theory T is decidable, we can define a computable function g that takes as arguments the index of a tree π and the index of a proposition A, and checks that π is a well-formed proof and that its root is a sequent $\Gamma \vdash B$ such that $B = A$ and such that all the elements of Γ are axioms in T. The function h such that $h(A)$ is the least natural number π such that $1 \overset{\cdot}{-} g(\pi, A) = 0$ composed with the constant function 1 is a semi-decision algorithm for the set of provable propositions in T. If A is provable in T, then $h(A) = 1$, otherwise h is undefined for A.   □

We have shown that the set of proofs is decidable, and the set of provable propositions is semi-decidable. These two results gave rise to two kinds of programs: *proof verification programs* and *programs for automated theorem proving*. The first kind of program takes as argument a tree π, and indicates whether π is a well-formed proof or not (this kind of program always terminates). The second kind of program takes as argument a proposition A and tries to find a proof π for A. If the proposition is not provable, this search may continue forever. We will see an example of this kind of program in Chap. 6.

5.5 Gödel's First Incompleteness Theorem

The definitions of the functions g and h in the proof of Proposition 5.9 could be modified. Instead of the function h, we could define a function h' that searches simultaneously for proofs of the proposition A and the proposition $\neg A$ in the theory T, and returns 1 or 0 depending on which proof it finds. Since each of the propositions can be provable or not provable, there are four different cases:

1. both A and $\neg A$ are provable propositions,
2. the proposition A is provable but $\neg A$ is not,
3. the proposition $\neg A$ is provable but A is not,
4. neither A nor $\neg A$ is provable.

If we assume that the theory T is consistent, case (1.) is not possible. In case (2.), $h'(A) = 1$, in case (3.), $h'(A) = 0$ and in case (4.) h' is undefined for A.

It is easy to find examples of propositions that satisfy case (2.) and also propositions that satisfy case (3.), but it is less clear whether there exists a proposition that satisfies case (4.). Is there a proposition A such that neither A nor $\neg A$ is provable in the theory T?

We show by contradiction that the answer to this question is positive for all the theories in which the set of provable propositions is undecidable: if there exists no proposition satisfying case (4.), the function h' defines a decision algorithm for provability in the theory T, contradicting our assumption that such an algorithm does not exist.

Definition 5.5 (Complete theory) Let $\mathcal{L}$ be a language. A theory T in $\mathcal{L}$ is *complete* if for each closed proposition A in $\mathcal{L}$, either A is provable in T or $\neg A$ is provable in T.

Proposition 5.10 *Let $\mathcal{L}$ be a language, N, Null, Succ, Plus, Mult and Eq propositions in $\mathcal{L}$, and T a theory with a decidable set of axioms and an $\mathbb{N}$-model. The theory T is incomplete: there exists a closed proposition G such that neither G nor $\neg G$ is provable in this theory.*

Proof Let g be the computable function that associates to the index of a tree π and the index of a closed proposition A the value 1 if π is a well-formed proof where the root is a sequent $\Gamma \vdash B$ such that $B = A$ and all the elements of Γ are axioms in T, and the value 0 otherwise. Let r be the computable function that associates to a proof with root $\Gamma \vdash B$ the proposition B. Let $\overset{\wedge}{\neg}$ be the function that associates the index of the proposition $\neg A$ to the index of the proposition A: $\overset{\wedge}{\neg}(x) = \ulcorner \neg \urcorner; (x; 0)$. Let $|$ be the Boolean function *or*: $x \mid y = x + y \overset{\cdot}{-} (x \times y)$ and $\chi_=$ the characteristic function of equality. Let h_1 be the computable function such that $h_1(A)$ is the least natural number π such that $1 \overset{\cdot}{-} (g(\pi, A) \mid g(\pi, \overset{\wedge}{\neg}(A))) = 0$. Let h' be the function $h'(A) = \chi_=(r(h_1(A)), A)$.

If the theory T is complete, h' is a decision algorithm for provability in T, contradicting Proposition 5.7.   □

Theorem 5.3 (Gödel's first incompleteness theorem) *Arithmetic, and all its extensions that have a model $(\mathbb{N}, 0, x \mapsto x + 1, +, \times, =)$ and a decidable set of axioms, are incomplete.*

Proof Define $N = \top$, $Null = (x = 0)$, $Succ = (y = S(x))$, $Plus = (z = x + y)$, $Mult = (z = x \times y)$ and $Eq = (x = y)$. The set of axioms of the theory is decidable and the model $\mathbb{N}$ is an $\mathbb{N}$-model of the theory, therefore we can apply Proposition 5.10.   □

This theorem can be generalised to all consistent extensions of arithmetic, that is, all the extensions of arithmetic that have a decidable set of axioms and a model, be it $\mathbb{N}$ or not. It is possible to prove in this way the incompleteness of some exotic extensions of arithmetic that are consistent even though $\mathbb{N}$ is not a model. We will not do it here.

It is important to note that this result does not extend to contradictory extensions of arithmetic. If we add the axiom $\bot$, for instance, then all the propositions become provable and therefore the theory is trivially complete. This result does not extend either to extensions of arithmetic where the set of axioms is undecidable. Thus, the theory that has as axioms all the propositions that are valid in the model $\mathbb{N}$ is a consistent and complete extension of arithmetic, but by Gödel's theorem the set of axioms in this theory is undecidable. Similarly, in the proof of Proposition 2.5, we showed that any theory $\mathcal{T}$ has a consistent and complete extension $\mathcal{U}$, but in general the set of axioms of this theory is not decidable.

Exercise 5.1 (An example of an undetermined proposition) Proposition 5.10 shows that there exists a closed proposition G such that neither G nor $\neg G$ is provable in the theory $\mathcal{T}$, but it does not give us an example. In this exercise we will show how to build such a proposition.

Let $\mathcal{L}$ be a language, N, *Null*, *Succ*, *Plus*, *Mult* and *Eq* propositions in $\mathcal{L}$ and $\mathcal{T}$ a theory with a decidable set of axioms and with an $\mathbb{N}$-model $\mathcal{M}$. Let $\mathcal{T}'$ be the theory $\mathcal{T} \cup \mathcal{T}_0$.

Let f be the computable function such that $f(n, p, q) = 1$ if $n = \ulcorner \pi \urcorner$, $p = \ulcorner A \urcorner$ and the tree π is a proof of the proposition $\forall w\ (N_q[w] \Rightarrow A)$ in $\mathcal{T}'$, otherwise $f(n, p, q) = 0$.

Let F be the proposition representing a program that implements this function. We denote by $F[t_1, t_2, t_3, u]$ the proposition $(t_1/x_1, t_2/x_2, t_3/x_3, u/y)F$.

By Proposition 5.3, the following three propositions are equivalent

- $f(n, p, q) = r$,
- the proposition

$$\forall x_1 \forall x_2 \forall x_3 \forall y\ (N_n[x_1] \wedge N_p[x_2] \wedge N_q[x_3] \wedge N_r[y] \Rightarrow F[x_1, x_2, x_3, y])$$

  is provable in $\mathcal{T}'$,
- in the model $\mathcal{M}$, $[\![F]\!]_{x_1=n, x_2=p, x_3=q, x_4=r} = 1$.

Let T be the proposition

$$\forall x \forall y\ ((N[x] \wedge N_1[y]) \Rightarrow \neg F[x, w, w, y])$$

$m = \ulcorner T \urcorner$ and G the closed proposition

$$\forall w\ (N_m[w] \Rightarrow T)$$

Show that if G is provable in $\mathcal{T}'$ then

1. $[\![G]\!] = 1$,
2. for any natural number n, $[\![F]\!]_{x_1=n, x_2=m, x_3=m, y=1} = 0$,
3. for any n, $f(n, m, m) = 0$,
4. the proposition $\forall w\ (N_m[w] \Rightarrow T)$ is not provable in $\mathcal{T}'$,
5. the proposition G is not provable in $\mathcal{T}'$.

Show that the proposition G is not provable in $\mathcal{T}'$ using the above.
Conclude that the proposition G is not provable in $\mathcal{T}$.
Show that if $\neg G$ is provable in $\mathcal{T}'$ then

1. $[\![\neg G]\!] = 1$,
2. there exists a natural number n such that $[\![F]\!]_{x_1=n, x_2=m, x_3=m, y=1} = 1$,
3. there exists a natural number n such that $f(n, m, m) = 1$,
4. the proposition $\forall w\ (N_m[w] \Rightarrow T)$ is provable in T',
5. the proposition G is provable in T',
6. the theory T' is contradictory.

Show that the proposition $\neg G$ is not provable in T' using the above.
Conclude that the proposition $\neg G$ is not provable in T.

Exercise 5.2 In this exercise we will admit that Matiyasevich's theorem holds, that is, we will assume that the set of provable arithmetic propositions that have the form $\exists x_1 \ldots \exists x_m\ (t = u)$ is undecidable.

1. Show that there exists a closed proposition A of the form $\exists x_1 \ldots \exists x_m\ (t = u)$ such that neither A nor $\neg A$ is provable in arithmetic.
2. Show that the proposition $\forall x_1 \ldots \forall x_m\ \neg(t = u)$ is not provable.
3. Show that if a is a closed arithmetic term, then there exists an integer n such that the proposition $a = \underline{n}$ is provable. Show that if n and p are two integers, then either the proposition $\underline{n} = \underline{p}$ or the proposition $\neg(\underline{n} = \underline{p})$ is provable. Show that if a and b are two closed arithmetic terms, then the proposition $a = b$ is provable or the proposition $\neg(a = b)$ is provable.
4. Consider an equation $t = u$ with variables among $x_1, \ldots, x_m$, and natural numbers $p_1, \ldots, p_m$ such that the proposition $(\underline{p_1}/x_1, \ldots, \underline{p_m}/x_m)(t = u)$ is provable. Show that the proposition $\exists x_1 \ldots \exists x_m\ (t = u)$ is provable. Show that if the proposition $\exists x_1 \ldots \exists x_m\ (t = u)$ is not provable, then for all $p_1, \ldots, p_m$, the proposition $(\underline{p_1}/x_1, \ldots, \underline{p_m}/x_m)(t = u)$ is not provable.
5. Show that if the proposition $\exists x_1 \ldots \exists x_m\ (t = u)$ is not provable, then for all $p_1, \ldots, p_m$, the proposition $(\underline{p_1}/x_1, \ldots, \underline{p_m}/x_m)\neg(t = u)$ is provable.
6. Show that there exists a proposition A of the form $\neg(t = u)$ with variables among $x_1, \ldots, x_m$ such that

   – for all $p_1, \ldots, p_m$ the proposition $(\underline{p_1}/x_1, \ldots, \underline{p_m}/x_m)A$ is provable,
   – the proposition $\forall x_1 \ldots \forall x_m\ A$ is not provable.

Chapter 6
Automated Theorem Proving

We have seen in Chap. 5 that provability in predicate logic is not decidable; it is actually semi-decidable. There exists a computable function f such that $f(\ulcorner \Gamma \vdash \Delta \urcorner) = 1$ if the sequent $\Gamma \vdash \Delta$ is provable and f is undefined for $\ulcorner \Gamma \vdash \Delta \urcorner$ otherwise. This function proceeds by enumerating all the numbers, and checking, for each of them, whether the number corresponds to the index of a proof of $\Gamma \vdash \Delta$ or not. If a proof exists, its index will eventually come up in the enumeration, otherwise the process will continue forever.

In this way one can show that provability in predicate logic is semi-decidable, but this method is too inefficient to be useful in practise. However, the underlying idea of enumeration and test can lead to less inefficient methods.

6.1 Sequent Calculus

6.1.1 Proof Search in Natural Deduction

We can try to find a proof for a given a sequent by enumerating all the rules that can be applied at each node in the proof tree, starting from the root. For example, if we search for a proof of the sequent $P \vdash Q \Rightarrow (P \wedge Q)$, we start by enumerating the rules that could be used in the last step of the proof. For instance, one of the options is $\Rightarrow$-intro

$$\frac{\Gamma, A \vdash B, \Delta}{\Gamma \vdash A \Rightarrow B, \Delta} \Rightarrow\text{-intro}$$

and in this case we must have $\Gamma = [P]$, $A = Q$, $B = P \wedge Q$ and $\Delta = [\ ]$. The premisse of this rule is the sequent $P, Q \vdash P \wedge Q$ and we proceed by enumerating all the rules that could be used in the last step of the proof of this sequent. For instance, the last rule could be $\wedge$-intro

$$\frac{\Gamma \vdash A, \Delta \quad \Gamma \vdash B, \Delta}{\Gamma \vdash A \wedge B, \Delta} \wedge\text{-intro}$$

G. Dowek, *Proofs and Algorithms*, Undergraduate Topics in Computer Science, DOI 10.1007/978-0-85729-121-9_6, © Springer-Verlag London Limited 2011

and in this case we must have $\Gamma = [P, Q]$, $A = P$, $B = Q$ and $\Delta = [\ ]$. The premisses of this rule are the sequents $P, Q \vdash P$ and $P, Q \vdash Q$. We look first for a proof of the first sequent, by enumerating the rules that could be used in the last step of the proof. For instance, the last rule could be the *axiom* rule, concluding the proof. The same rule proves the second sequent, and we have thus a complete proof

$$\dfrac{\dfrac{\overline{P, Q \vdash P}\ \text{axiom}\quad \overline{P, Q \vdash Q}\ \text{axiom}}{P, Q \vdash P \wedge Q}\ \wedge\text{-intro}}{P \vdash Q \Rightarrow (P \wedge Q)}\ \Rightarrow\text{-intro}$$

If we enumerate all the rules that could be used to prove the sequent $P \vdash Q \Rightarrow (P \wedge Q)$, we can see that the only introduction rule that could apply is $\Rightarrow$-intro. Indeed, the rule $\vee$-intro, for example, can only be applied to propositions of the form $A \vee B$ and cannot be used to prove an implication. However, any of the elimination rules could be used, for instance, $\wedge$-elim

$$\dfrac{\Gamma \vdash A \wedge B, \Delta}{\Gamma \vdash A, \Delta}\ \wedge\text{-elim}$$

Moreover, if we use this rule, the sequent $P \vdash Q \Rightarrow (P \wedge Q)$ to be proved suggests that we should take $\Gamma = [P]$, $A = Q \Rightarrow (P \wedge Q)$ and $\Delta = [\ ]$, but we have no clue as to which proposition we should take for B since it does not occur in the conclusion of the rule. We have to choose a proposition B blindly, and if we make the wrong choice, we have to keep trying with other propositions; in other words, we have to enumerate all the possibilities for B. Thus, when we try to prove the sequent $P \wedge Q \vdash P$, nothing indicates that we should use the rule $\wedge$-elim and choose $B = Q$ to obtain the proof

$$\dfrac{\overline{P \wedge Q \vdash P \wedge Q}\ \text{axiom}}{P \wedge Q \vdash P}\ \wedge\text{-elim}$$

6.1.2 Sequent Calculus Rules

In natural deduction, the form of the conclusion guides us in the choice of introduction rules, but it does not help us choose the right elimination rule. The idea behind the *sequent calculus* is to keep the introduction rules of natural deduction, which will now be called *right-hand side rules*, and replace the elimination rules by introduction rules for the hypotheses of the sequent: *left-hand side rules*. For example, the $\wedge$-elim rule is replaced by the rule

$$\dfrac{\Gamma, A, B \vdash \Delta}{\Gamma, A \wedge B \vdash \Delta}\ \wedge\text{-left}$$

In this way, the proof for the sequent $P \wedge Q \vdash P$ is very different from the natural deduction proof

$$\dfrac{\overline{P, Q \vdash P}\ \text{axiom}}{P \wedge Q \vdash P}\ \wedge\text{-left}$$

and when we look for a proof of this sequent, the form of the hypothesis $P \wedge Q$ guides us in the choice of left rule.

Each elimination rule in natural deduction is replaced by a left rule

$$\frac{}{\Gamma, \bot \vdash \Delta} \; \bot\text{-left}$$

$$\frac{\Gamma, A \vdash \Delta \quad \Gamma, B \vdash \Delta}{\Gamma, A \vee B \vdash \Delta} \; \vee\text{-left}$$

$$\frac{\Gamma \vdash A, \Delta \quad \Gamma, B \vdash \Delta}{\Gamma, A \Rightarrow B \vdash \Delta} \; \Rightarrow\text{-left}$$

$$\frac{\Gamma \vdash A, \Delta}{\Gamma, \neg A \vdash \Delta} \; \neg\text{-left}$$

$$\frac{\Gamma, (t/x)A \vdash \Delta}{\Gamma, \forall x \; A \vdash \Delta} \; \forall\text{-left}$$

$$\frac{\Gamma, A \vdash \Delta}{\Gamma, \exists x \; A \vdash \Delta} \; \exists\text{-left} \; x \text{ not free in } \Gamma, \Delta$$

We also need to add a contraction rule on the left in order to be able to use the hypotheses more than once.

As in natural deduction, the rule of the excluded middle can be expressed by a deduction rule, or, as we have done it here, by the use of sequents with multiple conclusions.

Finally, to show that the sequent calculus is equivalent to natural deduction we will add a rule called *cut*

$$\frac{\Gamma \vdash A, \Delta \quad \Gamma, A \vdash \Delta}{\Gamma \vdash \Delta} \; \text{cut}$$

but we will later show that this rule is superfluous.

The following definition summarises the rules.

Definition 6.1 (Sequent calculus rules)

$$\frac{}{\Gamma, A \vdash A, \Delta} \; \text{axiom}$$

$$\frac{\Gamma \vdash A, \Delta \quad \Gamma, A \vdash \Delta}{\Gamma \vdash \Delta} \; \text{cut}$$

$$\frac{\Gamma, A, A \vdash \Delta}{\Gamma, A \vdash \Delta} \; \text{contraction-left}$$

$$\frac{\Gamma \vdash A, A, \Delta}{\Gamma \vdash A, \Delta} \; \text{contraction-right}$$

$$\frac{}{\Gamma \vdash \top, \Delta} \; \top\text{-right}$$

$$\frac{}{\Gamma, \bot \vdash \Delta} \; \bot\text{-left}$$

$$\frac{\Gamma, A, B \vdash \Delta}{\Gamma, A \wedge B \vdash \Delta} \; \wedge\text{-left}$$

$$\frac{\Gamma \vdash A, \Delta \quad \Gamma \vdash B, \Delta}{\Gamma \vdash A \wedge B, \Delta} \wedge\text{-right}$$

$$\frac{\Gamma, A \vdash \Delta \quad \Gamma, B \vdash \Delta}{\Gamma, A \vee B \vdash \Delta} \vee\text{-left}$$

$$\frac{\Gamma \vdash A, B, \Delta}{\Gamma \vdash A \vee B, \Delta} \vee\text{-right}$$

$$\frac{\Gamma \vdash A, \Delta \quad \Gamma, B \vdash \Delta}{\Gamma, A \Rightarrow B \vdash \Delta} \Rightarrow\text{-left}$$

$$\frac{\Gamma, A \vdash B, \Delta}{\Gamma \vdash A \Rightarrow B, \Delta} \Rightarrow\text{-right}$$

$$\frac{\Gamma \vdash A, \Delta}{\Gamma, \neg A \vdash \Delta} \neg\text{-left}$$

$$\frac{\Gamma, A \vdash \Delta}{\Gamma \vdash \neg A, \Delta} \neg\text{-right}$$

$$\frac{\Gamma, (t/x)A \vdash \Delta}{\Gamma, \forall x \, A \vdash \Delta} \forall\text{-left}$$

$$\frac{\Gamma \vdash A, \Delta}{\Gamma \vdash \forall x \, A, \Delta} \forall\text{-right } x \text{ not free in } \Gamma, \Delta$$

$$\frac{\Gamma, A \vdash \Delta}{\Gamma, \exists x \, A \vdash \Delta} \exists\text{-left } x \text{ not free in } \Gamma, \Delta$$

$$\frac{\Gamma \vdash (t/x)A, \Delta}{\Gamma \vdash \exists x \, A, \Delta} \exists\text{-right}$$

Natural deduction sequents always have a unique conclusion whereas in system D' sequents can have one or several conclusions but they cannot have none. Indeed, system D' has rules that transform the conclusion of the sequents, as in natural deduction rules: something has to be transformed. In sequent calculus, hypotheses and conclusions play symmetric roles: a sequent may have no hypothesis, and similarly it may have no conclusion. Intuitively, the sequent $\Gamma \vdash$ is simply a variant of the sequent $\Gamma \vdash \bot$. In general, both in system D' and in sequent calculus, the sequent $\Gamma \vdash \Delta$ is provable if and only if the sequent $\Gamma \vdash \bot, \Delta$ is provable.

This explains the difference between the rule $\neg$-right in sequent calculus

$$\frac{\Gamma, A \vdash \Delta}{\Gamma \vdash \neg A, \Delta} \neg\text{-right}$$

where the conclusion of the premisse may be empty when Δ is empty, and the corresponding rule in system D'

$$\frac{\Gamma, A \vdash \bot, \Delta}{\Gamma \vdash \neg A, \Delta} \neg\text{-intro}$$

6.1.3 Equivalence with Natural Deduction

We will now prove that a sequent $\Gamma \vdash A$ is provable in natural deduction if and only if it is provable in sequent calculus. Since we have defined a sequent calculus where sequents may have multiple conclusions, we will show the equivalence with the corresponding natural deduction system, namely system D'.

We start by proving a weakening property for sequent calculus, which corresponds to Propositions 1.6 and 1.13.

Proposition 6.1 (Weakening) *If the sequent $\Gamma \vdash \Delta$ is provable in sequent calculus then the sequents $\Gamma, A \vdash \Delta$ and $\Gamma \vdash A, \Delta$ are also provable.*

Proof By induction over the structure of the proof of $\Gamma \vdash \Delta$.   □

Proposition 6.2 *If the sequent $\Gamma \vdash A$ is provable in system D' then it is provable in sequent calculus.*

Proof We show a more general property: if the sequent $\Gamma \vdash \Delta$ is provable in system D', then it is provable in sequent calculus. We proceed by induction on the structure of the proof for this sequent in system D'.

– If the proof has the form

$$\frac{\dfrac{\pi}{\Gamma \vdash \bot, \Delta'}}{\Gamma \vdash A, \Delta'} \bot\text{-elim}$$

then, by induction hypothesis and Proposition 6.1, there exists a sequent calculus proof π' for the sequent $\Gamma \vdash \bot, A, \Delta'$. We build the proof

$$\frac{\dfrac{\pi'}{\Gamma \vdash \bot, A, \Delta'} \quad \dfrac{}{\Gamma, \bot \vdash A, \Delta'} \bot\text{-left}}{\Gamma \vdash A, \Delta'} \text{cut}$$

– If the proof has the form

$$\frac{\dfrac{\pi}{\Gamma \vdash A \wedge B, \Delta'}}{\Gamma \vdash A, \Delta'} \wedge\text{-elim}$$

then, by induction hypothesis and Proposition 6.1, there exists a sequent calculus proof π' for the sequent $\Gamma \vdash A \wedge B, A, \Delta'$. We build the proof

$$\frac{\dfrac{\pi'}{\Gamma \vdash A \wedge B, A, \Delta'} \quad \dfrac{\dfrac{}{\Gamma, A, B \vdash A, \Delta'} \text{axiom}}{\Gamma, A \wedge B \vdash A, \Delta'} \wedge\text{-left}}{\Gamma \vdash A, \Delta'} \text{cut}$$

The case for the other rule $\wedge$-elim is similar.
– If the proof has the form

$$\frac{\dfrac{\pi_1}{\Gamma \vdash A \vee B, \Delta'} \quad \dfrac{\pi_2}{\Gamma, A \vdash C, \Delta'} \quad \dfrac{\pi_3}{\Gamma, B \vdash C, \Delta'}}{\Gamma \vdash C, \Delta'} \vee\text{-elim}$$

then, by induction hypothesis and Proposition 6.1, there are proofs π_1', π_2' and π_3' in sequent calculus for the sequents $\Gamma \vdash A \vee B, C, \Delta'$, $\Gamma, A \vdash C, \Delta'$ and $\Gamma, B \vdash C, \Delta'$, respectively. We build the proof

$$
\cfrac{
\cfrac{\pi_1'}{\Gamma \vdash A \vee B, C, \Delta'} \quad
\cfrac{\cfrac{\pi_2'}{\Gamma, A \vdash C, \Delta'} \quad \cfrac{\pi_3'}{\Gamma, B \vdash C, \Delta'}}{\Gamma, A \vee B \vdash C, \Delta'} \text{V-left}
}{\Gamma \vdash C, \Delta'} \text{cut}
$$

- If the proof has the form

$$
\cfrac{\cfrac{\pi_1}{\Gamma \vdash A \Rightarrow B, \Delta'} \quad \cfrac{\pi_2}{\Gamma \vdash A, \Delta'}}{\Gamma \vdash B, \Delta'} \Rightarrow\text{-elim}
$$

then, by induction hypothesis and Proposition 6.1, there are proofs π_1' and π_2' in sequent calculus for the sequents $\Gamma \vdash A \Rightarrow B, B, \Delta'$ and $\Gamma \vdash A, B, \Delta'$, respectively. We build the proof

$$
\cfrac{
\cfrac{\pi_1'}{\Gamma \vdash A \Rightarrow B, B, \Delta'} \quad
\cfrac{\cfrac{\pi_2'}{\Gamma \vdash A, B, \Delta'} \quad \cfrac{}{\Gamma, B \vdash B, \Delta'}\text{axiom}}{\Gamma, A \Rightarrow B \vdash B, \Delta'} \Rightarrow\text{-left}
}{\Gamma \vdash B, \Delta'} \text{cut}
$$

- If the proof has the form

$$
\cfrac{\cfrac{\pi_1}{\Gamma \vdash \neg A, \Delta'} \quad \cfrac{\pi_2}{\Gamma \vdash A, \Delta'}}{\Gamma \vdash \bot, \Delta'} \neg\text{-elim}
$$

then, by induction hypothesis and Proposition 6.1, there are proofs π_1' and π_2' in sequent calculus for the sequents $\Gamma \vdash \neg A, \bot, \Delta'$ and $\Gamma \vdash A, \bot, \Delta'$, respectively. We build the proof

$$
\cfrac{
\cfrac{\pi_1'}{\Gamma \vdash \neg A, \bot, \Delta'} \quad
\cfrac{\cfrac{\pi_2'}{\Gamma \vdash A, \bot, \Delta'}}{\Gamma, \neg A \vdash \bot, \Delta'} \neg\text{-left}
}{\Gamma \vdash \bot, \Delta'} \text{cut}
$$

- If the proof has the form

$$
\cfrac{\cfrac{\pi}{\Gamma \vdash \forall x\, A, \Delta'}}{\Gamma \vdash (t/x)A, \Delta'} \forall\text{-elim}
$$

then, by induction hypothesis and Proposition 6.1, there exists a proof π' in sequent calculus for the sequent $\Gamma \vdash \forall x\, A, (t/x)A, \Delta'$. We build the proof

$$
\cfrac{
\cfrac{\pi'}{\Gamma \vdash \forall x\, A, (t/x)A, \Delta'} \quad
\cfrac{\cfrac{}{\Gamma, (t/x)A \vdash (t/x)A, \Delta'}\text{axiom}}{\Gamma, \forall x\, A \vdash (t/x)A, \Delta'} \forall\text{-left}
}{\Gamma \vdash (t/x)A, \Delta'} \text{cut}
$$

– If the proof has the form

$$\frac{\dfrac{\pi_1}{\Gamma \vdash \exists x\, A, \Delta'} \quad \dfrac{\pi_2}{\Gamma, A \vdash B, \Delta'}}{\Gamma \vdash B, \Delta'} \exists\text{-elim}$$

then, by induction hypothesis and Proposition 6.1, there are proofs π'_1 and π'_2 in sequent calculus for the sequents $\Gamma \vdash \exists x\, A, B, \Delta'$ and $\Gamma, A \vdash B, \Delta'$. We build the proof

$$\frac{\dfrac{\pi'_1}{\Gamma \vdash \exists x\, A, B, \Delta'} \quad \dfrac{\dfrac{\pi'_2}{\Gamma, A \vdash B, \Delta'}}{\Gamma, \exists x\, A \vdash B} \exists\text{-left}}{\Gamma \vdash B, \Delta'} \text{cut}$$

– If the proof has the form

$$\frac{\dfrac{\pi}{\Gamma, A \vdash \bot, \Delta'}}{\Gamma \vdash \neg A, \Delta'} \neg\text{-intro}$$

then, by induction hypothesis, there exists a proof π' in sequent calculus for the sequent $\Gamma, A \vdash \bot, \Delta'$. We build the proof

$$\frac{\dfrac{\dfrac{\pi'}{\Gamma, A \vdash \bot, \Delta'} \quad \dfrac{}{\Gamma, A, \bot \vdash \Delta'} \bot\text{-left}}{\Gamma, A \vdash \Delta'} \text{cut}}{\Gamma \vdash \neg A, \Delta'} \neg\text{-right}$$

– If the proof has the form

$$\frac{\dfrac{\pi}{\Gamma \vdash A, \Delta'}}{\Gamma \vdash A \vee B, \Delta'} \vee\text{-intro}$$

then, by induction hypothesis and Proposition 6.1, there exists a proof π' in sequent calculus for the sequent $\Gamma \vdash A, B, \Delta'$. We build the proof

$$\frac{\dfrac{\pi'}{\Gamma \vdash A, B, \Delta'}}{\Gamma \vdash A \vee B, \Delta'} \vee\text{-right}$$

The case for the other rule $\vee$-intro is similar.
– The remaining cases are trivial: all the remaining rules in system D' are also sequent calculus rules.   □

To show that if the sequent $\Gamma \vdash A$ is provable in sequent calculus then it is provable in system D', we might want to prove that if the sequent $\Gamma \vdash \Delta$ is provable in sequent calculus then it is provable in system D'. Unfortunately this property does not hold if Δ is empty. We will show a weaker property: if the sequent $\Gamma \vdash \Delta$ is provable in sequent calculus, then the sequent $\Gamma \vdash \bot, \Delta$ is provable in system D'. We will then discard the proposition $\bot$ when the multiset Δ is a singleton.

We start by proving the following proposition.

Proposition 6.3 *If the sequents* $\Gamma, A \vdash \Delta$ *and* $\Gamma \vdash A, \Delta$ *are provable in system* D'
then so is the sequent $\Gamma \vdash \Delta$.

Proof We prove a more general property: if the sequents $\Gamma, \Sigma, A \vdash \Delta$ and $\Gamma \vdash A, \Delta$ are provable in system D', then the sequent $\Gamma, \Sigma \vdash \Delta$ is also provable. We proceed by induction over the structure of the proof of $\Gamma, \Sigma, A \vdash \Delta$. All the cases are trivial except the one for the *axiom*. In this case, if the proposition shared by Γ, Σ, A and Δ is an element of Γ, Σ, the sequent $\Gamma, \Sigma \vdash \Delta$ is provable using the rule *axiom*. If it is A, then, by Proposition 1.13, the sequent $\Gamma, \Sigma \vdash A, \Delta$ is provable and since the proposition A is in Δ, the sequent $\Gamma, \Sigma \vdash \Delta$ is provable using the rule *contraction*.   □

Proposition 6.4 *If the sequent* $\Gamma \vdash A$ *is provable in sequent calculus then it is also provable in system* D'.

Proof We prove that if the sequent $\Gamma \vdash \Delta$ is provable in sequent calculus then the sequent $\Gamma \vdash \bot, \Delta$ is provable in system D'. The result follows: if the sequent $\Gamma \vdash \bot, A$ has a proof π in system D', then the sequent $\Gamma \vdash A$ has the proof

$$\cfrac{\cfrac{\cfrac{\pi}{\Gamma \vdash \bot, A}}{\Gamma \vdash A, A} \bot\text{-elim}}{\Gamma \vdash A} \text{contraction}$$

We proceed by induction over the structure of the sequent calculus proof for the sequent $\Gamma \vdash \Delta$.

– If the proof has the form

$$\cfrac{\cfrac{\pi_1}{\Gamma \vdash A, \Delta} \quad \cfrac{\pi_2}{\Gamma, A \vdash \Delta}}{\Gamma \vdash \Delta} \text{cut}$$

then, by induction hypothesis, the sequents $\Gamma \vdash \bot, A, \Delta$ and $\Gamma, A \vdash \bot, \Delta$ are provable in system D'. Therefore the sequent $\Gamma \vdash \bot, \Delta$ is provable by Proposition 6.3.

– If the proof has the form

$$\cfrac{\cfrac{\pi_1}{\Gamma', A, A \vdash \Delta}}{\Gamma', A \vdash \Delta} \text{contraction-left}$$

then, by induction hypothesis, the sequent $\Gamma', A, A \vdash \bot, \Delta$ has a proof in system D'. We show by induction over the structure of this proof that the sequent $\Gamma', A \vdash \bot, \Delta$ has a proof in system D'.

– If the proof has the form

$$\cfrac{}{\Gamma', \bot \vdash \Delta} \bot\text{-left}$$

then, the sequent $\Gamma', \bot \vdash \bot, \Delta$ is provable in system D' using the rule *axiom*.

- If the proof has the form

$$\frac{\dfrac{\pi}{\Gamma', A, B \vdash \Delta}}{\Gamma', A \wedge B \vdash \Delta} \text{ ∧-left}$$

then, by induction hypothesis and Proposition 1.13, the sequent $\Gamma', A \wedge B, A, B \vdash \bot, \Delta$ is provable in system D'. The sequents $\Gamma', A \wedge B, B \vdash A, \bot, \Delta$ and $\Gamma', A \wedge B \vdash B, \bot, \Delta$ are provable using the rules *axiom* and ∧-elim. The sequent $\Gamma', A \wedge B \vdash \bot, \Delta$ is therefore provable, by Proposition 6.3.

- If the proof has the form

$$\frac{\dfrac{\pi_1}{\Gamma', A \vdash \Delta} \quad \dfrac{\pi_2}{\Gamma', B \vdash \Delta}}{\Gamma', A \vee B \vdash \Delta} \text{ ∨-left}$$

then, by induction hypothesis and Proposition 1.13, the sequents $\Gamma', A \vee B, A \vdash \bot, \Delta$ and $\Gamma', A \vee B, B \vdash \bot, \Delta$ are provable in system D'. The sequent $\Gamma', A \vee B \vdash \bot, \Delta$ is therefore provable with rules *axiom* and ∨-elim.

- If the proof has the form

$$\frac{\dfrac{\pi_1}{\Gamma' \vdash A, \Delta} \quad \dfrac{\pi_2}{\Gamma', B \vdash \Delta}}{\Gamma', A \Rightarrow B \vdash \Delta} \text{ ⇒-left}$$

then, by induction hypothesis and Proposition 1.13, the sequents $\Gamma', A \Rightarrow B \vdash \bot, A, B, \Delta$ and $\Gamma', A \Rightarrow B, B \vdash \bot, \Delta$ are provable in system D'. The sequent $\Gamma', A, A \Rightarrow B \vdash B, \bot, \Delta$ is provable using rules *axiom* and ⇒-elim. Hence, by Proposition 6.3, the sequent $\Gamma', A \Rightarrow B \vdash \bot, \Delta$ is provable.

- If the proof has the form

$$\frac{\dfrac{\pi}{\Gamma' \vdash A, \Delta}}{\Gamma', \neg A \vdash \Delta} \text{ ¬-left}$$

then, by induction hypothesis and Proposition 1.13, the sequent $\Gamma', \neg A \vdash \bot, A, \Delta$ is provable in system D'. The sequent $\Gamma', \neg A, A \vdash \bot, \Delta$ is provable using *axiom* and ¬-elim. Hence, by Proposition 6.3, the sequent $\Gamma', \neg A \vdash \bot, \Delta$ is provable.

- If the proof has the form

$$\frac{\dfrac{\pi}{\Gamma', (t/x)A \vdash \Delta}}{\Gamma', \forall x\, A \vdash \Delta} \text{ ∀-left}$$

then, by induction hypothesis and Proposition 1.13, the sequent $\Gamma', \forall x\, A, (t/x)A \vdash \bot, \Delta$ is provable in system D'. The sequent $\Gamma', \forall x\, A \vdash (t/x)A, \bot, \Delta$ is provable using *axiom* and ∀-elim. Hence, by Proposition 6.3, the sequent $\Gamma', \forall x\, A \vdash \bot, \Delta$ is provable.

– If the proof has the form

$$\frac{\dfrac{\pi}{\Gamma', A \vdash \Delta}}{\Gamma', \exists x\ A \vdash \Delta}\ \exists\text{-left}$$

then, by induction hypothesis and Proposition 1.13, the sequent $\Gamma', \exists x\ A, A \vdash \bot, \Delta$ is provable in system D'. The sequent $\Gamma', \exists x\ A \vdash \bot, \Delta$ is provable using *axiom* and $\exists$-elim.

– If the proof has the form

$$\frac{\dfrac{\pi}{\Gamma, A \vdash \Delta'}}{\Gamma \vdash \neg A, \Delta'}\ \neg\text{-right}$$

then, by induction hypothesis, the sequent $\Gamma, A \vdash \bot, \Delta'$ is provable in system D'. The sequent $\Gamma \vdash \neg A, \Delta'$ is therefore provable using rule $\neg$-intro and the sequent $\Gamma \vdash \bot, \neg A, \Delta'$, by Proposition 1.13.

– If the proof has the form

$$\frac{\dfrac{\pi}{\Gamma \vdash A, B, \Delta'}}{\Gamma \vdash A \vee B, \Delta'}\ \vee\text{-right}$$

then, by induction hypothesis, the sequent $\Gamma \vdash \bot, A, B, \Delta'$ is provable in system D'. The sequent $\Gamma \vdash \bot, A \vee B, \Delta'$ is therefore provable using rules *contraction* and $\vee$-intro.

– The remaining cases are trivial since all the remaining sequent calculus rules are also in system D'.

$$\square$$

Theorem 6.1 *The sequent $\Gamma \vdash A$ is provable in sequent calculus if and only if it is provable in system D' if and only if it is provable in natural deduction.*

Proof Consequence of Propositions 6.2, 6.4 and 1.12. $\square$

6.1.4 Cut Elimination

In sequent calculus, all the propositions that occur in premisses of left or right rules occur also in the conclusions of the rules. This makes proof search easier since there is no need to make a choice in order to apply a rule. However, the cut rule

$$\frac{\Gamma \vdash A, \Delta \quad \Gamma, A \vdash \Delta}{\Gamma \vdash \Delta}\ \text{cut}$$

used to prove the equivalence of sequent calculus and system D' does not satisfy this property: the proposition A occurs in the premisses of the rule but not in the conclusion. Thus, to apply this rule we need to choose a proposition A.

Fortunately, this rule is redundant in sequent calculus, as shown below.

Definition 6.2 (Sequent calculus without cuts) The *sequent calculus without cuts* includes all the rules in Definition 6.1 except the *cut* rule.

Obviously, if a sequent $\Gamma \vdash \Delta$ is provable in the sequent calculus without cuts then it is also provable in the sequent calculus. Our goal now is to prove the converse. If a sequent $\Gamma \vdash \Delta$ is provable in the sequent calculus, then it is also provable in the sequent calculus without cuts. For this, it is sufficient to prove the following property.

Proposition 6.5 *If the sequents $\Gamma, A \vdash \Delta$ and $\Gamma \vdash A, \Delta$ are provable in the sequent calculus without cuts, so is the sequent $\Gamma \vdash \Delta$.*

Proof We will prove a more general property: if the sequents $\Gamma, A^n \vdash \Delta$ and $\Gamma' \vdash A^m, \Delta'$ have proofs π and π' in the sequent calculus without cuts, then the sequent $\Gamma, \Gamma' \vdash \Delta, \Delta'$ has a proof in the sequent calculus without cuts. The proposition we aim to prove follows from the case $n = m = 1$, using the contraction rules.

The proof is by a double induction on the number of connectives and quantifiers of the proposition A, and the sum of the sizes of the proofs π and π'.

We consider the last rules in π and π'. In the first series of cases these two rules are applied to a proposition A, in which case $n \geq 1$ and $m \geq 1$.

– If the last rule in π is the *axiom* rule, then the multiset Δ contains the proposition A. The sequent $\Gamma' \vdash A^m, \Delta'$ has a proof, and by Proposition 6.1, so does the sequent $\Gamma, \Gamma' \vdash A^m, \Delta, \Delta'$. From this proof we can build a proof for the sequent $\Gamma, \Gamma' \vdash \Delta, \Delta'$ using the rule *contraction-right*. If the last rule of π' is the *axiom* the proof is similar.
– If the last rule in π or π' is a contraction rule, we apply the induction hypothesis.
– In the other cases, if the last rule in π is $\wedge$-left, then $A = (B \wedge C)$ and the last rule in π' is $\wedge$-right. Therefore π is of the form

$$\frac{\begin{array}{c} \rho \\ \Gamma, A^{n-1}, B, C \vdash \Delta \end{array}}{\Gamma, A^{n-1}, B \wedge C \vdash \Delta} \wedge\text{-left}$$

and π' of the form

$$\frac{\begin{array}{cc} \rho'_1 & \rho'_2 \\ \Gamma' \vdash B, A^{m-1}, \Delta' & \Gamma' \vdash C, A^{m-1}, \Delta' \end{array}}{\Gamma' \vdash B \wedge C, A^{m-1}, \Delta'} \wedge\text{-right}$$

The induction hypothesis applied to π and ρ'_1 first, then to π and ρ'_2, and finally to ρ and π' produces a proof of $\Gamma, \Gamma' \vdash B, \Delta, \Delta'$, $\Gamma, \Gamma' \vdash C, \Delta, \Delta'$ and $\Gamma, \Gamma', B, C \vdash \Delta, \Delta'$. The induction hypothesis applied to B and C and the contraction rules produce a proof of $\Gamma, \Gamma', C \vdash \Delta, \Delta'$, and then $\Gamma, \Gamma' \vdash \Delta, \Delta'$.
– If the last rule in π is $\vee$-left, then $A = (B \vee C)$ and the last rule in π' is $\vee$-right. Therefore π is of the form

$$\frac{\begin{array}{cc} \rho_1 & \rho_2 \\ \Gamma, A^{n-1}, B \vdash \Delta & \Gamma, A^{n-1}, C \vdash \Delta \end{array}}{\Gamma, A^{n-1}, B \vee C \vdash \Delta} \vee\text{-left}$$

and π' of the form

$$\frac{\displaystyle \begin{array}{c} \rho' \\ \hline \Gamma' \vdash B, C, A^{m-1}, \Delta' \end{array}}{\Gamma' \vdash B \vee C, A^{m-1}, \Delta'} \vee\text{-right}$$

The induction hypothesis applied to π and ρ' first, then to ρ_1 and π', and finally to ρ_2 and π' produces a proof of $\Gamma, \Gamma' \vdash B, C, \Delta, \Delta'$, $\Gamma, \Gamma', B \vdash \Delta, \Delta'$ and $\Gamma, \Gamma', C \vdash \Delta, \Delta'$. The induction hypothesis applied to B and C and the contraction rules produce a proof of $\Gamma, \Gamma' \vdash C, \Delta, \Delta'$, and then $\Gamma, \Gamma' \vdash \Delta, \Delta'$.

− If the last rule in π is $\Rightarrow$-left, then $A = (B \Rightarrow C)$ and the last rule in π' is $\Rightarrow$-right. Therefore π is of the form

$$\frac{\displaystyle \begin{array}{cc} \rho_1 & \rho_2 \\ \hline \Gamma, A^{n-1} \vdash B, \Delta \quad \Gamma, A^{n-1}, C \vdash \Delta \end{array}}{\Gamma, A^{n-1}, B \Rightarrow C \vdash \Delta} \Rightarrow\text{-left}$$

and π' of the form

$$\frac{\displaystyle \begin{array}{c} \rho' \\ \hline \Gamma', B \vdash C, A^{m-1}, \Delta' \end{array}}{\Gamma' \vdash B \Rightarrow C, A^{m-1}, \Delta'} \Rightarrow\text{-right}$$

The induction hypothesis applied to π and ρ' first, then to ρ_1 and π' and finally to ρ_2 and π' produces a proof of $\Gamma, \Gamma', B \vdash C, \Delta, \Delta'$, $\Gamma, \Gamma' \vdash B, \Delta, \Delta'$ and $\Gamma, \Gamma', C \vdash \Delta, \Delta'$. The induction hypothesis applied to B and C and the contraction rules produce a proof of $\Gamma, \Gamma' \vdash C, \Delta, \Delta'$, then $\Gamma, \Gamma' \vdash \Delta, \Delta'$.

− If the last rule in π is $\neg$-left, then $A = \neg B$ and the last rule in π' is $\neg$-right. Therefore π is of the form

$$\frac{\displaystyle \begin{array}{c} \rho \\ \hline \Gamma, A^{n-1} \vdash B, \Delta \end{array}}{\Gamma, A^{n-1}, \neg B \vdash \Delta} \neg\text{-left}$$

and π' of the form

$$\frac{\displaystyle \begin{array}{c} \rho' \\ \hline \Gamma', B \vdash A^{m-1}, \Delta' \end{array}}{\Gamma' \vdash \neg B, A^{m-1}, \Delta'} \neg\text{-right}$$

The induction hypothesis applied to π and ρ', then to ρ and π', produces a proof of $\Gamma, \Gamma', B \vdash \Delta, \Delta'$ and $\Gamma, \Gamma' \vdash B, \Delta, \Delta'$. The induction hypothesis applied to B and the contraction rules produce a proof of $\Gamma, \Gamma' \vdash \Delta, \Delta'$.

− If the last rule in π is $\forall$-left, then $A = \forall x\, B$ and the last rule in π' is $\forall$-right. Therefore π is of the form

$$\frac{\displaystyle \begin{array}{c} \rho \\ \hline \Gamma, A^{n-1}, (t/x)B \vdash \Delta \end{array}}{\Gamma, A^{n-1}, \forall x\, B \vdash \Delta} \forall\text{-left}$$

and π' of the form

$$\frac{\begin{array}{c}\rho'\\ \Gamma' \vdash B, A^{m-1}, \Delta'\end{array}}{\Gamma' \vdash \forall x\ B, A^{m-1}, \Delta'}\ \forall\text{-right}$$

Since x is not free in Γ', A or Δ', by substituting the variable x by the term t in the proof ρ', we obtain a proof ρ'_1 of $\Gamma' \vdash (t/x)B, A^{m-1}, \Delta'$. The induction hypothesis applied to π and ρ'_1, then to ρ and π' produces a proof of $\Gamma, \Gamma' \vdash (t/x)B, \Delta, \Delta'$, and $\Gamma, \Gamma', (t/x)B \vdash \Delta, \Delta'$. The induction hypothesis applied to $(t/x)B$ and the contraction rules produce a proof of $\Gamma, \Gamma' \vdash \Delta, \Delta'$.

- If the last rule in π is $\exists$-left, then $A = \exists x\ B$ and the last rule in π' is $\exists$-right. Therefore π is of the form

$$\frac{\begin{array}{c}\rho\\ \Gamma, A^{n-1}, B \vdash \Delta\end{array}}{\Gamma, A^{n-1}, \exists x\ B \vdash \Delta}\ \exists\text{-left}$$

and π' of the form

$$\frac{\begin{array}{c}\rho'\\ \Gamma' \vdash (t/x)B, A^{m-1}, \Delta'\end{array}}{\Gamma' \vdash \exists x\ B, A^{m-1}, \Delta'}\ \exists\text{-right}$$

Since x is not free in Γ, A or Δ, by substituting the variable x by the term t in the proof ρ, we obtain a proof ρ_1 of $\Gamma, A^{n-1}, (t/x)B \vdash \Delta$. The induction hypothesis applied to π and ρ', then to ρ_1 and π' produces a proof of $\Gamma, \Gamma' \vdash (t/x)B, \Delta, \Delta'$, and $\Gamma, \Gamma', (t/x)B \vdash \Delta, \Delta'$. The induction hypothesis applied to $(t/x)B$ and the contraction rules produce a proof of $\Gamma, \Gamma' \vdash \Delta, \Delta'$.

In a second series of cases, the last rule in π or π' applies to a proposition different from A. For example, if the last rule in π is $\wedge$-left, then $\Gamma = \Gamma_1, B \wedge C$ and π is of the form

$$\frac{\begin{array}{c}\rho\\ \Gamma_1, A^n, B, C \vdash \Delta\end{array}}{\Gamma_1, A^n, B \wedge C \vdash \Delta}\ \wedge\text{-left}$$

we apply the induction hypothesis to ρ and π' to obtain a proof of $\Gamma_1, \Gamma', B, C \vdash \Delta, \Delta'$. Using the same rule, that is, $\wedge$-left, we obtain a proof of $\Gamma_1, \Gamma', B \wedge C \vdash \Delta, \Delta'$, that is, $\Gamma, \Gamma' \vdash \Delta, \Delta'$. The other cases are similar. $\square$

Exercise 6.1 Show that the sequent $P(c) \vee Q(c) \vdash P(c)$ does not have a proof in the sequent calculus without cuts. Conclude that it has no proof in natural deduction.

Proposition 6.6 *If we restrict the rule axiom to the case in which all the propositions in the sequent proved are atomic, we obtain a system equivalent to the sequent calculus without cuts.*

Proof We show, by induction on the number of connectives and quantifiers of $\Gamma \vdash \Delta$, that in the restricted system the sequents of the form $\Gamma \vdash \Delta$, where Γ and Δ share a proposition, are provable. $\square$

6.2 Proof Search in the Sequent Calculus Without Cuts

In the sequent calculus without cuts, all the propositions occurring in premisses of
rules occur also in the conclusions, thus proof search in the sequent calculus without
cuts does not require choosing a proposition amongst the infinite set of propositions
in the language. However, not all the choices have been eliminated, as we will see.

6.2.1 Choices

If we are looking for a proof of the sequent $P \wedge Q(c) \vdash P \wedge \exists x \ Q(x)$, for instance,
we can choose to apply a rule to the proposition $P \wedge Q(c)$ or to the proposition
$P \wedge \exists x \ Q(x)$: we are faced with a *proposition choice*. If we choose the proposition
$P \wedge \exists x \ Q(x)$, we can apply either the rule $\wedge$-right or the rule *contraction-right*: we
are faced with a *rule choice*. If we decide to apply $\wedge$-right, two new sequents need to
be proved: $P \wedge Q(c) \vdash P$ and $P \wedge Q(c) \vdash \exists x \ Q(x)$. Again we have a choice: we can
start looking for a proof of the first sequent or for a proof of the second, that is, we
have a *sequent choice*. Finally, if we try to prove the sequent $P \wedge Q(c) \vdash \exists x \ Q(x)$
by applying the rule $\exists$-right, we have to choose the term to be substituted for the
variable x; this is a *term choice*.

In general, at each step in the process of proof search, we have a set of sequents
to prove and we have to choose which one we prove first. Afterwards, we have
to choose a proposition in this sequent, and once we have chosen the proposition,
two or three rules may apply: the rule that corresponds to the main quantifier or
connective and to its side, the left- or right-contraction rule, and sometimes the
axiom rule. Finally, if the chosen rule is $\exists$-right or $\forall$-left, we also need to choose a
term to substitute.

6.2.2 Don't Care Choices and Don't Know Choices

If during a process of search we are faced with a choice (for example, take the path
A or the path B), two scenarios are possible. In the first one, if we choose the path
A and it turns out that it is blocked, we have to backtrack and explore the path B.
This is a typical situation when we are searching for the way out of a labyrinth. If
the path A may be infinite, we might start exploring the path B even if the path A is
not blocked. This is called a *don't know choice*. In the other scenario, if the path A
leads to a failure, we might already know that the path B will also fail; in this case
we say that it is a *don't care choice*. For example, to cook eggs mimosa style, we
can start by making a mayonnaise or by cooking the eggs. If we decide to start by
the mayonnaise and we fail, it is useless to cook the eggs since this will not help us
improve the mayonnaise.

In the search for a proof in sequent calculus, the choice of sequent is of
course a don't care choice: the order in which the sequents $P \wedge Q(c) \vdash P$ and

$P \wedge Q(c) \vdash \exists x \ Q(x)$ are proved is not important, each proof search is independent. However, the other three choices are don't know choices. The following example illustrates a don't know proposition choice. We search for a proof of the sequent $\exists x \ P(x), \forall y \ (P(y) \Rightarrow Q) \vdash Q$. If we start by applying rule $\exists$-left to proposition $\exists x \ P(x)$, we obtain the sequent $P(x), \forall y \ (P(y) \Rightarrow Q) \vdash Q$ and we can apply rule $\forall$-left to proposition $\forall y \ (P(y) \Rightarrow Q)$, choose the term x, and finish. But if we apply first rule $\forall$-left to proposition $\forall y \ (P(y) \Rightarrow Q)$, with the same term x, we obtain the sequent $\exists x \ P(x), P(x) \Rightarrow Q \vdash Q$, which is not provable. In particular, since the variable x occurs free in the sequent, to apply the rule $\exists$-left to the proposition $\exists x \ P(x)$ we need to rename the bound variable x to x', obtaining the sequent $P(x'), P(x) \Rightarrow Q \vdash Q$, which is not provable.

The following is an example of a don't know rule choice. We search for a proof of the sequent $\vdash \exists x \ (P(x) \Rightarrow P(f(x)))$. If we apply the rule *contraction-right* first, followed by two applications of the rule $\exists$-right with the terms c and $f(c)$ we obtain the sequent $\vdash P(c) \Rightarrow P(f(c)), P(f(c)) \Rightarrow P(f(f(c)))$, which is easy to prove. However, if we apply the rule $\exists$-right, we obtain a sequent of the form $\vdash P(t) \Rightarrow P(f(t))$, which is not provable.

A don't know term choice is illustrated by the following example. To prove the sequent $P(f(f(c))) \vdash \exists x \ P(f(x))$, we must apply the rule $\exists$-right with the term $f(c)$, certainly not with c.

6.2.3   Restricting the Choices

One of the choices discussed above, term choice, requires choosing a term amongst an infinite set of terms. The other two choices (proposition choice and rule choice) are both finite choices. It is therefore important to restrict first the number of choices for terms.

When looking for a proof of the sequent $P(f(f(c))) \vdash \exists x \ P(f(x))$, if we apply rule $\exists$-right to proposition $\exists x \ P(f(x))$, we can substitute the variable x by many different terms: $c, f(c), f(f(c)), f(f(f(c))), \ldots$. Of course, only the term $f(c)$ will lead to a success. Instead of enumerating all the terms that can be substituted and trying them one by one, we can delay the choice by substituting x by a special variable X. A comparison of the propositions in the resulting sequent, that is, $P(f(f(c)))$ and $P(f(X))$, will suggest the substitution $f(c)/X$ in a second phase.

Thus, we will partition the variables into two infinite sets: *ordinary variables*, denoted by a lower case letter, and *metavariables* denoted by capital letters.

Definition 6.3 (Proof schema) A *proof schema* is a proof built in a variant of the sequent calculus without cuts where

- the rules $\exists$-right and $\forall$-left are restricted so that the substituted term t is always a metavariable,

- the *axiom* rule is replaced by a rule *axiom'* which will allow us to prove any
sequent where the propositions are atomic

$$\frac{}{\Gamma \vdash \Delta} \text{ axiom}' \; \Gamma, \Delta \text{ atomic}$$

For example, the tree

$$\frac{\dfrac{}{P(f(f(c))) \vdash P(f(X))} \text{ axiom}'}{P(f(f(c))) \vdash \exists x \; P(f(x))} \text{ ∃-right}$$

is a proof schema.

Proposition 6.7 *Let $\Gamma \vdash \Delta$ be a sequent and h a natural number. The sequent $\Gamma \vdash \Delta$ has a finite number of proof schemas whose height is less than h.*

Proof By induction on h.   □

Definition 6.4 If σ is a substitution and Γ a multiset of propositions, the multiset $\sigma \Gamma$ is obtained by applying the substitution σ to each element of Γ.

If σ is a substitution and π a proof or proof schema, the proof or proof schema $\sigma \pi$ is obtained by applying the substitution σ to each node in π.

Definition 6.5 A substitution σ that associates the terms $t_1, \ldots, t_n$ to the metavari-ables $X_1, \ldots, X_n$ *perfects* a proof schema π if the tree $\sigma \pi$ is a proof in the sequent calculus without cuts where the rule *axiom* is restricted to sequents where all the propositions are atomic, that is, if

- for each sequent $\Gamma \vdash \Delta$, proved using the rule *axiom'*, the multisets $\sigma \Gamma$ and $\sigma \Delta$ share a proposition
- and each time a rule ∃-left or ∀-right is used in π, the freshness condition for the variables is satisfied in $\sigma \pi$, this means that if a node in π is of the form

$$\frac{\Gamma \vdash A, \Delta}{\Gamma \vdash \forall x \; A, \Delta} \text{ ∀-right}$$

or

$$\frac{\Gamma, A \vdash \Delta}{\Gamma, \exists x \; A \vdash \Delta} \text{ ∃-left}$$

then the variable x is not free in $\sigma \Gamma$ or $\sigma \Delta$. In other words, x is not free in Γ, Δ and if Y is free in Γ, Δ, then x is not free in σY.

For example, the substitution $f(c)/X$ perfects the proof schema above and pro-duces the proof

$$\frac{\dfrac{}{P(f(f(c))) \vdash P(f(f(c)))} \text{ axiom}}{P(f(f(c))) \vdash \exists x \; P(f(x))} \text{ ∃-right}$$

Given a proof schema π, it is possible to decide whether or not there exists a substitution that perfects it. Indeed, if suffices to find a substitution σ and, for each sequent $\Gamma \vdash \Delta$ proved by the rule *axiom'*, a pair of an atomic proposition A in Γ and an atomic proposition B in Δ such that $\sigma A = \sigma B$. Since in π there is only a finite number of sequents proved by the rule *axiom'*, and for each of them there is a finite number of pairs, we can enumerate all the possible choices of atomic pairs for each sequent. Then, for each choice we need to find out whether there exists a substitution σ such that for each pair (A, B), $\sigma A = \sigma B$.

For example, in the schema above we have only one sequent proved by the rule *axiom'*, and only one choice for the pair of atomic propositions from Γ and Δ. We need to find a substitution σ such that $\sigma(P(f(X))) = \sigma(P(f(f(c))))$, that is, a substitution σ that solves the equation

$$P(f(X)) = P(f(f(c)))$$

This equation is a *unification problem*. To solve this problem we proceed as follows. The solutions of the problem

$$P(f(X)) = P(f(f(c)))$$

coincide with those of

$$f(X) = f(f(c))$$

which are the same as those of

$$X = f(c)$$

and this problem has a solution: the substitution $f(c)/X$.

Definition 6.6 A *unification problem* is a system of equations of the form $t = u$. A solution of a unification problem is a substitution σ such that for each equation $t = u$ in the problem, the terms σt and σu are identical.

We can solve unification problems using Robinson's unification algorithm, which is similar in some respects to Gaussian elimination.

Definition 6.7 (Robinson's unification algorithm) Choose an equation in the system.

- If the equation is of the form $f(t_1, \ldots, t_n) = f(u_1, \ldots, u_n)$ where f is a predicate symbol, a function symbol or a variable, replace it with the equations $t_1 = u_1, \ldots, t_n = u_n$ and solve the resulting system.
- If the equation is of the form $f(t_1, \ldots, t_n) = g(u_1, \ldots, u_m)$ where f and g are different symbols, the algorithm fails.
- If the equation is of the form $X = X$, discard it and continue solving the remaining equations.
- If the equation is of the form $X = t$ or $t = X$, where X occurs in t and is different from t, the algorithm fails.

- If the equation is of the form $X = t$ or $t = X$ and X does not occur in t, substitute X by t in the remaining equations and solve the resulting system, obtaining a substitution σ; the result is then $\sigma \cup \{\sigma t / X\}$.

The only non-trivial case is the fourth: an equation of the form $X = f(X)$, for instance, does not have a solution. This can be proved by contradiction: if we assume that there is a solution, for example the term u, then u should be equal to $f(u)$ and the number of symbols in u should satisfy the equation $n = n + 1$. This is called an *occur check*, it is essential to ensure the termination of the unification algorithm. Indeed, in the fifth case, termination follows from the fact that the variable X disappears when X is substituted by t and therefore the recursive calls to the algorithm work on a system with less variables. This unification algorithm always terminates. It fails if the system does not have a solution, and returns a solution if the system is solvable.

A unification problem may have several solutions. For example, the equation $X = f(Y)$ has, amongst others, the solutions

$$f(c)/X, c/Y$$

$$f(f(c))/X, f(c)/Y$$

$$f(Z)/X, Z/Y$$

$$f(Y)/X$$

A solution σ is said to be *most general* if for each solution τ there exists a substitution η such that $\tau = \eta \circ \sigma$. For example, the last two substitutions above are most general solutions, but the first two are not. It can be shown that any solvable unification problem has a most general solution, and the substitution returned by the unification algorithm is a most general solution. Also, if σ is a most general solution of a unification problem and τ is an arbitrary solution, then the set of variables in τX is included in the set of variables of σX. To decide whether there exists a solution τ for a unification problem such that some constraint of the form "x does not occur in τY" holds, it is sufficient to check whether the most general solution σ, computed by the unification algorithm, satisfies this constraint.

In this way, it is possible to decide whether there exists a substitution that perfects a proof schema, which means that the set of sequents having a proof in the sequent calculus without cuts of height less than h is decidable.

There are also many ways to restrict the choice of proposition and the choice of rule. We give some examples in Exercise 6.4.

Definition 6.8 A *prenex* proposition is a proposition of the form $\mathcal{Q}_1 x_1 \ldots \mathcal{Q}_n x_n\ C$ where $\mathcal{Q}_1, \ldots, \mathcal{Q}_n$ are quantifiers, $\forall$ or $\exists$, and C is a proposition without quantifiers. An *existential* proposition is a proposition of the form $\exists x_1 \ldots \exists x_n\ C$ where C is a proposition without quantifiers. A *universal* proposition is a proposition of the form $\forall x_1 \ldots \forall x_n\ C$ where C is a proposition without quantifiers.

A proposition without quantifiers is in *conjunctive normal form* if it is of the form $\top$ or $C_1 \wedge (\cdots \wedge C_n)$ where each proposition C_i is of the form $\bot$ or $D_1 \vee (\cdots \vee D_m)$ where each D_i is an atomic proposition or the negation of an atomic proposition.

Exercise 6.2 (Transforming sequents: quantifiers) This exercise relies on Exercise 1.5, which should be done prior to this one.

1. Show that if the sequent $\vdash A \Leftrightarrow A'$ is provable then the sequent $\Gamma, A \vdash \Delta$ is provable if and only if the sequent $\Gamma, A' \vdash \Delta$ is provable and the sequent $\Gamma \vdash A, \Delta$ is provable if and only if the sequent $\Gamma \vdash A', \Delta$ is provable.

2. Show that if x is not a free variable in B, the propositions $((\forall x\ A) \wedge B) \Leftrightarrow \forall x\ (A \wedge B)$, $(B \wedge (\forall x\ A)) \Leftrightarrow \forall x\ (B \wedge A)$, $((\exists x\ A) \wedge B) \Leftrightarrow \exists x\ (A \wedge B)$, $(B \wedge (\exists x\ A)) \Leftrightarrow \exists x\ (B \wedge A)$, $((\forall x\ A) \vee B) \Leftrightarrow \forall x\ (A \vee B)$, $(B \vee (\forall x\ A)) \Leftrightarrow \forall x\ (B \vee A)$, $((\exists x\ A) \vee B) \Leftrightarrow \exists x\ (A \vee B)$, $(B \vee (\exists x\ A)) \Leftrightarrow \exists x\ (B \vee A)$, $((\forall x\ A) \Rightarrow B) \Leftrightarrow \exists x\ (A \Rightarrow B)$, $(B \Rightarrow (\forall x\ A)) \Leftrightarrow \forall x\ (B \Rightarrow A)$, $((\exists x\ A) \Rightarrow B) \Leftrightarrow \forall x\ (A \Rightarrow B)$, $(B \Rightarrow (\exists x\ A)) \Leftrightarrow \exists x\ (B \Rightarrow A)$, $(\neg(\forall x\ A)) \Leftrightarrow \exists x\ \neg A$ and $(\neg(\exists x\ A)) \Leftrightarrow \forall x\ \neg A$ are provable.

   Show that for any proposition A there exists a prenex proposition A' such that the proposition $A \Leftrightarrow A'$ is provable.

   Show that the sequent $\vdash A$ is provable if and only if the sequent $\vdash A'$ is provable.

3. Recall that, by Proposition 1.7, the sequent $\vdash A$ is provable if and only if the sequent $\vdash \neg\neg A$ is provable.

   Show that the sequent $\vdash A$ is provable if and only if the sequent $\neg A \vdash$ is provable.

   Show that for any proposition A there exists a prenex proposition A' such that the sequent $A' \vdash$ is provable if and only if the sequent $\vdash A$ is provable.

4. Show that for any proposition A there exists a universal proposition A' such that the sequent $A' \vdash$ is provable if and only if the sequent $\vdash A$ is provable. Hint: use Skolem's Theorem 2.3.

   Show that for any proposition A there exists an existential proposition A' such that the sequent $\vdash A'$ is provable if and only if the sequent $\vdash A$ is provable.

Exercise 6.3 (Transforming sequents: connectives) This exercise relies on Exercise 6.2, which should be done prior to this one.

1. Show that the propositions $(A \Rightarrow B) \Leftrightarrow (\neg A \vee B)$, $(\neg\top) \Leftrightarrow \bot$, $(\neg\bot) \Leftrightarrow \top$, $(\neg(A \wedge B)) \Leftrightarrow ((\neg A) \vee (\neg B))$, $(\neg(A \vee B)) \Leftrightarrow ((\neg A) \wedge (\neg B))$ and $(\neg\neg A) \Leftrightarrow A$ are provable.

   Show that for any proposition A without quantifiers there exists a proposition A' also without quantifiers and moreover without any occurrence of the symbol $\Rightarrow$ and with negation applied only to atomic propositions, such that the proposition $A \Leftrightarrow A'$ is provable.

2. Show that the propositions $((A \wedge B) \wedge C) \Leftrightarrow (A \wedge (B \wedge C))$, $((A \vee B) \vee C) \Leftrightarrow (A \vee (B \vee C))$, $(A \vee (B \wedge C)) \Leftrightarrow (A \vee B) \wedge (A \vee C)$, $((A \wedge B) \vee C) \Leftrightarrow (A \vee C) \wedge (B \vee C)$, $(\top \vee A) \Leftrightarrow \top$, $(A \vee \top) \Leftrightarrow \top$, $(\bot \vee A) \Leftrightarrow A$ and $(A \vee \bot) \Leftrightarrow A$ are provable.

   Show that for any proposition A without quantifiers there exists a proposition A' in conjunctive normal form such that the proposition $A \Leftrightarrow A'$ is provable.

3. Show that for any proposition A there exists a universal proposition A' of the form $\forall x_1 \ldots \forall x_n$ C, where C is a proposition in conjunctive normal form such that the sequent $A' \vdash$ is provable if and only if the sequent $\vdash A$ is provable.

Show that the proposition $(\forall x\ (A \wedge B)) \Leftrightarrow ((\forall x\ A) \wedge (\forall x\ B))$ is provable. Show that the sequent $\Gamma, A \wedge B \vdash \Delta$ is provable if and only if the sequent $\Gamma, A, B \vdash \Delta$ is provable.

Show that for any proposition A there are propositions $C_1, \ldots, C_p$ of the form $\bot$ or $\forall x_1 \cdots \forall x_n\ (D_1 \vee (\ldots \vee D_m))$, where each D_i is an atomic proposition or the negation of an atomic proposition, such that the sequent $\vdash A$ is provable if and only if the sequent $C_1, \ldots, C_p \vdash$ is provable.

Exercise 6.4 This exercise relies on Exercise 6.2, which should be done prior to this one.

1. Show that by restricting the *contraction-left* rule to propositions of the form $\forall x\ A$ and the *contraction-right* rule to propositions of the form $\exists x\ A$ we obtain a system which is equivalent to the sequent calculus without cuts.
2. Show that proofs of existential propositions in the sequent calculus without cuts never use the rules $\exists$-left and $\forall$-right. Show that in the sequent calculus without cuts and without the rules $\exists$-left and $\forall$-right the proposition choice is don't care.
3. Write a program to search for proofs in the sequent calculus.

Exercise 6.5 (Herbrand's Theorem) Let A be a closed prenex proposition of the form $\mathcal{Q}_1 x_1 \ldots \mathcal{Q}_n x_n\ C$. A *closed instance* of A is a closed proposition of the form σC, where σ is a substitution with domain $x_1, \ldots, x_n$.

Let $A_1, \ldots, A_n$ be closed existential propositions, and Γ and Δ multisets of closed propositions without quantifiers. Show that if the language contains at least one constant then the sequent $\Gamma \vdash A_1, \ldots, A_n, \Delta$ is provable in the sequent calculus without cuts if and only if there are closed instances $A_1^1, \ldots, A_1^{p_1}$ of $A_1, \ldots, A_n^1, \ldots, A_n^{p_n}$ of A_n, such that the sequent without quantifiers $\Gamma \vdash A_1^1, \ldots, A_1^{p_1}, \ldots, A_n^1, \ldots, A_n^{p_n}, \Delta$ is provable in the sequent calculus without cuts.

Let $A_1, \ldots, A_n$ be closed existential propositions. Show that if the language contains at least one constant then the sequent $\vdash A_1, \ldots, A_n$ is provable in the sequent calculus without cuts if and only if there are closed instances $A_1^1, \ldots, A_1^{p_1}$ of $A_1, \ldots, A_n^1, \ldots, A_n^{p_n}$ of A_n, such that the sequent without quantifiers $\vdash A_1^1, \ldots, A_1^{p_1}, \ldots, A_n^1, \ldots, A_n^{p_n}$ is provable in the sequent calculus without cuts.

Let $A_1, \ldots, A_n$ be closed universal propositions. Show in the same way that if the language contains at least one constant then the sequent $A_1, \ldots, A_n \vdash$ is provable in the sequent calculus without cuts if and only if there are closed instances $A_1^1, \ldots, A_1^{p_1}$ of $A_1, \ldots, A_n^1, \ldots, A_n^{p_n}$ of A_n, such that the sequent without quantifiers $A_1^1, \ldots, A_1^{p_1}, \ldots, A_n^1, \ldots, A_n^{p_n} \vdash$ is provable in the sequent calculus without cuts.

Exercise 6.6 (Resolution) This exercise relies on Exercises 6.2, 6.3 and 6.5, which should be done prior to this one.

A *clause* is a finite set of propositions where each proposition is either atomic or it is the negation of an atomic proposition.

If $C = \{A_1, \ldots, A_n\}$ is a clause, we denote by $\overline{\forall}C$ the proposition $\forall x_1 \ldots \forall x_p (A_1 \vee \cdots \vee A_n)$, where $x_1, \ldots, x_p$ are the free variables of $A_1, \ldots, A_n$ and $\overline{\forall}\emptyset = \bot$ by definition.

Let E be a set of clauses. Below we consider the set G of clauses inductively defined by the following three rules.

- if C is in E, then C is in G,
- if C is in G, then $(t/x)C$ is in G,
- if $C_1 \cup \{A\}$ and $C_2 \cup \{\neg A\}$ are in G, then $C_1 \cup C_2$ is in G.

The notation $E \rightsquigarrow C$ will be used to state that the clause C is in the set G.

1. Let E be a set consisting of four clauses

$$P(a, b)$$

$$P(b, c)$$

$$\neg P(x, y), \neg P(y, z), G(x, z)$$

$$\neg G(a, c)$$

   Give a derivation for $E \rightsquigarrow \emptyset$.

2. Show that for any proposition A, there exists a set $C_1, \ldots, C_n$ of clauses, such that the sequent $\vdash A$ is provable if and only if the sequent $\overline{\forall}C_1, \ldots, \overline{\forall}C_n \vdash$ is provable. Which set of clauses is associated to the following proposition?

$$(P(a, b) \wedge P(b, c) \wedge \forall x \forall y \forall z ((P(x, y) \wedge P(y, z)) \Rightarrow G(x, z))) \Rightarrow G(a, c)$$

3. Our aim is to prove that if $C_1, \ldots, C_n \rightsquigarrow \emptyset$, then the sequent $\overline{\forall}C_1, \ldots, \overline{\forall}C_n \vdash$ is provable. We will prove a more general property: if $C_1, \ldots, C_n \rightsquigarrow D$, then the sequent $\overline{\forall}C_1, \ldots, \overline{\forall}C_n \vdash \overline{\forall}D$ is provable.

   Show that if $D = (t/x)C$, then the sequent $\overline{\forall}C \vdash \overline{\forall}D$ is provable.

   Show that if $C_1 = C_1' \cup \{A\}$, $C_2 = C_2' \cup \{\neg A\}$ and $D = C_1' \cup C_2'$, then the sequent $\overline{\forall}C_1, \overline{\forall}C_2 \vdash \overline{\forall}D$ is provable.

   Let $C_1, \ldots, C_n$ be a set of clauses. Show that if $C_1, \ldots, C_n \rightsquigarrow D$, then the sequent $\overline{\forall}C_1, \ldots, \overline{\forall}C_n \vdash \overline{\forall}D$ is provable.

   Show that if the sequent $\Gamma \vdash \bot$ is provable, then the sequent $\Gamma \vdash$ is also provable.

   Show that if $C_1, \ldots, C_n \rightsquigarrow \emptyset$, then the sequent $\overline{\forall}C_1, \ldots, \overline{\forall}C_n \vdash$ is provable.

4. We now wish to prove the converse, that is, prove that if the sequent $\overline{\forall}C_1, \ldots, \overline{\forall}C_n \vdash$ is provable, then $C_1, \ldots, C_n \rightsquigarrow \emptyset$.

   Let E be a set of clauses and C and D two clauses. Show that if $E \rightsquigarrow C$ and $E \cup \{C\} \rightsquigarrow D$, then $E \rightsquigarrow D$.

   Let D be a closed clause, $E = \{C_1, \ldots, C_n\}$ and $E' = \{C_1', \ldots, C_n'\}$ two sets of closed clauses closes such that for all i, C_i' is either the clause C_i or the clause $C_i \cup D$ and C is a closed clause. Show that if $E \rightsquigarrow C$, then either $E' \rightsquigarrow C$ or $E' \rightsquigarrow C \cup D$. Show that if $E \rightsquigarrow \emptyset$, then either $E' \rightsquigarrow \emptyset$ or $E' \rightsquigarrow D$. Show that if C and C' are two closed clauses and $E \cup \{C\} \rightsquigarrow \emptyset$ and $E \cup \{C'\} \rightsquigarrow \emptyset$, then $E, (C \cup C') \rightsquigarrow \emptyset$.

Let $C_1, \ldots, C_n$ be closed clauses and $P_1, \ldots, P_m$ closed atomic propositions. Show that if the sequent $\overline{\forall} C_1, \ldots, \overline{\forall} C_n \vdash P_1, \ldots, P_m$ is provable, then $C_1, \ldots, C_n, \neg P_1, \ldots, \neg P_m \rightsquigarrow \emptyset$. Show that if the sequent $\overline{\forall} C_1, \ldots, \overline{\forall} C_n \vdash$ is provable, then $C_1, \ldots, C_n \rightsquigarrow \emptyset$.

Let $C_1, \ldots, C_n$ be arbitrary clauses. Show that if the sequent $\overline{\forall} C_1, \ldots, \overline{\forall} C_n \vdash$ is provable, then $C_1, \ldots, C_n \rightsquigarrow \emptyset$. Hint: use Herbrand's theorem.

Let $C_1, \ldots, C_n$ be arbitrary clauses. Show that the sequent $\overline{\forall} C_1, \ldots, \overline{\forall} C_n \vdash$ is provable if and only if $C_1, \ldots, C_n \rightsquigarrow \emptyset$.

5. The three rules given above cannot be used yet as a proof search algorithm, because the second rule requires that we choose a term from an infinite set. To avoid this choice, we will introduce another set of rules, which will be called *resolution rules*.

   Let E be a set of clauses. We define the set G of clauses inductively, using the following two rules.

   – if C is in E, then C is in G,
   – if $C \cup \{A_1, \ldots, A_n\}$ and $C' \cup \{\neg B_1, \ldots, \neg B_m\}$ are two clauses in G that do not share variables (it is always possible to rename their variables so that no variable is shared), and σ is a most general solution of the unification problem $A_1 = \cdots = A_n = B_1 = \cdots = B_m$, then the clause $\sigma(C \cup C')$ is in G.

   The notation $E \hookrightarrow C$ will be used to state that C is in the set G.

   Let E be the set of clauses defined in question (1.). Give a derivation of $E \hookrightarrow \emptyset$.

   Let E be a set of clauses. Show that if $E \hookrightarrow D$, then $E \rightsquigarrow D$. Show that if $E \hookrightarrow \emptyset$, then $E \rightsquigarrow \emptyset$.

   Show that if there exists a set E' containing clauses of the form σC, where C is a clause in E and σ a substitution, such that $E' \rightsquigarrow D'$, then there exists a clause D and a substitution τ such that $E \hookrightarrow D$ and $D' = \tau D$. Show that if $E \rightsquigarrow \emptyset$, then $E \hookrightarrow \emptyset$.

   Let E be a set of clauses. Show that $E \rightsquigarrow \emptyset$ if and only if $E \hookrightarrow \emptyset$.

   Let A be a proposition and $C_1, \ldots, C_n$ a set of clauses, such that the sequent $\vdash A$ is provable if and only if the sequent $\overline{\forall} C_1, \ldots, \overline{\forall} C_n \vdash$ is provable. Show that the sequent $\vdash A$ is provable if and only if $C_1, \ldots, C_n \hookrightarrow \emptyset$.

6. Write a resolution-based proof-search program.

Chapter 7
Decidable Theories

We have seen in Chap. 5 that provability in predicate logic is not decidable. However, not all is lost: provability in predicate logic is semi-decidable in general, and by adding axioms it is sometimes possible to obtain a decidable theory.

In Chap. 6 we developed algorithms to search for proofs, which, since the problem is semi-decidable, sometimes do not terminate when the proposition that we are trying to prove is not provable.

In this chapter we will study an example of an algorithm that can be used to decide provability in a specific theory.

Several different methods can be used to decide provability within a theory. For instance, one of the methods is based on the fact that if a proposition is not provable in the theory, then there exists a finite model of the theory that invalidates the proposition. Thus, by enumerating both the proofs and the models we can be sure that we will eventually find a proof, if the proposition is provable, or a model if it is not. Another method, the so-called *quantifier elimination method* relies on proving, first, that for closed propositions without quantifiers provability can be decided simply by analysing the proposition, and second, that any closed proposition can be transformed into an equivalent closed proposition without quantifiers. We will use this method to prove the decidability of the set of propositions in the language 0, 1, $+$, $-$, $\leq$ that are valid in $\mathbb{Z}$. Once we prove that this set is decidable, we can use it to define a theory where the axioms are the elements of this set. The resulting theory is consistent, complete and decidable.

To prove this theorem we will extend the language adding unary predicates $Mult_n$, for each natural number n different from 0, to characterise the multiples of n.

Definition 7.1 Let $\mathcal{L}$ be the language consisting of the constants 0 and 1, binary function symbols $+$ and $-$, a binary predicate symbol $\leq$, and a unary predicate $Mult_n$ for each natural number n different from 0.

We will use the following shorthand notations: if n is a positive integer, we use n to denote the integer $1 + 1 + \cdots + 1$ where the symbol 1 occurs n times, and if

G. Dowek, *Proofs and Algorithms*, Undergraduate Topics in Computer Science,
DOI 10.1007/978-0-85729-121-9_7, © Springer-Verlag London Limited 2011

n is negative, we denote by n the integer $0 - 1 - 1 - \cdots - 1$ where the symbol 1 occurs $-n$ times. Similarly, we write $1.x$ for the term x, $2.x$ for $x + x$, $3.x$ for $x + x + x, \ldots, (-1).x$ for $0 - x$, $(-2).x$ for $0 - x - x, \ldots$ and $0.x$ represents the term 0.

Definition 7.2 (The model $\mathbb{Z}$) The model $\mathbb{Z}$ consists of the set $\mathbb{Z}$, the integers 0 and 1, the addition and subtraction operations on $\mathbb{Z}$, the ordering relation over $\mathbb{Z}$ and, for each natural number n different from 0, the characteristic function of the set of multiples of n.

Let us start with an example. Consider the proposition $1 \leq 3.x \wedge x \leq 7 - x$, which we will call A, with a unique free variable, x. Our goal is to decide whether the proposition $\exists x\, A$ is valid or not in $\mathbb{Z}$. In order to do this, we transform each inequation, so that all the x are on one side of the symbol $\leq$ and the other terms on the other. Then we multiply the first inequation by 2 and the second by 3, to have the same coefficient for x in each inequation. We obtain the equivalent proposition $\exists x\, (2 \leq 6.x \wedge 6.x \leq 21)$. Now we change the variable, and obtain the equivalent proposition $\exists x'\, (2 \leq x' \wedge x' \leq 21 \wedge Mult_6(x'))$. We have to decide whether there exists a multiple of 6 in the interval between 2 and 21, and the answer is positive.

If the proposition A had other variables, we would not be able to decide whether the proposition $\exists x\, A$, which has free variables, is valid or not, but we could transform it into an equivalent proposition without quantifiers and with the same variables. Consider, for instance, the proposition $1 \leq 3.x \wedge x \leq y - x$. We start as before by moving all the x to one side of the symbol $\leq$ and the other terms to the other. Then we multiply each inequality to obtain the same coefficient for x in each inequation and we change the variable, obtaining a proposition equivalent to $\exists x\, A$, namely $\exists x'\, (2 \leq x' \wedge x' \leq 3.y \wedge Mult_6(x'))$. Let us call A' the proposition $2 \leq x' \wedge x' \leq 3.y \wedge Mult_6(x')$.

Fix a value q for y and assume that there exists a natural number p that satisfies this proposition. Two cases may arise. Either all the numbers greater than p and congruents with p modulo 6 satisfy it too, or, as in this example, they do not. In this case, there exists an integer p' that satisfies the proposition and such that $p' + 6$ does not. This means that there exists an inequation, here $x' \leq 3.y$, which changed between p' and $p' + 6$. Therefore $p' \leq 3.q < p' + 6$. There exists then a natural number j between 0 and 5 such that $3.q = p' + j$ and hence $p' = 3.q - j$ satisfies the proposition give above. In other words, the proposition A' where we substitute y by q and x' by $3.q - j$ for some j between 0 and 5 is valid in $\mathbb{Z}$.

Let B be the proposition without quantifiers $(3.y/x')A' \vee ((3.y - 1)/x')A' \vee ((3.y - 2)/x')A' \vee ((3.y - 3)/x')A' \vee ((3.y - 4)/x')A' \vee ((3.y - 5)/x')A'$. The proposition B, where we substitute y by q, is valid in $\mathbb{Z}$. Conversely, if this proposition is valid in $\mathbb{Z}$, then so is $\exists x'\, A'$.

The following proposition generalises this construction.

Proposition 7.1 *Let A be a proposition without quantifiers in the language $\mathcal{L}$. There exists a proposition B without quantifiers such that the proposition $(\exists x\, A) \Leftrightarrow B$ is valid in the model $\mathbb{Z}$.*

Proof We start by replacing in A all propositions of the form $C \Rightarrow D$ (that is, all the implications) by the equivalent proposition $\neg C \vee D$. Then we eliminate all the negations by replacing the propositions of the form $\neg \top$ by $\bot$, $\neg \bot$ by $\top$, $\neg (C \wedge D)$ by $\neg C \vee \neg D$, $\neg (C \vee D)$ by $\neg C \wedge \neg D$, $\neg \neg C$ by C, $\neg\, t \leq u$ by $u + 1 \leq t$ and $\neg\, Mult_n(t)$ by $Mult_n(t+1) \vee \cdots \vee Mult_n(t+n-1)$ until the symbol $\neg$ disappears. The resulting proposition can only contain the connectives $\top$, $\bot$, $\wedge$, $\vee$ and atomic propositions of the form $t \leq u$ or $Mult_n(t)$.

The next step consists of moving all the x to one side of the symbol $\leq$ in each inequation, leaving the other terms in the other side. We can then replace each proposition of the form $t \leq u$ by the equivalent proposition $k.t \leq k.u$, where k is a strictly positive integer, and each proposition of the form $Mult_n(t)$ by $Mult_{kn}(k.t)$, in order to obtain the same coefficient s for x in all the atomic propositions. Then all the terms of the form $s.x$ can be replaced by a variable x', adding the atomic proposition $Mult_s(x')$. The result is a proposition of the form $\exists x'\, A'$, equivalent to the proposition $\exists x\, A$, where A' uses the connectives $\top$, $\bot$, $\wedge$, $\vee$ and atomic propositions of the form $x' \leq t$, $t \leq x'$, $0 \leq t$, $Mult_n(x' + t)$ and $Mult_n(t)$ such that t does not contain any occurrence of the variable x'.

Let r be a common multiple of all the integers n such that the atomic proposition $Mult_n(x' + t)$ occurs in A'.

If we fix the value of the variables different from x', the truth value of such a proposition is a function of the value of x', which is periodic (with period r) from a certain point. Indeed, there is a certain value such that for any greater value all propositions of the form $x' \leq t$ are false and all propositions of the form $t \leq x'$ are true, only those of the form $Mult_n(x' + t)$ change their value, with period r.

Let E be the set of terms t such that the atomic proposition $x' \leq t$ occurs in A'. Let A'' be the proposition obtained by replacing in A' all the propositions of the form $x' \leq t$ by $\bot$ and all the propositions of the form $t \leq x'$ by $\top$. Let B be the disjunction of all the propositions of the form

- $(i/x')A''$ where i is an integer between 0 and $r - 1$,
- $((t - j)/x')A'$ where t is a term in E and j an integer between 0 and $r - 1$.

Let us now prove that the proposition $(\exists x'\, A') \Leftrightarrow B$ is valid in $\mathbb{Z}$.

Let $y_1, \ldots, y_n$ be the variables in A' different from x'. We denote by $A'[p, q_1, \ldots, q_n]$ the proposition $(p/x', q_1/y_1, \ldots, q_n/y_n)A'$, by $A''[p, q_1, \ldots, q_n]$ the proposition $(p/x', q_1/y_1, \ldots, q_n/y_n)A''$ and by $B[q_1, \ldots, q_n]$ the proposition $(q_1/y_1, \ldots, q_n/y_n)B$. We will show that for all $q_1, \ldots, q_n$, there exists an integer p such that $A'[p, q_1, \ldots, q_n]$ is valid if and only if $B[q_1, \ldots, q_n]$ is valid.

Assume that there exists an integer p such that $A'[p, q_1, \ldots, q_n]$ is valid. In this case, either $A'[p + vr, q_1, \ldots, q_n]$ is valid for all v, or not.

In the first case, there are integers p' (arbitrarily large) such that $A'[p', q_1, \ldots, q_n]$ is valid, and for some p' sufficiently large $A'[p', q_1, \ldots, q_n]$ is equivalent to $A''[p', q_1, \ldots, q_n]$. Therefore, there exists an integer p' such that $A''[p', q_1, \ldots, q_n]$ is valid. Also, for all p $A''[p, q_1, \ldots, q_n]$ is equivalent to $A''[p - r, q_1, \ldots, q_n]$. Thus, there exists an integer i between 0 and $r - 1$ such that $A''[i, q_1, \ldots, q_n]$ is valid. The proposition $B[q_1, \ldots, q_n]$ is therefore valid.

In the second case, there exists an integer p' such that $A'[p', q_1, \ldots, q_n]$ is valid but $A'[p' + r, q_1, \ldots, q_n]$ is not. There exists an atomic proposition of the form $x' \leq t$ satisfied by p' but not by $p' + r$. Let us write $t[q_1, \ldots, q_n]$ for the term $(q_1/y_1, \ldots, q_n/y_n)t$. We have $p' \leq t[q_1, \ldots, q_n]$, but $t[q_1, \ldots, q_n] < p' + r$. Therefore, there exists an integer j between 0 and $r - 1$ such that $p' = t[q_1, \ldots, q_n] - j$. The proposition $B[q_1, \ldots, q_n]$ is therefore valid.

Conversely, if $B[q_1, \ldots, q_n]$ is valid, then, either there exists an integer i such that $A''[i, q_1, \ldots, q_n]$ is valid or there exists an element t in E and a number j such that $A'[t[q_1, \ldots, q_m] - j, q_1, \ldots, q_n]$ is valid. In the second case, there exists an integer p such that $A'[p, q_1, \ldots, q_n]$ is valid. In the first case, for all p such that $A''[p, q_1, \ldots, q_n]$ is equivalent to $A''[p + r, q_1, \ldots, q_n]$, there are integers p arbitrarily large such that $A''[p, q_1, \ldots, q_n]$ is valid, and for p sufficiently large $A''[p, q_1, \ldots, q_n]$ is equivalent to $A'[p, q_1, \ldots, q_n]$. Therefore, there exists an integer p such that $A'[p, q_1, \ldots, q_n]$ is valid. $\square$

Proposition 7.2 *Let A be a proposition in the language $\mathcal{L}$. There exists a proposition B without quantifiers such that $A \Leftrightarrow B$ is valid in $\mathbb{Z}$.*

Proof The propositions of the form $\forall x\, C$ can be replaced by the equivalent proposition $\neg \exists x \neg C$, and a proof by induction over the structure of the obtained proposition allows us to conclude, using Proposition 7.1 in the case of the existential quantifier. $\square$

Theorem 7.1 *The set of propositions in the language $0, 1, +, -, \leq$ that are valid in $\mathbb{Z}$ is decidable.*

Proof Validity of closed propositions without quantifiers is obviously decidable, and for arbitrary propositions it can be derived from Proposition 7.2. $\square$

We can state a similar result for natural numbers.

Theorem 7.2 (Presburger) *The set of propositions in the language $0, S, +, =$ that are valid in $\mathbb{N}$ is decidable.*

Proof To each proposition A in the language $0, S, +, =$ we associate a proposition $|A|$ in the language $0, 1, +, -, \leq$ such that for every closed proposition A, A is valid in $\mathbb{N}$ if and only if $|A|$ is valid in $\mathbb{Z}$.

- $|0| = 0$, $|x| = x$, $|S(t)| = |t| + 1$, $|t + u| = |t| + |u|$,
- $|t = u| = |t| \leq |u| \wedge |u| \leq |t|$,
- $|\top| = \top$, $|\bot| = \bot$, $|\neg A| = \neg |A|$, $|A \wedge B| = |A| \wedge |B|$, $|A \vee B| = |A| \vee |B|$, $|A \Rightarrow B| = |A| \Rightarrow |B|$,
- $|\forall x\, A| = \forall x\, (0 \leq x \Rightarrow |A|)$, $|\exists x\, A| = \exists x\, (0 \leq x \wedge |A|)$.

$\square$

Chapter 8
Constructivity

If a set of natural numbers contains 0, but not 2, we can show that there exists a natural number in this set such that its successor is not in the set. Indeed, if we enumerate the natural numbers, at some point the sequence leaves the set. We can even show that the natural number we are looking for is either 0 or 1, but we cannot show that it is 0, or that it is 1, because we do not know whether the number 1 is in the set or not.

In predicate logic, the corresponding sequent

$$\Gamma \vdash \exists x \ (P(x) \wedge \neg P(S(x)))$$

where $\Gamma = P(0), \neg P(2)$ is provable

$$\cfrac{\cfrac{\vdots}{\Gamma \vdash P(1) \vee \neg P(1)} \quad \cfrac{\cfrac{\vdots}{\Gamma, P(1) \vdash P(1) \wedge \neg P(2)}}{\Gamma, P(1) \vdash \exists x \ (P(x) \wedge \neg P(S(x)))} \quad \cfrac{\cfrac{\vdots}{\Gamma, \neg P(1) \vdash P(0) \wedge \neg P(1)}}{\Gamma, \neg P(1) \vdash \exists x \ (P(x) \wedge \neg P(S(x)))}}{\Gamma \vdash \exists x \ (P(x) \wedge \neg P(S(x)))}$$

However, for each term t, the sequent $P(0), \neg P(2) \vdash P(t) \wedge \neg P(S(t))$ is not provable. Indeed, take $\mathcal{M} = \mathbb{N}$; if we interpret 0 and S in the obvious way and P first by the characteristic function of the pair $\{0, 1\}$ and then by that of the singleton $\{0\}$, we obtain two models in which the term t has the same denotation, and that refute the sequent above (the first in the case where the denotation of t is 0 and the second in the case where it is different from 0).

Definition 8.1 (Witness Property) A set of propositions satisfies the *witness property* if for each proposition of the form $\exists x \ A$ in the set, there is also a proposition $(t/x)A$, for some term t, in the set.

It follows from the discussion above that the set of propositions that are provable in the theory $P(0), \neg P(2)$ does not satisfy this property. We can prove in a similar way that the set of propositions that are provable in the empty theory does not have the witness property either. For example, consider the proposition

$$\exists x \ ((P(0) \wedge \neg P(2)) \Rightarrow (P(x) \wedge \neg P(S(x))))$$

G. Dowek, *Proofs and Algorithms*, Undergraduate Topics in Computer Science, 143
DOI 10.1007/978-0-85729-121-9_8, © Springer-Verlag London Limited 2011

Exercise 8.1 Show that the proposition $\exists x \ (P(x) \vee \neg P(S(x)))$ is provable but there is no term t such that $P(t) \vee \neg P(S(t))$ is provable.

In the proof of the sequent $P(0), \neg P(2) \vdash \exists x \ (P(x) \wedge \neg P(S(x)))$, it seems essential to rely on the rule of excluded middle to prove the proposition $P(1) \vee \neg P(1)$. The question arises as to whether a proof can be built without using the rule of excluded middle. It turns out that the answer is negative, because the set of propositions that are provable in predicate logic without using the rule of excluded middle have the witness property, as we will see below.

Definition 8.2 (Constructive proof) A natural deduction proof is *constructive* if it does not use the rule of *excluded middle*. A proof in the system D' is *constructive* if it contains only sequents of the form $\Gamma \vdash \Delta$ where Δ is a singleton. A sequent calculus proof is *constructive* if it contains only sequents of the form $\Gamma \vdash \Delta$ where Δ is a singleton or the empty multiset. We eliminate from the sequent calculus the rule *contraction-right* and we modify some of the other rules, as follows. The rule $\vee$-right is replaced by the rules

$$\frac{\Gamma \vdash A}{\Gamma \vdash A \vee B} \ \vee\text{-right}$$

$$\frac{\Gamma \vdash B}{\Gamma \vdash A \vee B} \ \vee\text{-right}$$

the rule $\Rightarrow$-left by

$$\frac{\Gamma \vdash A \quad \Gamma, B \vdash C}{\Gamma, A \Rightarrow B \vdash C} \ \Rightarrow\text{-left}$$

the rule $\neg$-left by

$$\frac{\Gamma \vdash A}{\Gamma, \neg A \vdash B} \ \neg\text{-left}$$

and the rule *cut* by the rule

$$\frac{\Gamma \vdash A \quad \Gamma, A \vdash B}{\Gamma \vdash B} \ \text{cut}$$

It can be shown that a sequent $\Gamma \vdash A$ has a constructive proof in natural deduction if and only if it has a constructive proof in sequent calculus. The proof of this property follows the same lines as the proofs given in Chap. 6.

Similarly, it can be shown that a sequent $\Gamma \vdash A$ has a constructive proof in the sequent calculus if and only if it has a constructive proof without cuts.

Proposition 8.1 *If a sequent $\vdash A$ has a proof without cuts in the sequent calculus, then the last rule in the proof is a right rule.*

Proof Since the left-hand side of the sequent is empty, none of the left rules can apply, and neither can the *axiom* rule. Since the proof has no cuts, the last rule cannot be a *cut* either. Therefore, it must be a right rule. □

Proposition 8.2 *The set of propositions that have a constructive proof has the witness property.*

Proof If the sequent $\vdash \exists x\ A$ has a constructive proof in sequent calculus, it also has a constructive proof without cuts. The last rule in this proof is a right rule, and since the *contraction-right* rule is not part of the constructive sequent calculus, it can only be the rule $\exists$-right. The proof has then the form

$$\frac{\begin{array}{c} \pi \\ \vdash (t/x)A \end{array}}{\vdash \exists x\ A}\ \exists\text{-right}$$

and the proposition $(t/x)A$ has a constructive proof. □

In the proof above, the fact that the left-hand side of the sequent is empty is crucial. The theorem does not hold in arbitrary theories. For example, the set of propositions that have a constructive proof in the theory $\exists x\ P(x)$ clearly does not have the witness property. However, the theorem does extend to arithmetic and also to some versions of set theory.

Thanks to the witness property, constructive proofs can be used as programs. For example, the proposition

$$\forall x \exists y\ (x = 2 \times y \vee x = 2 \times y + 1)$$

has a constructive proof π in arithmetic. Using this proof it is easy to build a proof of the proposition

$$\exists y\ (25 = 2 \times y \vee 25 = 2 \times y + 1)$$

$$\frac{\begin{array}{cc} \pi & \dfrac{\Gamma, \exists y\ A[25, y] \vdash \exists y\ A[25, y]}{\Gamma, \forall x \exists y\ A[x, y] \vdash \exists y\ A[25, y]}\ \begin{array}{l}\text{axiom}\\ \forall\text{-left}\end{array} \\ \Gamma \vdash \forall x \exists y\ A[x, y] & \end{array}}{\Gamma \vdash \exists y\ A[25, y]}\ \text{cut}$$

where A is the proposition $x = 2 \times y \vee x = 2 \times y + 1$ and where $A[t, u]$ denotes the proposition $(t/x, u/y)A$. By eliminating the cuts in this proof we obtain a witness: 12.

The proof π is therefore a program that divides its input 25 by 2, and cut elimination is the mechanism used to execute this program. By construction, this program is correct with respect to the specification

$$x = 2 \times y \vee x = 2 \times y + 1$$

Exercise 8.2 We will define types for the terms in the lambda-calculus. Types are closed expressions in a language consisting of an infinite set of constants $\rho_0, \rho_1, \rho_2, \ldots$ and a binary symbol $\to$. A *typing context* is a finite set of declarations of the form $x : \alpha$ where x is a variable and α a type, such that if $x : \alpha$ and $x : \beta$ are both in the set, then $\alpha = \beta$. A typing judgement is a triple consisting of a typing context Γ, a term t and a type α. The judgement $\Gamma \vdash t : \alpha$ states that the term t has the type α in the context Γ. For example, the term $fun\, x \to (f\, x\, x)$ has the type $\rho_0 \to \rho_0$ in the context $f : \rho_0 \to \rho_0 \to \rho_0$. The set of *derivable judgements* is inductively defined by the following rules

$$\frac{}{\Gamma \vdash x : \alpha} \quad \text{if } x : \alpha \text{ is in } \Gamma$$

$$\frac{\Gamma, x : \alpha \vdash t : \beta}{\Gamma \vdash (fun\, x \to t) : \alpha \to \beta}$$

$$\frac{\Gamma \vdash t : \alpha \to \beta \quad \Gamma \vdash u : \alpha}{\Gamma \vdash (t\, u) : \beta}$$

1. Write a term of type $\rho_0 \to \rho_1 \to \rho_0$ in the empty context, and a term of type $\rho_0 \to \rho_1 \to \rho_1$.

   The fragment of predicate logic consisting of the proposition symbols $P_0, \ldots, P_n$ and implication is called minimal propositional logic.
2. Which natural deduction rules can be used to prove propositions in this fragment? Write a proof for the proposition $P_0 \Rightarrow P_1 \Rightarrow P_0$ and another for the proposition $P_0 \Rightarrow P_1 \Rightarrow P_1$.

   The following function ϕ associates a lambda-calculus type to each proposition in minimal propositional logic.

$$\phi P_i = \rho_i$$

$$\phi(A \Rightarrow B) = (\phi A) \to (\phi B)$$

3. What is the type associated to the proposition $P_0 \Rightarrow P_1 \Rightarrow P_0$?
4. Show that there exists a proof π for the sequent $A_1, \ldots, A_p \vdash B$ if and only if there exists a term t of type ϕB in the context $x_1 : \phi A_1, \ldots, x_p : \phi A_p$.
5. Let Γ be the context $A, A \Rightarrow B, B \Rightarrow C, C \Rightarrow D$. Give the term associated to the proof

Is this term terminating? What is its irreducible form? Which proof is associated to this irreducible form?

6. What is the form of the proofs associated to redexes? And what is the proof associated to the term obtained by reducing a redex?

Exercise 8.3 This exercise relies on Exercise 1.5 which should be done prior to this one.

1. Let A be an arbitrary proposition. Give a sequent calculus proof—not necessarily constructive—of the proposition

$$A \vee \neg A$$

Give a constructive proof of the proposition

$$\neg\neg(A \vee \neg A)$$

To each proposition A in predicate logic we associate a proposition $|A|$ defined by induction over the structure of A as follows

- $|P| = \neg\neg P$
- $|T| = \neg\neg T$
- $|\bot| = \neg\neg\bot$
- $|A \wedge B| = \neg\neg(|A| \wedge |B|)$
- $|A \vee B| = \neg\neg(|A| \vee |B|)$
- $|A \Rightarrow B| = \neg\neg(|A| \Rightarrow |B|)$
- $|\neg A| = \neg\neg\neg|A|$
- $|\forall x\ A| = \neg\neg\forall x\ |A|$
- $|\exists x\ A| = \neg\neg\exists x\ |A|$

2. Write down the proposition associated to $|\exists x\ (P(x) \wedge \neg P(S(x)))|$.
3. To each proposition A in predicate logic we associate a proposition $\|A\|$ similar to $|A|$ except that negations at the root are eliminated

- $\|P\| = \neg P$
- $\|T\| = \neg T$
- $\|\bot\| = \neg\bot$
- $\|A \wedge B\| = \neg(|A| \wedge |B|)$
- $\|A \vee B\| = \neg(|A| \vee |B|)$
- $\|A \Rightarrow B\| = \neg(|A| \Rightarrow |B|)$
- $\|\neg A\| = \neg\neg|A|$
- $\|\forall x\ A\| = \neg\forall x\ |A|$
- $\|\exists x\ A\| = \neg\exists x\ |A|$

Show that if the sequent $\Gamma \vdash \Delta$ has a proof—not necessarily constructive—in the sequent calculus without cuts, then the sequent $|\Gamma|\|\Delta\| \vdash$ has a constructive proof without cuts.
4. Let A be a proposition. Show that if A has a proof—not necessarily constructive —, then $|A|$ has a constructive proof.

5. Show that for any proposition B, the proposition $B \Leftrightarrow \neg\neg B$ has a proof—not necessarily constructive. Show that the proposition $A \Leftrightarrow |A|$ has a proof—not necessarily constructive. Show that if the proposition $|A|$ has a constructive proof then the proposition A has a proof—not necessarily constructive.

    Show that the proposition $|A|$ has a constructive proof if and only if the proposition A has a proof—not necessarily constructive.

6. Give a constructive proof of the sequent

$$|P(0)|, |\neg P(2)| \vdash |\exists x \ (P(x) \wedge \neg P(S(x)))|$$

7. Give a constructive proof of the sequent

$$P(0), \neg P(2) \vdash \neg\neg\exists x \ (P(x) \wedge \neg P(S(x)))$$

Chapter 9
Epilogue

In this book we have explored some of the links between proofs and algorithms, through the theorem of undecidability of provability in predicate logic first, then through the decidability result for well-formedness of proofs (which ensures the semi-decidability of provability in predicate logic and leads also to proof verification algorithms and to automated theorem proving), and also through some decidability results in specific theories. Finally, the notion of contructivism highlights another link between proofs and algorithms, which leads to methods to prove that an algorithm satisfies a specification, amongst other results.

On the way, we have discovered four main concepts that are central in contemporary logic: the notions of proof, algorithm, model and set. These four notions define the four branches of logic: proof theory, computability theory, model theory and set theory. This classification is useful, but we should not lose sight of the fact that all these notions are used, in different degrees, in each of these branches.

Until the end of the 19th century, the notion of proof was quite rudimentary, the notions of set and algorithm were informal, and there was no notion of model. Logic underwent a total makeover when these four notions were clarified in the 1870's and later in the 1930's.

We have also described in this book a number of applications of logic in mathematics, with independence and relative consistency results, and also in a more unexpected way with results in algebra for which it was not obvious *a priori* that logic tools would be necessary. However, it is in computer science where logic finds its most prominent field of application. For instance, we have seen applications in programming language theory, where two new families of languages emerged: functional languages, based on the lambda-calculus, and logic languages based on automated theorem proving algorithms. There are also applications in machine architecture, where circuits are represented as propositions in propositional logic, in complexity theory, where we can cite for example the notion of non-deterministic Turing machine, in database theory, where the notion of query language is based on finite model theory, and also in verification, more precisely, through the design of tools to prove the correctness of circuits and programs with respect to their logic specification.

G. Dowek, *Proofs and Algorithms*, Undergraduate Topics in Computer Science, DOI 10.1007/978-0-85729-121-9_9, © Springer-Verlag London Limited 2011

The central rôle of the notion of algorithm in logic could certainly make us think that there should be applications in computer science, but nobody would have thought that there would be so many applications and at the level we are seeing nowadays. In a sense, logic seems to be for computer science what differential calculus is for physics.

And it is not clear whether we have completely grasped yet the reasons why logic is so unreasonably effective in computer science.

References

1. Cori, R., Lascar, D.: Mathematical Logic: A Course with Exercises. Oxford University Press, London (2000)
2. David, R., Nour, K., Raffalli, C.: Introduction à la logique: théorie de la démonstration. Dunod, Paris (2001)
3. Girard, J.-Y., Lafont, Y., Taylor, P.: Proofs and Types. Cambridge University Press, Cambridge (1989)
4. Krivine, J.-L.: Lambda-Calculus, Types and Models. Ellis Horwood, Chichester (1993)
5. Krivine, J.-L.: Théorie des ensembles. Cassini, Paris (1998)

G. Dowek, *Proofs and Algorithms*, Undergraduate Topics in Computer Science, DOI 10.1007/978-0-85729-121-9, © Springer-Verlag London Limited 2011

Index